A Mirror of Your Soul

You may think you're composing a thank you note or a shopping list, but each stroke of your pen sends a hidden message—to someone who knows how to read it. Your pen strokes reveal how you feel about yourself and others ... your talents and abilities ... how you're likely to react under stress ... even facts about yourself that you aren't aware of. Truth be told, your script is a mirror of your soul.

Your handwriting also reveals talents and potentials that can help you choose a career—or, if you're doing the hiring, a quick look at an application can help you choose the right employee.

P. Scott Hollander's *Handwriting Analysis* teaches you how to analyze handwriting, how to counsel others, and how to best use the subject once you learn it. You'll start at the beginning and discover, step by step, everything you need to know to analyze a sample of script—and how to use that analysis once you have it. You'll also learn how to analyze the writing of children, identify medical problems, and change your life by changing your own writing.

About the Author

P. Scott Hollander was a certified graphologist with fifteen years of experience in personal counseling. She wrote a regular column in a bimonthly magazine answering readers' questions based on an analysis of their script. She also wrote two correspondence courses on graphology.

P. Scott Hollander was a professional freelance writer who wrote mostly fiction for adults and children. She was also the editor/publisher of her own magazine-style newsletter, *The Wiccan Advertiser*, a business publication for the Wiccan/Pagan community. P. Scott Hollander passed away in 1996.

A complete self-teaching guide

Handwriting Analysis

P. Scott Hollander

1998
Llewellyn Publications
St. Paul, Minnesota 55164-0383, U.S.A.

SECOND EDITION
First Printing, 1998
(Previously titled *Reading Between the Lines*)

Cover art by Lisa Novak
Book design by Terry Buske

Library of Congress Cataloging-in-publication Data
Hollander, P. Scott
     Handwriting Analysis : a complete self-teaching guide / P. Scott Hollander. - -2nd ed.
     p.   cm.
Previously published: Reading between the lines. 1st ed. 1991
     ISBN 1-56718-390-5
     1. Graphology I. Hollander, P. Scott— Reading between the lines. II. Title.
BF891.H812   1998   CIP
155.2′82—dc20

Publisher's note:
Llewellyn Worldwide does not participate in, endorse, or have any authority or responsibility concerning private business transactions between our authors and the public.
All mail addressed to the author is forwarded but the publisher cannot, unless specifically instructed by the author, give out an address or phone number.

Printed in the United States of America

Llewellyn Publications
A Division of Llewellyn Worldwide, Ltd.
P.O. Box 64383, Dept. K390-5
St. Paul, MN 55164-0383

Dedication

This book is dedicated to my uncle, Sol Present—because
without his help, it could never have been written.

Acknowledgments

Except for Schoolform lettering used as illustrations, all handwriting samples in this text were written by real people. To disguise the identity of those people, any signatures shown in this text have been designed by a graphic artist to mimic actual handwriting styles. All names used are aliases.

The author would like to thank everyone who contributed handwriting samples for your permission to use those samples as illustrations in this text—and for the feedback you took the time and trouble to give me on your analyses.

Contents

Preface

This book is designed to teach you the fundamentals of handwriting analysis. Each chapter concentrates on one (or one group) of the trait indicators found in script. For each of these script and penstroke formations you will be told (a) the name and definition of the formation; (b) how to recognize and measure it; (c) what it means in its various forms; and (d) how its meaning affects and is affected by other formations in script. Each chapter also includes examples of the handwriting styles described in the text.

At the end of each chapter there is a list of the important principles that you will need in order to do the analysis. You will also find a short "quiz": a group of handwriting samples for you to analyze so that you can test your analysis skills. (Answers to the test samples are given in Appendix B.) How well you do on your test analyses will help you determine how well you understood each lesson and what you need to review. The information in this text is cumulative. You should make certain that you understand and can use the principles outlined in each chapter before you go on to the next.

When you have completed the instruction section of this book, you will have all the information you need to do a basic analysis of anyone's handwriting. But how adept you become at using what you've learned depends entirely on you.

Handwriting analysis is a skill, and the best way to learn any skill is to *practice*. In this sense, it's not much different from learning a new language or a musical instrument. If you are serious about becoming a handwriting expert, then from the start you should apply what you learn in each chapter of this book.

Begin now to collect samples of handwriting from as many different people in as many different professions as possible. Ask for samples from your family, your friends, your neighbors, your co-workers. In exchange for their cooperation, you can offer to do an analysis of their writing. As you progress through the text, add to your analysis of each sample using the principles outlined in each section. Your practice and their feedback will help you make sense of what you are learning in this book.

As much as possible, try to insist on certain guidelines for your samples. (Think of them as laboratory specimens—because that's what they are!). They should be:

• **written** (and you *must* have script: printing is useless for analysis purposes. (If they can sign their name, they can write.);
• on a **full** (8 1/2 x 11), **unlined** sheet of paper (give your subject plenty of room, and plenty of leeway, for self-expression);
• using a **ballpoint pen** (a common writing tool that most people will use more naturally, and which will also make it easier for you to measure pen pressure).

Date each sample when you get it, and make a note of the subject's age, sex, and current occupation.

The words don't matter. A graphologist very rarely reads the verbal message in a sample. The following test line will give you all the script formations you will need for a preliminary analysis:

> *This is a sample of the way I normally write. I would like you to tell me what my handwriting reveals.*

Their Signature

Be sure you get a full signature; and then ask your subject to print their full name below it (this is for your benefit: in case their signature is illegible).

Besides fulfilling your technical requirements, using a standardized test line for your preliminary analysis has several other advantages. Since all your samples have the same format; it will make it easier for you to compare differences and similarities in people's script styles. It will also mean that, no matter how illegible someone's handwriting, you will know exactly what they wrote (and therefore what letter formations you are looking at). And it will answer the inevitable question: "Well, what do you want me to write?"

It will also give you your first analysis clue. Your instructions for the sample were specific, were they not? Now look at the sample you got. Can your subject follow simple directions?

Let's find out why or why not.

Introduction

What are you really saying when you write?

You may think that you're composing a thank you note, telling a friend the latest news, or even just jotting down a reminder to yourself about some unfinished business. Whatever the case, all you're concerned with are the words; the verbal message.

But each stroke of your pen also sends a hidden message—to someone who knows how to read it. And the way you combine those penstrokes reveals what kind of person you really are: how you feel about yourself and others around you; what kinds of talents and abilities you have, and whether or not you can or will make use of them; how you're likely to react in different situations, especially under stress; even facts about yourself that you may not be aware of until they're pointed out. To someone who knows how to read penstrokes, your writing is the mirror of your soul.

What Is Graphology?

Graphology is the study of character and personality through the analysis of penstroke formations used in handwriting.

So much for scientific definition. What it means, quite simply, is that you can use graphology to find out what people are like under their masks; and you can use graphology to help people cope with their hurts. Is the life of the party really as happy and self-confident as she seems? And how about that guy over there in the corner. Is he really stuck up, or just painfully shy? Penstrokes can tell you what people can't: how they really feel.

The connection between your thoughts and feelings and the way you form your handwriting is one you can prove for yourself before you even begin this book. Try this:

Copy the test sentence given in the Preface. Write it when you're angry. Write it again when you're happy, or feeling tired, or feeling fine, or feeling nothing in particular at all. The subject of the sentence will have nothing to do with what you're thinking. But when you compare the different samples you'll be able to see noticeable differences in penstroke usage, even though your handwriting style remains basically the same.

Your handwriting shows what you *feel*: about yourself, about the people around you, about your environment, about your life. And because it reveals what kind of person you really are, an accurate analysis of your script can also tell you what to *do* to help you improve your life.

But before you get the idea that handwriting analysis has the answer to all your questions, let's take a look at some of the questions it doesn't answer.

Some Limitations of Graphology

There are certain facts about a person that you cannot tell by analyzing their handwriting.

A person's handwriting does not reveal chronological age. It does reveal mental age (or, level of maturity), which is a very different thing; and with it, the ability of the individual to arrive at his own conclusions and make his own decisions.

A person's handwriting does not reveal sex. Masculine and feminine traits—at least, as defined by society—are found in both men and women. Handwriting only reveals which of these traits are present and/or dominant, but it won't tell you whether the writer is a woman or a man.

It also won't tell you the writer's sexual preference (i.e., hetero- or homosexuality, etc.). But it does point out quite vividly the writer's comfort with or guilt feelings about sexual activities.

A person's handwriting does not reveal profession. Analysis does point out talents, abilities, proclivities, and may often suggest the potential for a real skill in specific fields. It also makes clear the kind of work environment in which a particular writer would feel most comfortable. But there is no way to tell from the handwriting what profession the writer *chose* to follow: and as we know, many people are working at jobs which in no way use or reflect their real capabilities.

A person's handwriting does not reveal race or ethnic origin. The writing styles taught in different school systems produce "intonations" in script which are just as identifiable, for someone trained to recognize them, as accents in speech can be to a trained semanticist. But the kind of person you become depends on your own individual experiences and your own individual reactions to those experiences. A graphologist who has chosen to specialize in national or regional writing styles can sometimes tell where you come from by the way you write; or at least where and when you were taught to write. But there is no indicator in script which can tell even the most expert graphologist the color of the hand that's doing the writing.

A person's handwriting does not reveal their future. Because an accurate analysis of someone's handwriting does uncover essential traits, it is possible to draw reasonable conclusions about what that writer is likely to do in any given future situation. But that's as far as it goes: you cannot predict, by analyzing someone's handwriting, what those future situations might turn out to be.

You also cannot uncover a writer's past, so if you're looking for skeletons in someone's closet, graphology is not the key. As you will learn, even someone suffering from massive guilt feelings may not have ever done anything to deserve those feelings. You can project what kind of background the writer must have come from to feel the way he does; given a good enough sample, you may even be able to tell, from his reactions, what kind of confrontations he must have faced in the past. But all you know for certain are the writer's *feelings* about those events: you won't know, unless he tells you, what those events actually were—or what he actually did about them.

Now that you know what you can't do with graphology, let's find out what you can do.

Some Uses of Graphology

Graphology can help you understand yourself. Having an accurate means of uncovering and understanding basic character and personality traits has many advantages; knowing yourself is not the least of them. An analysis of your own handwriting can help you gain insights into your own strengths and weaknesses. And though you may have to face some unpleasant truths, it will at least enable you to make wiser decisions for your personal and professional life.

Graphology can help you understand other people. Under normal circumstances, it could take years to really get to know someone, and most of us don't have that kind of time or opportunity. With handwriting analysis, you have a quick, sure means of discovering what someone else is like, what their expectations are, and what's the best way to approach them, and this can make your family, social, and business contacts that much easier. (Why marry someone to find out whether you can live with them—or live with them to find out whether you should marry them—when a careful comparison of your handwriting and theirs will tell you where or whether you are compatible, and where or whether conflicts could arise!)

Graphology can help you choose a career. Vocational analysis can help guide you, and those for whom you do an analysis, in the choice of a career or profession. By pointing out talents, abilities, and preferences, it gives you a means of deciding what type of work would best suit you, and, just as important, what kind of employment situation to avoid. (Note, however, that this type of analysis does require either a background in vocational guidance or the assistance of an employment counselor. Your analysis of someone's writing can uncover skills or potentials that even the writer was unaware of, but you also need a knowledge of available employment to decide just how those skills could be marketable.)

Handwriting analysis is also useful to an employer; it can help a personnel manager determine whether or not a job applicant is suitable for a particular position, and/or where it's best to place someone. Because handwriting knows no sexual or racial distinctions, graphology is truly an equal opportunity placement tool.

And finally, graphology can *be* a career; especially now, when this art-science is being recognized by more and more institutions as the accurate counseling and investigative tool it is. There are openings in business, police departments, hospitals and mental health centers, to name but a few. And there is also the possibility of becoming an independent consultant. A word of warning, however: you'd better be good at it. Many people are beginning to give handwriting analysis the credit it deserves, but for most people, you will still have to prove you're not a charlatan every time you do an analysis.

Graphology can help you guard your health. Your handwriting and your physical health are closely related. When you're ill or injured, it affects the smoothness and coordination of your script, and very often an impending illness will show up in handwriting before you're even aware that something is happening to you. As you know, the earlier an illness is spotted, the easier it is to deal with it; and with graphology, you may be the reason someone gets to a doctor for a checkup before a disease has a chance to take hold.

Graphology can help you change your life. Knowing your weaknesses isn't enough, if you have to keep living with them. The question is, can you change what's wrong with your life? The answer is an emphatic *yes*.

Just as your thoughts and feelings can affect the way you form your handwriting, the way you form your handwriting can change your thoughts and feelings. Graphotherapy can be used to effect character and personality changes in anyone who can write. This is not a miracle process: both the preparatory analysis and the therapy procedure take time, and require concentration and hard work on the part of the writer (and, please note, a solid psychological background on the part of the therapist!). But you are how you write—and you can write how you want to be.

When You Are Doing an Analysis

Some Do's:

You will find it helpful to know your subject's age, sex, and present occupation before you start your analysis (though you can work without these, or any facts, if necessary).

What someone is doing with his life can give you clues to the possible causes of stress you may find in his writing; if a writer's lifestyle is in conflict with strong likes and dislikes, he's not going to be able to function adequately.

Knowing the writer's physical sex (male or female) can give you the same kind of information in relation to that person's probable upbringing; it can also reveal points of conflict between what was expected of that person, and what he or she became. Someone who is working in a non-traditional job is going to be taking flak from a less than understanding society, which will affect their personal or professional performance no matter how well they deal with it. The same is true of someone who behaves in a non-traditional manner: in this society, for example, a gentle man or an aggressive woman are also very likely to be in conflict with "what people think." You need to be aware of possible outside pressures on the individual, because they can often be the cause of internal conflict—no matter how well suited that person may be for the lifestyle he or she has chosen.

Of the three, chronological age is the most useful piece of data (though it may sometimes be the hardest to get). A childish script used by a 12-year-old obviously does not have the same implications as a childish script used by someone who is fifty. Even a rough estimate of the writer's age (or age group) can give you some clues as to what might be causing his problems, and also tell you whether those problems are ingrained, or just growing pains. (And a word of caution here, too. *Never* underestimate problems you may find in a child's handwriting. Emotional turmoil can be shattering to someone too young to know how to deal with it—and too inexperienced to know that it can be dealt with.)

It could also be helpful for you to know whether or not the writer was educated in this country (and/or just how literate your correspondent is). Lack of familiarity with the language, or with the skill of writing, can produce variations in script which might be misinterpreted as stress signs or other problem areas. If, for whatever reason, the writer is not familiar with the English script alphabet, you will be limited in at least some of the conclusions you can draw from a sample of his script.

If you can get a longer sample than just the test line, you'll find that useful, too. The more writing, the more data you'll have to work from; also, the more the person writes, the more natural (i.e., the more unselfconscious) his style is likely to be, or become.

To answer a question often asked, it is *not* necessary to know whether your subject is right- or left-handed. The only time handedness does affect the form or style of script is when the writer has been given a hard time about being left-handed—which, fortunately, is happening less and less in our school systems—and in that case it would show up as a sign of emotional stress, or some similar problem in communication.

Some Don'ts:

You will be limited, to some extent, in the conclusions you can draw from the samples you'll be collecting for this study. In the first place, no matter how cooperative your subjects are trying to be be, they will be aware that the sample is for analysis, and are likely, consciously or unconsciously, to be "on their best behavior" when writing it. Essential indicators in a style of handwriting do not change, however, and eventually—with practice, and with the feedback you'll be getting from your subjects—you will learn to compensate for any inadequacies in your samples. But, as you have just proven for yourself, the surface characteristics of handwriting do change; and you should always be cautious about the conclusions you draw from a single, and especially a very short, sample of script.

Since most of your samples will probably come from friends and family, you should also be aware that even for an experienced graphologist, the most difficult analysis to do is of someone you *think* you know very well. Never correct an analysis according to what you think you know somebody "must be like," and certainly, never take the word of a third party. Make every effort to base your conclusions *only* on the handwriting; and whenever your analysis points out traits you feel a particular person "couldn't possibly have," check with the writer. More often than not, your subject will confirm that the analysis was more accurate than your personal impressions.

In the same respect, never base any conclusions on the *content* of a sample of handwriting. If there is a sudden radical change in style in the middle of a longer sample, sometimes reading the words may tell you what caused it. But even that is chancy; you have no way of knowing what really caused the variation, and it could be something totally unrelated to the content. People do write shopping lists even when they're worried about the health of someone close to them, and very often have great difficulty finding the words for what is really bothering them. Again: base your analysis *only* on the formations in the script, and on your knowledge of what those formations mean.

And always be aware that handwriting changes: not just with age, but from moment to moment, mood to mood, sickness to health. Your sample, accurately analyzed, will tell you everything you need to know about the person who wrote it *at the moment of writing*.

Conclusion

Handwriting is a motor-reflex skill which requires eye-hand coordination and fine-muscle control. Like most other motor skills, such as tying your shoelaces, riding a bicycle, or driving a car, it may be easier for some people to learn and more difficult for others. But once it is learned, it becomes automatic, and it is at that point that the individual's character and personality begin to superimpose themselves on the "right way" to perform the skill.

Handwriting changes, but the meanings of the basic penstroke formations which make up the alphabet do not. And once you learn those meanings, you can apply them to any style of script, no matter how unique the writer's means of self-expression.

Principles of the Analysis

No two handwriting styles are alike: the way you form your script is as individual as your fingerprints.(Even without a background in graphology, you can identify the writer of a familiar sample of script). Despite the differences in form and style, there is one consistent factor which applies to any sample of handwriting. Whatever a given individual may know about himself consciously, and however much may be buried in his subconscious, the moment someone picks up a pen and puts it to paper he is aware that this physical gesture is an act of communication. *Handwriting is a means of relating to others*, and the style of your script is influenced both by what you want to say and can't, and what you try to leave unsaid.

In Chapter One we'll be taking a look at what the writer is telling you with his handwriting style.

PART I

The Fundamentals of Handwriting Analysis

1

Organization—
The Style of Script

Who or what runs *your* life? If it isn't you, then no matter what you think you want, your needs and your goals will always take second place. Even if you approve of the monkey on your back (and some people do!), it is still vital that you know exactly what it is, and exactly what it's making you do.

The **organization** or lack of it in a handwriting sample is a picture of the clarity or confusion of the writer's mind at the time of writing. A *well-organized script* indicates that the writer is more likely to make use of his virtues and compensate for his faults, and is therefore more capable of fulfilling his own individual potential. A *disorganized* writer is likely to create conflicts where none exist, or to react inappropriately and sometimes even irrationally, when a choice is called for. In short: a writer who is in control of himself has greater control over his own personal destiny.

(Just for the record: keep in mind that good organization does not necessarily mean a "good" person. *It means that the writer is capable of good planning and self-determination*—traits Moriarty no doubt possessed to the same degree as did Sherlock Holmes! The test for organization asks only one question: *Who's in the driver's seat?* How much control does this writer have over his own mental processes?)

Definition

Organization is the overall arrangement of a script sample. The *internal organization* is made up of the trait indicators and penstroke formations which we will be studying in detail in the following chapters. The way the writer puts all these factors together creates his script *style*.

A judgement of good organization is not necessarily based on legibility, schoolbook neatness, or the artistic quality of the letterforms, though these are all factors which must be taken into account. The criterion for judging organization is *control*. In the purely physical sense, this means control of the pen (the ability to form penstrokes into readable letters and words). In the mental

3

and emotional sense, it means the writer's control over his own behavior: whatever script style the writer has adopted, it must show that he is capable of effectively performing a task (in this case, writing a message) which he has set for himself.

Measuring Organization

Because the purpose of writing is communication, anything which interferes with the writer's ability to communicate should be considered at least a potentially negative organizational factor. From the viewpoint of handwriting analysis, you are actually concerned with how the writer manages to perform a simple task which has a single, definite purpose—and from that, to determine how he is likely to perform a more complicated task which may or may not have an identifiable purpose.

Efficiency is not the sole criterion for judging script, of course, or anything else for that matter. But whenever something irrelevant to an action interrupts, interferes with, or prevents the primary purpose of that action, it most certainly gives an analyst a clear picture of your priorities or problems. Your style of writing is a pattern of behavior; a picture of how you think, and therefore what you are likely to do, under given circumstances.

Here's what you're looking for:

1. A well-organized script shows consistent usage.

Consistency is measured by comparing similar penstrokes or letterforms *to each other*. For example: you compare the angle (or slant) of one letter in script to the angle of other letters; the pen pressure in one part of the sample to the pen pressure in other parts; the penstrokes used to form any given letter to the penstrokes used to form similar letters.

A script style that maintains its own chosen shape or form simply shows someone who knows his own mind. If there are obvious inconsistencies (variations and/or contradictions) in the trait indicators or penstroke usage, you are looking at a picture of mental confusion; if the variations are severe enough, the writer may not even know what is causing his problems.

Variation in penstroke usage can show up in many or all parts of script, such as:

letter size and shape:

slant (or angle):

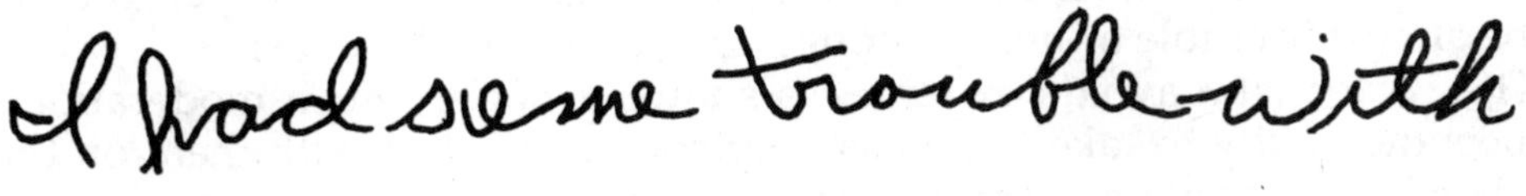

I had some trouble with

pen pressure:

for so many years

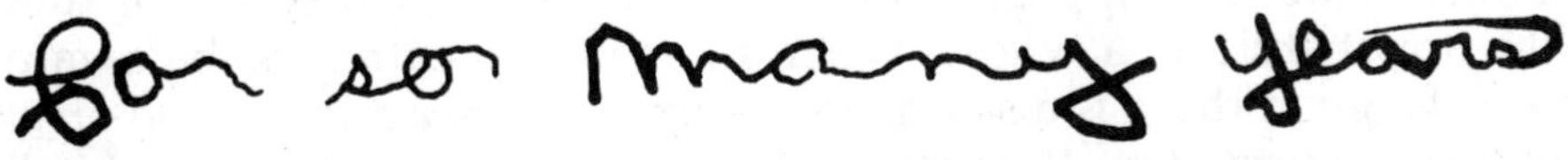

and so forth. If the variation affects only one kind of formation in the handwriting, then the writer is experiencing problems in only that one area of his life. When persistent variations show up in many or all parts of script you are looking at evidence of changeability, inconsistency, instability—in short, a writer who is unpredictable, often even to himself.

Your analysis of each script formation will tell you the cause of the writer's confusion. But an erratic style, and the erratic behavior it illustrates, is one of the surest signs in handwriting of someone who is under stress and unable to cope.

FIGURE 1
Two samples from the opposite ends of the spectrum

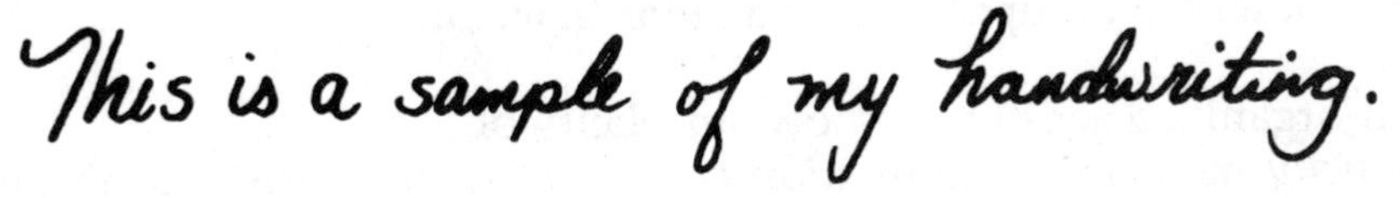

This is a sample of my handwriting.

A clear, well-organized script, showing original formations (i.e., original thought) and definitely independent opinions.

this is a sample of how I

This handwriting has some original formations, too, but we would have to characterize it as confused and disoriented. In this case, poor physical health is at least one of the causative factors, but it is obvious even to the untrained eye that something is troubling this writer.

2. A well-organized script avoids extremes.

An *extreme* in script can be on either side of center. For example: an extreme tilt is one that leans all the way to the right or all the way to the left; extreme size means filling the page or submicroscopic; extreme pen pressure can be almost invisible or heavy enough to cut holes in the paper.

The writer who avoids extremes is showing not so much moderation as balance; the ability to take things as they come, and deal with them on their own level of importance. Any extreme in script, even when it is consistent, shows a writer who is over-reacting to situations or events.

An extreme in handwriting means the same thing as an extreme in behavior, dress, or speech; it identifies a person who has a tendency to go overboard in his actions or reactions, certainly in that area and possibly in others. Like variation, extremes can appear in one or in many parts of script, or they can affect the script style as a whole. When interpreting extremes, be aware that too much of a good thing is also an over-reaction. *Even extremely well-organized script* will show signs that the writer has relinquished control over his life to someone or something else.

FIGURE 2
Extreme Organization

I rather like such a

A formal, stylized script, much more concerned with appearances ("What will people think?") than with content. The organization here is almost professional—I would let this writer engrave my invitations any day—but when it is used in writing a letter it should make you wonder whether or not the writer is sincere. Note the strong right tilt: which contradicts, as you will learn, loops that start in the upper zone (variation in intent).

3. A well-organized script will show simplicity of form.

Simplicity means the elimination of unnecessary or distracting penstroke formations.

Complications in the script (any unnecessary strokes or additions to the letterform) show mental confusion translated into action: the person who cannot get anything done because he is too involved with non-essentials.

For example: knots and ties, fanciful scrolls or curlicues, extra lead-in or ending strokes—any unnecessary ornamentation or accessories to the basic letter form are all things which interfere with the smooth flow of thought. Most people think faster than they can write: if the writer has time to add these unnecessary decorations to his script, then something matters more to him than what he's doing.

The interpretation of script accessories depends on which ones they are and how they're used, but in a general sense, "stalling strokes," and/or distracting ornamentation are signs of indecision, pretense, or confusion on the part of the writer.

FIGURE 3
Unnecessary Accessories to Script

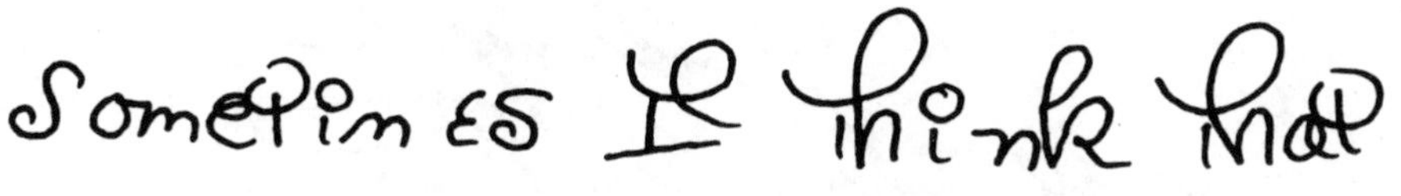

Sometimes I think that (handwritten)

Extra strokes and an attempt, at least, at elegance. The circled i-dots are something this writer has probably seen somewhere else and copied as a way of being artistic and different. The script style shows someone who will try anything to be noticed.

4. A well-organized script will show an overall clarity of style.

The *style* of a script sample is a graphic picture of the writer's thought processes. Clearly formed, clearly legible script shows clarity of thought and a desire to be understood (and very often someone whose script is normally illegible will resort to print to get an important message across). Tangled, scribbled over, or jerky writing shows tangled, confused, or erratic thought (though note: some jerky pen strokes can also be a sign of physical pain). Missing t-bars and i-dots and missing or improper punctuation (in a writer who knows the rules of grammar) are signs of carelessness and a lack of attention to details. An illegible scrawl, no matter how well organized, indicates that the writer doesn't give a damn whether or not you understand him; a form that is too correct, on the other hand, may show immaturity or conformity (in either case, an inability or unwillingness to think for yourself). A flourished script that is nonetheless smooth-flowing and readable shows originality and flair; if it's crude, it can show anything from insecurity to dishonesty.

Look at the overall style of a handwriting sample as though it were a self-portrait drawn by the writer to illustrate his thoughts: a picture of the mind at work.

FIGURE 4
Sample Styles, and the Picture They Draw

you think and because sometimes (handwritten)

Tangled script, showing confusion, depression, instability.

this is how I write (handwritten)

Cooperative and conforming; also somewhat immature.

Flamboyant but crude. This writer is putting up a front.

Sensitive, reserved, defensive.

Conclusion

The general organization of a script sample, good or bad, tells you how the writer manages to integrate all his traits, abilities, and characteristics and make them work—for him, or against him.

Graphology rates character and personality traits as being positive or negative *for that writer*. A given trait is considered **positive** if it is *beneficial* to the writer; i.e., if it helps the writer to cope with events and/or achieve his goals. A trait is **negative** if it is *detrimental* to that writer; if it interferes with his ability to function effectively. You are not concerned here with moral judgements (whether the trait makes the writer a "good" person or a "bad" person); only with whether or not a given trait is good or bad *for that writer*.

Poor organization in script means that positive traits will be less effective, negative traits more prominent—and sometimes actively dangerous, both to the writer and to those with whom he comes in contact. The *control* mirrored in good organization is not a matter of self-restraint, but of self-determination: the general style of a sample tells you whether or not the writer is in charge of his own life, and how well he can work within his own capabilities and limitations.

Principles of the Analysis

A slip of the pen, like a slip of the tongue, can be revealing; but it can also be a simple mistake that has no significance whatsoever. In judging script organization, you will be forming a conclusion about the writer which will influence the rest of your analysis. That being the case, there is one basic rule of thumb you should always keep in mind. *No one indicator in script is signifi-*

cant in and of itself. Minor irregularities in form, occasional variations in style, and even illegible writing under certain circumstances, can all be classed as controlled script. Each individualized variation is a clue to character and personality, but all these clues have to be put together to form a coherent picture of the writer as a person.

Every script sample you see will show some of the signs of disorganization we have discussed in this chapter. People do not have a machine-like precision over their control of the pen, after all, and everybody has problems of one kind or another. So before you judge any formation significant, it should be *habitual* on the part of the writer (repeated throughout the entire script). Unless there are at least three and preferably more *consistently* negative signs in a script, the handwriting would still qualify as having good organization.

Review

Well-organized script shows consistent and moderate formations and evenness of pen pressure; simplicity of form (lack of ornamentation); the inclusion of necessary accessories (i-dots and t-bars, and clarifying punctuation); clarity of style; and general readability.

Poorly-organized script shows continual variations in some or many formations (stress); extremes of any kind (over-reacting to life); missing punctuation and/or i-dots (carelessness, lack of concentration, lack of attention to detail); and/or tangled script, blotched, full of corrections, or crude in formation (confused thought, careless indifference, poor planning, perhaps even feelings of guilt).

Any script can show minor variations and still be considered well-organized: for a script to be rated poorly organized, it must consistently show three or more negative traits.

Beginning the Analysis—Handwriting Organization

Theoretical knowledge is all well and good, but this is a how-to text. Let's see how the theory applies to actual samples of handwriting.

The following examples were all done according to the technical guidelines laid down in the Preface. Since they were written for analysis, keep in mind that they might be a little more careful than the writers' natural style (i.e., the writers were probably on their "best behavior" when writing these samples).

All four writers are about the same age (late 20s to early 30s); two are men and two are women. That's all you need to know for now. Let's see what just their handwriting tells us.

SAMPLE ONE (see page 10)

This is certainly a controlled script, by all the standards you've just been given. There are very slight variations in the way the letters slant; the difference in size between the d or t and other tall letters is traditional (American Schoolbook teaches that variation as the "right way" to do it). No complica-

SAMPLE ONE

This is a sample of the way I normally write.

I would like to know what my handwriting tells

about me.

SAMPLE TWO

This is a sample of the way I normally

write. I would like to know what my

handwriting tells about me.

tions, no ornamentation, and except for the size, no extremes; and all necessary accessories (punctuation, i-dots and t-bars, etc.) are precisely in place. The only formation that stands out as different is the undersized pronoun I in the first sentence, but since identity words are measured in a slightly different manner than other formations in script, we're going to leave that out of our calculations for now. Based only on what you know this is excellent organization, and you would have to conclude that this writer has him (or her)self well under control—if maybe too well.

SAMPLE TWO (see page 10)

This writing appears uneven and irregular at first glance, but if you look closely you will notice that, despite the over-blown letters and the general ungainliness in the style, the script is reasonably consistent and contains no unnecessary complications. This writer may give the appearance of not having it all together, but despite signs that s/he is occasionally under stress (minor variations in style), seems to be handling it well. You are looking at another example of good organization.

SAMPLE THREE (see page 12)

This is a very graceful, flowing script, but the only thing consistent in it is the pressure. Variations are minor and not immediately obvious, but they exist in almost every factor in the script. Note: variations in letter size, word spacing, and slant; original but unnecessary loops and curls; and even a tendency to illegibility ("handwritiy"?), which in this case must be called carelessness. This writer's problems are not so severe that s/he can't handle them, and s/he is covering up well (the graceful script begins to look like someone who's putting a good face on a bad job!); but very few things in his/her life are going the way s/he wants them to. Because the poor organization is not extreme, we can assume that writer number three is still on top of things, but this is a situation that could go either way.

SAMPLE FOUR (see page 12)

Stress signs in this script are largely identity problems (variation in style). Note the capital-letter insertions, especially in the middle of a word ("aBout"). Occasional missing i-dots show some carelessness, and we would have to consider at least the possibility of a communication problem (note the tight little knots on some of the lower case letters, and the extra strokes on the ends of some words). We also have to consider that for someone in the 20- to 30-age range, this is a very immature style (Schoolform usage), so whatever this writer's problems, s/he is not growing to meet them. It's not exactly poor organization, but neither is this the handwriting of someone capable of running his/her own life.

SAMPLE THREE

This is a sample of the way I normally write —
I would like to know what my handwriting
tells about me.

SAMPLE FOUR

This is a sample of the way I normally
write. I would like to know what my
handwriting tells about me.

Exercise for Chapter One

Classify each sample of script you have collected as having good or poor organization (and remember that you need more "proof" for a negative judgement).

Answer the question: Do you think each of your writers is in charge of his or her own life, or does it look like something else may be calling the shots?

In the following chapters, we will break down script style into its component parts: the major trait indicators, and the penstroke formations. We'll also begin to build an outline that you can use in doing your own analyses.

TEST YOURSELF

For each of the five script samples given below, identify at least one positive and one negative organizational indicator and give its meaning. Our answers are in Appendix B.

SAMPLE ONE

I wanted to see if I could

SAMPLE TWO

Today I feel so good about

SAMPLE THREE

my main problem is dueed

SAMPLE FOUR

I need to know if they are

SAMPLE FIVE

I sometimes wonder if anyone

2

Direction—
The Baseline of Script

How do you feel about the way your life is going? And, more important, how do you feel about your ability to decide where it's going to go?

The **baseline** of a handwriting sample tells you whether or not the writer has *adequate guidelines*: if he feels competent to make decisions, and if he feels secure in the decisions he has made.

The *shape* of the baseline tells you whether or not the writer feels he can succeed at whatever he tries to do (i.e., how much he trusts his ability to run his own life, make decisions, and perform tasks). The *direction* of the baseline tells you how he feels about the way life in general is likely to treat him (i.e., whether or not he believes that "fate" is likely to influence or interfere with what he tries to do).

Definition

The baseline of any line of writing (script, print, or type) is that part of letters or words which *should* rest on the line if the writer were using lined paper. It includes the base (or bottom) of most letters of the alphabet, plus the connecting strokes which form them into words. Those letters which have lower loops (called *descenders*), such as g, y, and p, normally drop below the baseline: descenders are ignored when measuring this script indicator.

The internal formation of a handwritten line is rarely as straight as a line of type, even on lined paper. That means its baseline is not straight either. *The baseline of a sample of script is the path followed across the page by the base (or bottom) of individual letters, excluding descenders, and their connecting penstrokes.*

Measuring Baseline

There are two measurements for baseline: the overall formation (the **direction** of the line of writing as a whole), and the internal formation (the **shape** of the baseline; or the actual path the individual letters take across the page).

15

To measure the overall formation, place the straight edge of a ruler against the base of the first letter and the base of the last letter in a line of script, and draw a light pencil rule across the page, connecting those two points. This will give you the *direction* of the baseline: up, down, or level.

Almost all script samples will vary internally to some degree from that straight line. To get a clearer picture of the *shape* of the baseline, draw another light pencil rule that touches the bottom of each letter (excluding descenders) in the line of script. (See: Figure 1, below.)

(*Study Note*: It is a good idea to draw in all measuring lines described in this section; you'll find that they highlight discrepancies in the script that you might have missed without them. However, you will also find that just the measuring lines described in the first few chapters will pretty much scribble up your samples! Fortunately, there is a way for you to have your cake and eat it too. Use a piece of fine (very clear) tracing paper as a cover sheet for your samples. Tape the tracing paper across the top of each page only; this will hold it in place, and still allow you to lift it to look at your sample. Draw your measurement lines only on the tracing paper to preserve the integrity of your originals.)

What You Are Measuring

You are trying to determine (a) if and how far the letters stray from the overall baseline (the straight line); and (b) whether or not the overall baseline is parallel to the top and bottom of the page.

FIGURE 1
Sample Baselines

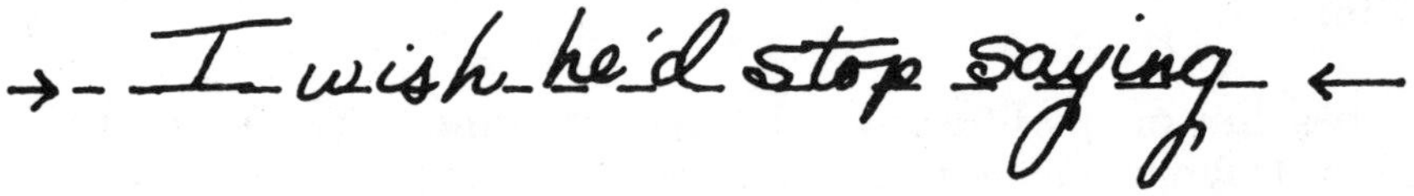

A Steady Baseline

An Erratic Baseline

Organizational Factors

All other things being equal, a steady, level baseline is considered a positive organizational indicator.

A *steady* baseline (where the internal shape remains fairly straight) indicates that the writer has a clear sense of objectives. A *level* baseline (one which stays fairly parallel to the top and bottom of the page) indicates a realistic approach to life's situations. The person who writes this way may encounter as many problems as anyone else, but he believes in his ability—and, more important, he believes in his right—to make decisions that will affect the course of his own life.

Negative organizational factors for all the major trait indicators will be either extremes or variations. For baseline, when the internal shape is too straight (i.e., rigid), that constitutes an **extreme**, and should be considered a potentially negative organizational indicator. Like any other extreme, it's an over-reaction: the writer who uses a rigid baseline is someone who needs to believe that his guidelines are the only right answer.

Variation is also an internal measure: when the baseline wavers along its length, it indicates feelings of insecurity. As with all other script factors, this is a matter of degree. Even the most successful people will have occasional self-doubts; it's also possible for someone who has always felt secure in his choices suddenly to begin to experience such doubts following a radical change in his life (such as retirement, illness, or divorce). In Figure 1 above, the slight tendency to indecision shown in the first sample is still an indication that this writer has good control over his life; the erratic baseline in the second sample shows confusion, emotional ups and downs and self-doubt, and the inability to cope with challenges or change—and it would qualify as a factor indicating poor organization.

An upslant or downslant in the overall direction of the baseline should also be interpreted as a variation; in this case indicating that the writer expects life to somehow influence its own course independent of his control. A level baseline is considered a positive organizational factor, since it shows that the writer's moods or feelings are usually less influenced by outside events, or by his expectations of what whose events are likely to be.

These are the types of baselines and their meanings:

A. The Shape of the Baseline: Internal Organization
1. *Rigid*: The baseline is as perfectly straight as a line of type.

This is hard to do even on lined paper, and it takes a special effort to make the baseline so absolutely perfect. The person who writes this way never allows himself to doubt, never questions his own motives, never hesitates in making a decision. It must be nice to always be so sure of yourself! But what do you do if you are suddenly confronted by a situation in which your rules don't work?

The rigid baseline indicates a writer who is literally walking a tightrope. He cannot afford a single misstep, because he cannot permit himself to be wrong.

2. *Steady* (or *Firm*): The baseline is fairly straight, though there may be either slight or occasional irregularity.

→ *I wish he'd stop saying* ←

This slight waver is normal, especially on unlined paper. And occasional self-doubts are also normal, and even healthy, since it never hurts once in a while to question your own motives or critically review your own progress.

Within the line of script, the firmer the baseline, the firmer the writer's sense of objectives: the more clearly he can visualize what he wants to do, and the more certain he is that what he is doing and the way he is doing it is right for him, and these are the requisites for doing it well. Most baselines will vary to some extent, or at least some of the time: within a steady baseline, however, a slight irregularity means that the writer can make a mistake, and is aware of it.

3. *Waver*: Some letters dip below the line or float above it. The baseline is still fairly steady (the writer is obviously aware of and is following an invisible guideline), but the irregularity is more pronounced.

→ *About me. I will be glad* ←

When the baseline wavers, it means that the writer has doubts or questions about his goals, profession, or lifestyle. As we discussed above, a baseline waver can occur following a radical change in the person's life; most often, it indicates conflict with established guidelines (i.e., the person who has chosen a lifestyle or goals which are in conflict with society's norms). When enough people tell you you're wrong, you may still do what you think is right, but you are going to feel that you're on shaky ground! And it's also a fact that when you step outside established rules, you have to create your own guidelines, and a person in this position may always question just how valid and useful those guidelines are. *These minor doubts are normal*, and if not extreme (see below, Erratic), they do not impede the writer's ability to function. But they do mean that the writer has serious questions about his ability to succeed, and however successful he may actually be, there will always be that undercurrent of self-doubt.

4. *Temporary Fluctuations*: One-time or occasional variations inside a given baseline shape.

a. *Baseline Bounce*: A section of the line, perhaps even an entire word or phrase, curves or jumps upward; the remainder of the baseline keeps its usual form.

— love that town ! How's your —

You may see a lot of this in your samples. A sudden baseline bounce is the script equivalent of a giggle. It means that at the moment of writing, the writer experienced a feeling of elation, or just thought something was funny.

b. *Baseline Sag*: A section of the line curves or dips below the baseline.

sometimes means just

This is a sign of *depression*: at the moment of writing, the writer was reminded of something that is making him unhappy.

Note that both the bounce and the sag are smooth formations, and that the rest of the baseline retains whatever is its normal shape. In either case, then, we are talking about an *event*: a specific set of circumstances that the writer can probably identify for you. You can mention in passing that you see the writer finds something funny (bounce), or that something's got him down in the dumps (sag), but unless these formations start showing up regularly, they do not indicate any questions or doubts about the way he's running his life.

What if they do show up regularly? The bounce means happiness; the sag means depression. The more often they appear, and/or the more pronounced they are when they do appear, the greater the importance of the event or set of circumstances in the writer's life which is causing them.

4. *Erratic*: The baseline jumps all over the place. [*Note*: the pronounced waver is judged erratic when the baseline variation begins to affect the internal organization of the sample (letter formation and usage).]

→ But for me it's not enough ←

Ever ride a roller-coaster? Even when you do it for fun, it's still a scary experience. Imagine what it would be like if the entire direction of your life continually felt that way, and you couldn't even be sure if there was anybody or anything at the controls! The erratic baseline shows confusion, emotional ups and downs and self-doubt, and the inability to cope with challenge or change. The feeling is called *insecurity*, and it's the most common form of fear there is. The person who writes like this feels that his life has no coherent direction at all; and that he has no idea what to do about it.

B. The *Direction* of the Baseline: Overall Formation.

This measurement considers the general direction of the entire line of script, no matter what the internal organization. There are three possible directions a baseline can take:

1. *Level*: The line of script is horizontal, and both the beginning and the end of the line are roughly parallel to the top and bottom of the page.

This writer is realistic, and he tends to be as level-headed about fate and luck as his writing shows. He understands that life normally has its ups and downs, and he depends on his own efforts to get him where he wants to go. And if he does not succeed, his attitude is likely to be that he has no one to blame but himself.

The level baseline is also considered good organization because it is the "right," and logical, way to place a line of writing on a page. It is evidence of planning ability: the line of writing follows the shape of the page on which it's written.

2. *Upswing*: The line of script slants or curves upward; it ends higher on the page than it began.

This writer is an optimist. No matter what goes on in his life, he believes that eventually everything is going to work out for the best. Depending on other factors in his script, this may mean that he is more able to take disappointments in stride. He may also be kidding himself.

3. *Downswing*: The line of script slants or curves downward; it ends lower on the page than it began.

This writer is a pessimist. He suspects that no matter what his efforts, the bottom is likely to drop out from under him; no matter what happens in his life, he expects the worst. As a result, he is hardly ever disappointed. He is also hardly ever content.

Variant Samples

Under this heading, whereever applicable, we will discuss samples which are not written to test-line specifications. These are called "natural" samples: the writer's own message using his own materials and writing tools. You'll be seeing more of these, in the course of your career as a graphologist, than you will the "laboratory" samples written for you to study. And you have to know how to interpret them.

There is a reason we ask for the study samples to be written on unlined paper. On lined paper, the writer has guidelines to help him do the job "right": the rules are both a crutch and a restraint. A sample written on unlined paper is more natural, and both baseline problems and individual idiocyncrasies will show up more clearly when the writer is winging it.

Some people normally prefer to use lined paper, or may simply use it because it's available. So: how do you read a sample written on lined paper?

1. The person who prefers to write on lined paper has a greater need for guidelines in performing a task (*Note*: This does not mecessarily mean that he can't think for himself. It's a case of either/or: he may be someone who is afraid or unable to function without guidelines in any area of his life; or, he may be a complete innovator in his personal and/or professional life and revert to guidelines for simple tasks, like writing, because enough is enough! Other signs in the script will reveal which is the case.)

2. Any irregularities in the baseline on lined paper should be considered more extreme than the same irregularities on unlined paper. It means that the person has trouble following the guidelines he has elected to use.

3. An erratic baseline on lined paper means the writer is in a lot of trouble. He can't cope even when he has clear guidelines to follow; either because he doesn't understand how to use them, or because he's fighting them hysterically. The use of lined paper is a recommended therapy technique for an erratic baseline; and many people who can't write a straight line instinctively choose to use lined paper for just that reason. If the rules don't straighten out the baseline, then your subject needs more help than you can give.

4. The same guideline conflict judgement holds true for paper that has a printed marginal rule: but again, it's a matter of degree. If your subject occa-

sionally over-writes a right marginal rule, it can be minor evidence of poor planning (i.e., the writer misjudged the length of his line). Left marginal rules, however, are as much evidence of established guidelines as the baseline: the writer who consistently uses paper with a left marginal rule and then consistently ignores it has an unconscious, and sometimes spiteful, grudge against "authority."

Conclusion: *Interpreting Baseline*

Internal formations (shape) and overall formations (direction) should be considered as two separate indicators: any or all of the internal formations we've described can appear within any or all of the overall line directions. (The bounce and sag should be considered separately; they can appear inside the internal formations.) In doing the analysis, you combine the meanings of these two indicators by adding the interpretation of the one to the interpretation of the other. For example:

1. Baseline waver (some self-doubts or questions) inside a level line (realistic outlook): "I might blow it, but I've got as good a chance of winning as losing."

2. Baseline waver inside an upswing line (generally optimistic attitude): "I may not always know what I'm doing, but I'm sure things will work out okay anyway."

3. Baseline waver inside a downswing line (general pessimism): "I'm not sure I'm doing this right, and eventually I'm going to be in big trouble."

The meaning of the indicator by itself does not change. A baseline waver *always* means some self-doubt—how much self-doubt depending on how pronounced the waver. The interpretation of line directions also stays the same. But, as you can see, how indicators are combined does affect what they mean in terms of *that writer*.

When you are doing the analysis, remember that no one trait stands alone. Two problems can make each other worse; a strength can modify or even overcome a weakness. Each trait the writer has will influence and slightly alter the effect of every other trait you find in his handwriting.

Principles of the Analysis

Direction: The baseline of script tells you if the writer feels he knows where his life is going. Your analysis will reveal whether or not the writer has guidelines he can trust and follow; and whether those guidelines are too strict, too loosely defined, or too far removed from his reality to be of any use to him.

The question you are trying to answer is this: Does this person feel he has achievable goals? And does he believe in his ability to achieve them?

To Review

Let's begin to build an outline that you can use as a guideline in doing your own analyses:

ANALYSIS OUTLINE

I. BASELINE (Does this person feel able to run his own life?)
  A. Internal Formations (How is he coping with events in his life?)
    1. Rigid (Does not permit himself any doubts)
    2. Steady (Clear sense of objectives; able to live with and learn from his mistakes)
    3. Waver (Some doubts or questions about his decisions or general goals)
    4. Temporary Fluctuations (Passing moods)
      a. Bounce (A feeling of elation; a memory of something that makes him happy or amuses him)
      b. Sag (A feeling of depression; a memory of something that is going wrong or saddens him)
    5. Erratic (Emotional ups and downs; confusion about goals; self-doubt; insecurity)
  B. Overall Formations (How does he feel about life in general?)
    1. Level (Realistic)
    2. Upswing (Optimistic)
    3. Downswing (Pessimistic)

Doing the Analysis—Baseline

Let's add baseline to our analysis of our volunteer subjects:

SAMPLE ONE (see page 24)

Baseline Shape: *rigid*
Baseline Direction: *level*
We suggested that this writer might have himself too well under control; the rigid baseline certainly confirms that. This is a person who sets his own standards and believes in them implicitly. He is realistic about the way life is likely to treat him (level), but he cannot allow *himself* the luxury of making any mistakes.

SAMPLE TWO (see page 24)

Baseline Shape: *pronounced sag; otherwise steady*
Baseline Direction: *level (but downslant last line)*
This writer knows pretty much what he wants out of life, but he is not particularly happy about the way things are going. The more pronounced the sag, the more important the cause of the depression, remember; that, combined with the slight tendency to downslant in the last line would seem to indicate that whatever is wrong, this writer does not expect it to get much better. We would have to say that this person knows what he wants and is sure it's right for him, but that some very significant element in his life is not going well.

SAMPLE ONE

This is a sample of the way I normally write.

I would like to know what my handwriting tells

about me.

SAMPLE TWO

This is a sample of the way I normally

write. I would like to know what my

handwriting tells about me.

SAMPLE THREE (see page 26)

Baseline Shape: *fairly steady; waver is mostly sag*
Baseline Direction: *slight (controlled) upswing, all lines*
Again, this is someone who feels that he knows how to run his own life, but is not particularly happy about something important; unlike our second writer, though, this person does believe that somehow, someway, things will work out for the best.

We rated this script as possibly poor organization, though, because of variations, however slight, which affect almost every indicator. That makes the sag in the baseline more significant (i.e., it may be that what he's unhappy about is the way that his life is going in general). It also makes the upswing a possibly more negative factor than it's mild nature might suggest; if writer number three is half-expecting the cavalry to come over the hill, we might wonder if he's doing anything positive to deal with his problems.

SAMPLE FOUR (see page 26)

Baseline Shape: *firm with occasional sag*
Baseline Direction: *level*
We noted stress signs in this script; we also noted elements of immaturity. Now we add that this writer believes his life is going the way it should (the single sag in the first line, with the very slight repetition in the second line would indicate that whatever this writer is unhappy about, it's probably situational). If this writer does have problems, they are not with his goals; right now his life is going where he wants it to.

Exercise for Chapter Two
For each sample you have collected, draw in the baseline. State the type of internal formation (shape) and what it means; state the type of overall formation (direction) and what it means. Combine the two indicators and write out your analysis conclusions.

Describe how your analysis of the baseline supports, contradicts, or explains your judgement of script organization. In the next chapter, we'll find out how our subjects deal with other people.

SAMPLE THREE

This is a sample of the way I normally write—

I would like to know what my handwriting

tells about me.

SAMPLE FOUR

This is a sample of the way I normally

write. I would like to know what my

handwriting tells about me.

TEST YOURSELF

For each of the five script samples given below, draw in the baseline (direction *and* shape). Name the baseline type(s) and give their meanings. Our answers are in Appendix B.

SAMPLE ONE

I wonder if perhaps he

SAMPLE TWO

This is a sample of the way I

SAMPLE THREE

For my part, I want to thank

SAMPLE FOUR

My house lies on a half

SAMPLE FIVE

tell me what my handwriting

3

Communication— The Angle of Script

Is anybody out there listening to you? What do you want them to hear?

The **angle** of script tells you how the writer feels about his ability to deal with other people. And the ability to deal with other people is not the same as the ability to make friends or even the desire to have them. It is the essence of your ability to *communicate*: to send and receive clear signals that put you in touch with the people who make up your world.

The *direction* of the tilt (right, left, or vertical) tells you the writer's need to relate to others, or avoid them; the *degree* of tilt (moderate to extreme) tells you the intensity of that need.

Definition

The angle of handwriting (also called tilt or slant) is the direction in which the letters lean: to the right, to the left, or vertical. When the top, or highest point, of the letters in a line is further right than the bottom of those same letters, the script is called right-angle; when the top of letters is left of their bottom points, the script is left-angle. The letters on this typewritten page are vertical (straight up and down).

Measuring Angle

Script angle is measured from the baseline. To determine the degree of tilt, first draw the overall baseline (as explained in Chapter Two). The straight baseline is your horizontal measure, and the direction and degree of tilt will be measured only against that horizontal:

FIGURE 1
Angle is measured from the Baseline

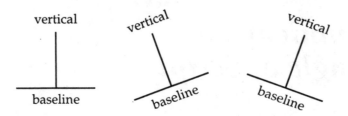

Next, lay your ruler down alongside script *ascenders* (the upper zone; such as the top part of the d, l, or t) and *descenders* (the lower zone; such as the bottom loop of the g) and draw a light rule showing the direction and degree of tilt. For letters without ascenders or descenders, those with at least one straight side, such as the a, i, m, and n can also be measured for tilt if necessary. It's a good idea to take the angle measure at several points in each line of script, since the angle can vary. (Caution: don't draw your rule *through* the letter itself; this will interfere with your analysis of letter shape and form later on. See Figure 2, below.)

What You Are Measuring

You are trying to determine which way most of the letters lean (direction), and how far they tilt away from the vertical (degree).

FIGURE 2
Sample Angle Measurements

This is how I form my writing. Baseline

A Right-Angle Script

I like working with my hands and Baseline

A Left-Angle Script

If you like, you can make your own Angle Measure by tracing the diagram in Figure 3 below on a piece of clear plastic; the measure can be laid down on top of a line of script to give you a quick estimate of the degree of tilt. Match the baseline in the measure with the baseline of your sample, and be sure to follow any upslant or downslant in order to get a correct reading.

FIGURE 3
Angle Measure

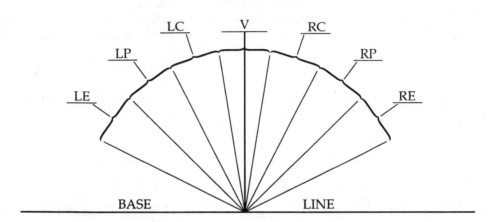

Briefly, a right tilt is other-oriented, the vertical tilt tends to be self-sufficient, and a left-leaning tilt shows a writer who is drawing back from outside contacts. Within the direction of the tilt, right or left, we rate the degree as being either *controlled* (RC/LC), *pronounced* (RP/LP), or *extreme* (RE/LE). The further right a script tilts, the more important other people are to the writer; the further left it leans, the more that writer is shutting other people out of his life.

(Note: The sharp division pictured between the degrees of tilt is somewhat hypothetical; the Angle Measure is not an exact tool but a general guide. Whenever you're in doubt as to the "exact" measure of the angle, you will have to pick up clues from other signs in the script to confirm or correct your tilt analysis.)

Organizational Factors

For Angle, a consistent tilt somewhere between LC and RC would be classified as good organization. Not everybody wants other people in their lives, so a slight left tilt, though it indicates negative communication, is not necessarily a negative organizational factor. Any controlled tilt indicates that the writer can cope with the demands other people make on his life and still maintain his own sense of identity and purpose.

An **extreme tilt** shows someone who is overreacting to the effects of their contacts with others. There is more leeway in a right tilt (i.e., a tilt to the left becomes extreme before a tilt to the right) because this language, and especially in this country, encourages a right tilt to begin with (even in printing. Which way do you slant italics?). In the case of a right tilt, over-reaction means increased dependence on others, in the case of left tilt, it means increased withdrawal.

A **variable tilt** is a picture of what psychology calls an "approach-avoidance" conflict: the writer who cannot make up his mind whether to be outgoing or reserved. Most scripts will waver to some extent, and for no other reason than that the writer's hand is in a different position against the paper as his pen moves across the line. So before you judge a tilt variable, it should show a pronounced swing from right to left and back again.

Now let's take a more careful look at what each degree of tilt tells us about the writer. As with the Baseline, we'll look at the script in terms of the people who are writing it:

A. Angle Right

A right-angled script is used by writers who are other-oriented: interested in people and events outside themselves.

1. *Controlled Right:*

The controlled-right tilt shows someone who gets along well with other people; this writer is able to express his own ideas, and is interested in the ideas of others. Such a person is basically friendly, and can be warm and affectionate; but his behavior is controlled by his intelligence, rather than his emotions, and his self-image is internal, rather than dependent on support or approval from others.

Graphology calls this the "ideal" tilt (and "ideal" does not mean nicest, or smartest, or best: it simply indicates a greater ability to cope). The controlled-right shows rational behavior and unoppressive self-control. The person who writes this way may have as many problems communicating as anyone else, but he basically likes others and gets along reasonably well with them. If included in social activities, he can enjoy himself without going overboard; and if he can't make a connection with someone else, he doesn't take it as a reflection on his own value as a person.

2. *Pronounced Right:*

With a pronounced-right tilt, you have a writer who is much more interested in others, much more expressive of his thoughts and feelings, and who has a greater need for the company of others. He likes parties, social and community activities, and getting involved. Such a writer can also be sympathetic and affectionate, but while the pronounced tilt still retains a fair measure of self-control, its user also tends to be more emotional, and more likely to indulge in impulsive behavior. Depending on other signs in the script (and remember: you can *want* to jump in but be afraid you can't swim!), these writers are people who generally prefer to spend their energies on activities involving others; they do not like to be alone, need lots of praise and a return of the attention and affection they give; and they tend to judge both others and themselves more by feelings than by facts.

3. *Extreme Right*

The extreme-tilt writer is less rational and more excitable. He doesn't simply want other people in his life; he depends on them for ego-support and for guidelines in building his own self-image. Insecurity is a dominant trait which can be expressed in many ways, and jealousy is often one of them: most people who write this way (but not all; check for other signs) are also extremely sensitive. The extreme-right tilt shows a writer who laughs and cries easily, is much more impulsive in decisions and reactions, and much more demonstrative about likes and dislikes. Such people can be unstable and unpredictable in behavior; they are trying to pick up their cues on how they "should" act from what they sense as the approval or disapproval of the people around them, and they are much more likely to put on a mask (to adopt a personality they think others will admire). This writer can latch onto someone else with a smothering grip, and can therefore sometimes be forcibly rejected; he needs help in understanding that the security he's are looking for must come from within, not from others.

4. *Very Extreme Right*

Even extremes have extremes: the further right the tilt, the more totally dependent the writer is on other people for ego-support. When the right tilt lays down flat, you're dealing with someone who has lost control. Unless there are tempering positive signs in other elements of the script, this type of writer can be an hysteric, capable of intense and sometimes dangerous emotional outbursts, unpredictable and erratic behavior, and violent jealousy. Such people are ruled almost entirely by their emotions, which can range from intense excitement to black despair; they wear themselves out and demand too much of others. They get over-involved, over-stimulated, over-excited. The problem is that they don't really know what it is they are running to, they just know they want to get there in the fastest way possible; it's also very important to them to make sure they are not "left out" of anything. They are exhausting to live with, and it's difficult if not impossible to explain to them that they are actively alienating, by the intensity of their emotional demands, the very people whose attention and support they are trying to gain. This writer should be dealt with carefully: it won't take much to push him over the edge.

B. Angle Vertical

The vertical writer is self-sufficient, and usually self-contained. This is not to say that he has no interest in anyone or anything else. But he can get along without you very well and often prefers to.

The qualifying factor in a vertical script (moderate to extreme) cannot be determined from the tilt; it must be deduced from emotional signs, such as self-doubt (baseline), sensitivity (loops, Chapter 7), or self-limiting factors (size, Chapter 4).

Vertical writers tend to be impersonal in their dealings with others. Whatever they may feel, their actions are totally controlled by intellect; they have a reason for everything they do, and their aim is to make sense out of their environment. Such writers are not only in control of themselves, but generally tend to have greater control over people and events about them as well. They are not necessarily domineering—you have to feel involvement with something in order to want to run it! They are simply more effective, because they are less personally affected, when dealing with outside events. Vertical writers can appear friendly and sociable when necessity demands it, but they tend to keep their own feelings out of most relationships, and both warmth and enthusiasm are restricted to special people and special events. Dominant traits in this script are independence and pride; interests tend to be intellectual and reactions business-like; and for many people, the vertical writer is difficult to really get to know.

C. Angle Left

A left-angled script is used by writers who prefer not to let others get too close. They may be shy, or they may be cold, or they may be frightened; but they are drawing away from close personal contacts: "None for me, thanks."

1. *Controlled Left*

The controlled-left tilt is not badly inhibited; in fact, such writers may not even be aware that they're introverted. Certainly other people will not be aware of it; this writer tends to be judged by others as cold, uninvolved, uncaring. And nothing could be further from the truth. The controlled-left writer can sometimes make himself appear outgoing on the surface, but, unlike the vertical writer who will be friendly when such behavior is plausible, the left-tilt writer finds outgoing behavior uncomfortable. Such writers are very cautious in establishing relationships with others; they feel isolated in crowds, and they find it difficult to communicate and difficult to trust other people. Shyness and reticence are among their traits, and as a result most other people will see them as unfriendly.

2. *Pronounced Left*

As the tilt goes further left, the discomfort in crowds and dislike of social activity becomes almost claustrophobic. With the pronounced-left tilt, we begin to see signs of fear as a reason for inhibition and introversion. Remember that you are dealing with a problem in communication: these writers often cannot tell anyone how they feel; they're certain that they will be misunderstood, and because of their reticence often are, which only adds to their feelings of rejection. The pronounced-left writer experiences greater insecurity, is more uncomfortable around people, and is literally defending himself against any possible hurt by pulling back from outside contact.

3. *Extreme Left*

Once the tilt left becomes extreme, fear—of others, and of being hurt—becomes a dominant factor in behavior and reactions. This writer often finds it difficult if not impossible to express himself adequately or function effectively; dealing with others, even on impersonal topics, is a painful and emotionally agonizing experience. The person who writes inward may also, very often, turn feelings of rejection inward ("There must be something wrong with me."); so in addition to the inability to communicate, this person will be unhappy and despondent. In an otherwise well-organized script, the writer may be aware of the reasons for his loneliness, but the awareness doesn't help much. In a less well-organized script, the extreme-left writer can be very suspicious of others. Whichever the case, such writers almost always have the feeling that they are not really wanted or liked.

4. *Very Extreme Left*

When the extreme-left tilt lies down flat, the writer *knows* he's not wanted. Here you are dealing with someone who is afraid of others and afraid of life, and certain only that whatever else happens, and whatever he may do, he's going to get hurt. This script comes close to total withdrawal; such writers find it almost impossible to function at all in either personal or business relationships, and only rarely do they find the strength or the conviction to make a success of what they try to do. Like the very extreme-right tilt, you are looking at someone who has lost control of himself, and who feels that he has lost control of his environment; but in this case, since the condemnation is turned inward, the very extreme-left tilt pictures a writer who is fearful and unhappy, usually extremely self-critical, and sometimes even suicidal.

D. Angle Variable

An inconsistent tilt shows someone who can't make up his mind what kind of person he should be; how he should feel about others, or how he should react.

As we noted above, any tilt may vary slightly just as the pen moves across the page; you judge the tilt variable if it changes direction more often than it stays the same. Tilt variation can be either moderate or extreme.

1. *Moderate Variation*

A moderate variation is one that stays inside a single direction, but varies from controlled to pronounced, from pronounced to extreme, or even from controlled to extreme.

In effect, this writer is trying to find his center of balance. He may know that he basically likes others (right variable) or basically distrusts others (left variable), but he can't decide how much.

A variation around the vertical (controlled-right to vertical to controlled-left) is most often used by the person who is trying to maintain the vertical attitude (self-sufficiency). He sometimes needs people and is sometimes afraid of them, and feels that the solution to his problem is to stop caring about them at all.

2. *Extreme Variation*

An extreme variation in one in which the script swings in all directions (as in our sample above), and you see a combination of two or even all three tilts, as far right and as far left as pronounced and extreme.

The extreme variation is the tilt equivalent of an erratic baseline, in terms of relationships with other people. This writer finds it very difficult to know what to do or how to behave with others. In a sense, he has his signals crossed: he can't grasp what other people are all about, and therefore doesn't know how to react to them, or even how to feel about them.

Writers with this type of conflict are unpredictable, even to themselves; they don't know if they do or should like other people, are not certain if they're liked in return, and often feel that they're running in circles in most things they try to do. Usually such writers want to like and trust others, but are not certain if they are liked in return, and therefore are also uncertain how to respond to others. The reasons for this type of conflict will be found in other parts of the script; it's often caused by outside pressures (or, by the writer's confused perceptions of those pressures), and always, like any other pronounced variation, it results in stress.

Conclusion: *Interpreting Angle*

Angle direction and degree are a single trait indicator: direction is what, and degree is how much. Let's take a look at how the writer's reactions to other people can affect or be affected by his basic feelings of security (baseline).

1. Baseline waver (some doubts or questions) inside a level line (realistic outlook), with a pronounced-right tilt (needs approval and attention): "I'm not sure how to run my life, but as long as you love me, I'll be fine."

2. Baseline waver inside a level line, with a vertical angle (self-sufficient): "I'm well aware that I can make mistakes, but I prefer to make my own, and I'd appreciate it if you'd butt out."

3. Baseline waver inside a level line, with a pronounced-left tilt (fear of others; feelings of being unloved): "The reason nobody likes me is because I keep screwing up all the time."

Our interpretations here are somewhat simplistic, but you should get the idea. For writer number one, his need for others may be a cause of his emotional insecurity (or vice versa!); we don't know which yet, but we can project that if he is rejected by others, it may increase his feelings of insecurity. For writer number two, the vertical script can be either a defense mechanism (i.e., a "so-what" attitude to other people's opinions of his mistakes), or it may be the reason the baseline waver isn't worse. Writer number three has two negative indicators (two traits which are harmful to him), and you know that whatever the cause, he is condemning himself for anything that goes wrong. Again: the meaning of the indicator by itself never changes, but every trait a writer has will be affected by every other trait.

Note: When writing up your analysis, you should bear in mind that many people are not aware of either differences or similarities between themselves and others. Especially when it comes to communication, most people only see their own difficulties in relating, and however well they do it, they don't feel they're doing it well enough. Avoid using words like "extrovert" or "introvert": as a graphologist, you know that person RC communicates better than person LC, because you are in contact with both of them, but you may have difficulty convincing even the most well-adjusted right-tilt writer that the word extrovert applies to him! Explain instead that a judgement of outgoing or withdrawn does not in any way depend on the extent of the writer's involvement in social activities, but on *how the writer feels about other people*: the right-tilt writer likes and trusts others—even if sometimes too much—the left-tilt writer is more likely to be fearful and suspicious, and the vertical writer tends to remain personally uninvolved.

Principles of the Analysis

Communication: The angle of script tells you if the writer feels he can make himself understood. Your analysis will reveal how important other people are to the writer, and how he deals with their effect on his life.

The question you are trying to answer is: How does this person relate to others, and does his attitude help or hurt him?

ANALYSIS OUTLINE (continued)
II. ANGLE (How does this person feel about others? What effect do
other people have on his life?)
  A. Angle Right (Leans toward others)
    1. Controlled (Basically likes and trusts others)
    2. Pronounced (Really needs attention and approval of others)
    3. Extreme (Totally depends on others)
  B. Angle Vertical (Self-sufficient; doesn't need others)
  C. Angle Left (Draws away from others)
    1. Controlled (Shy or diffident; or may possibly dislike others; in any
       case, unsure of their feelings toward him)
    2. Pronounced (Distrusts or is nervous around others; feels unwanted)
    3. Extreme (Is afraid of others, feels unlikeable)
  D. Angle Variable (Uncertain how to feel or react)
    1. Moderate:

     a. Right Variation (Not sure how much of himself to give)
     b. Vertical Variation (Not sure how much to withhold)
     c. Left Variation (Not sure how far to run away)
  2. Extreme (Stress, confusion, indecision. Does not know how to deal with others; does not know what he wants from them; does not know what they expect from him.)

Doing the Analysis—Angle

A tilt toward the right means an expressive liking of others, but is the person still warm and friendly if the rest of the handwriting shows an inability to communicate? The potential for sociability may still be there, and the desire to relate to others, but the writer may be so tied up in his own problems that he can't make use of it.

Each chapter in this text describes what could be called the "pure" meaning of a trait indicator: what that indicator means in and of itself with nothing else influencing it, and in most cases, what it means in the most well-organized script. As you add more and more information to your analysis, however, you have to combine these trait meanings, and this is where your own insight and common-sense judgement come into play. Because it's not simple addition; you're going to have to draw your own conclusions about how traits and characteristics affect and modify each other when they come together in one integrated personality.

In Chapters 1 and 2 we constructed a general overview of character and personality, with no real specifics except purposefulness of direction (baseline). Let's add the "pure meaning" of script angle to what we know about organization and baseline and see how that affects our original conclusions about the nature of these writers:

SAMPLE ONE (see page 40)

Angle: A controlled-right tilt.

Here's how one factor influences another. The controlled-right is graphology's "ideal" tilt: the best indicator of the ability to cope with other people. What does it mean in conjunction with a rigid baseline and overall tight self-control? It means that however much this writer likes other people, for some reason we have not yet determined, he's holding himself in check; and we'd have to wonder if he can indeed tell anyone else how he really feels. If we look at each indicator alone, we have a writer who can control his behavior (organization), is self-assured (baseline), and can deal with others but still maintain his independence (angle). When we put them together, we have a confirmation of our organizational conclusions: this writer has himself on much too tight a leash.

This is a sample of the way I normally write.

I would like to know what my handwriting tells about me.

SAMPLE TWO

This is a sample of the way I

write. I would like to know what my

handwriting tells about me.

SAMPLE TWO (see page 40)

Angle: Pronounced-right.

Here we have a writer with a strong need for the company and approval of others. Since the general style also shows stress and self-doubt, let's tentatively consider the possibility that writer number two may not be getting that approval, while we wait for additional data. Because the tilt is consistent, all we know right now is that this writer feels certain that other people are important in his life. Because the baseline sags, we know that something important is going very wrong. We don't know yet if the two factors are connected, but it's a definite possibility.

SAMPLE THREE (see page 42)

Angle: Moderate variation; mostly pronounced-right, with sporadic extreme-right, sporadic controlled-right.

Within a variation, you take the measurement which occurs most of the time as the writer's norm; variation from that norm indicates any conflict. This writer has a strong need for others in his life; sometimes that need gets away from him (extreme), and sometimes he fights it (controlled). We can say that this writer likes and needs others, but that he may not always be certain as to what kinds of responses might be appropriate. Remember, too, that we rated this handwriting as mildly disorganized, and we found the slight baseline waver is caused by a sag which this writer pulls back to the true. For writer number three, his control might be shaky, but whatever his problems are, he's fighting them.

SAMPLE FOUR (see page 42)

Angle: Variable tilt. Mostly pronounced-right tilt; the pronoun I always pulls back to vertical; occasional variation in other letters to vertical or controlled-right.

What do we have so far? Identity problems, immaturity, and a sag in an otherwise firm baseline. That gives us a writer who knows what he wants to be when he grows up, but who hasn't grown up yet. We add to that a tilt which overall shows a strong need for others, but which also shows an occasional strong need to pull away. The fact that the extreme variation occurs mostly in the pronoun I tells us, again, that it has something to do with the writer's sense of identity, but just what it tells is something we don't know yet. We can hypothesize that this writer's need for others may be a symptom of his immaturity; if so, he may be asking too much of others, or perhaps not getting as much as he needs (baseline sag). Certainly he is aware that something is wrong in his relationships (slant variation), but at this point we don't know what, if anything, he intends to do about it.

SAMPLE THREE

This is a sample of the way I normally write —
I would like to know what my handwriting
tells about me.

SAMPLE FOUR

This is a sample of the way I normally
write. I would like to know what my
handwriting tells about me.

Exercise For Chapter Three

Classify each sample of script you have collected as right, left, or vertical; include a judgement of angle extremes.

When there is a variation of tilt, use the most dominant angle as your guide; i.e., is the script mostly right, mostly left, or mostly vertical? Be sure to notice whether the variation is pronounced or only occasional; and in either case, see if it follows a pattern. For example: is it only certain letters, or certain parts of letters, which tilt differently; or does the variation just happen where it happens?

Answer the question: How does this writer feel about other people? How does this alter or support the conclusions you have already made based on your study of organization and baseline?

The pieces of the puzzle begin dropping into place. In Chapter 4, we'll add another specific.

TEST YOURSELF

For each of the five script samples given below, draw in the angle measure. Specify both direction and degree of angle, and give their meanings. Our answers are in Appendix B.

SAMPLE ONE

This is a sample of my handwriting.
you can understand it

SAMPLE TWO

This is how I write. I would like
what my writing shows.

SAMPLE THREE

This is a sample of my handwriting. I hope
you can read it.

SAMPLE FOUR

This is the way I normally write. I would

SAMPLE FIVE

This is a sample of my handwriting I
understand it

4

Limitation—
The Size of Script

How much personal space do you need? And how much actual space do you allow yourself in which to live, and move, and grow?

The **size** of script tells you the writer's *range* of feelings and interests: the variety or specialization of thought and expression. And while it does not tell you what his specific talents may be, it does give you your first clues as to what kind of work the writer might be happiest doing.

Letter height (large, small, or medium) tells you what kind of lifestyle the writer would prefer, and/or what kind of professional environment would suit him best. *Letter width* and *spacing* of letters and words (wide, narrow, or proportional) tells you how much room the writer currently has or still needs.

Definition

Script size is just what it sounds like: how big or how small the writing actually is. Defining the overall size is a bit more complicated, however. The measure of script size takes two main factors into account: the height of each individual letter, and the amount of space the writing as a whole takes up on the page. This second measure includes letter width and spacing (between letters, between words, and between lines); both measurements must be combined in order to get an accurate reading.

Measuring Size

You begin by taking a measure of letter *height*. For script size to be consistent, the *width* of individual letters, and the *spacing* of words, letters, and lines must be proportional to the height measure; otherwise, you have a size variation.

1. *Script height* can be measured with a ruler. This is a two-zone measurement: you work only with lower-case letters which have ascenders or descenders (but not both: don't include the "f"). Lay your ruler along the letter's slant to get the full length. Measure from the baseline to the highest point of the ascender on

letters such as the b, h, or l; or measure from the top of the letter to the bottom of the descender on letters such as the g, j, or y (crossing the baseline):

FIGURE 1
Size Measure

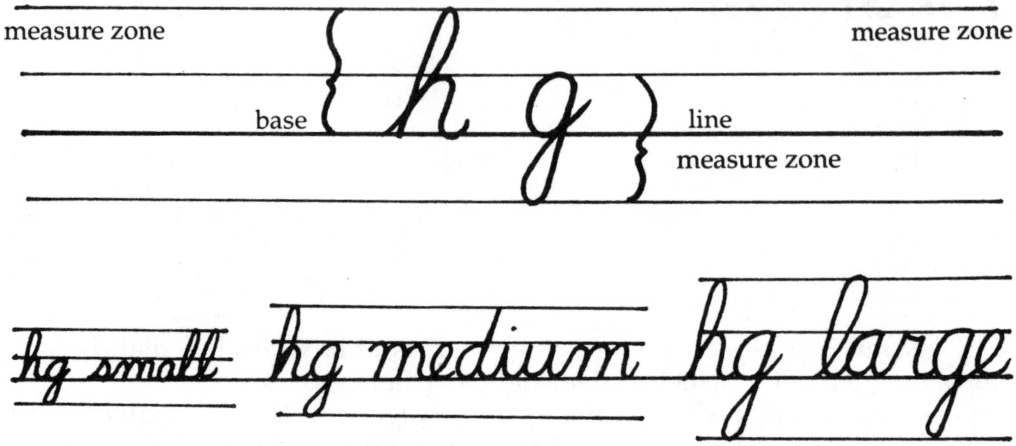

There is no real hard-and-fast rule here, but basically when the *total height* of any two-zone letter is 1/4 inch or less it would classify as small script; between 1/4 inch and 3/8 inch is medium, or average size writing; and taller than 3/8 inch is large. Use your judgement, however; remember that you're only measuring two zones: if the zones are not balanced you may get an incorrect height measure. For example, letters such as the a or c are single-zone formations; the bottom half of the b or h, and the top half of the g or y are also a single zone. A script which is large in this middle zone but has very short ascenders and descenders would measure as small by the rule we gave, but it would not be a small script. The middle zone of writing should be half the actual letter height, so in a case like this you can measure just the middle zone, then double that measurement to determine what should be the letter height. You will get a feel for actual script size as you compare more and more samples.

2. For *letter width* to be proportional, it should be about 1/2 the letter height. If the width of individual letters is very much wider or very much narrower, you are looking at a size variation. Measure letter width only in the middle zone, not by the loops of ascenders or descenders.

3. *Space between letters* in a word should be about 1/2 the letter width. Space between words should be about equal to the letter width. Note here that even if the the letter width is too wide or too narrow, word spacing is considered consistent if it fairly well matches the letter width. What you are primarily looking for is word spreads (extra space between words), or words which are crowded too close together.

4. *Line spacing* is measured by the number of lines to a full (8 1/2 x 11) page. On the average, and assuming enough space between lines so that let-

ters do not run into each other, the medium-size writer will be able to fit 24 to 30 lines of writing on a full-size sheet of paper, with a proportionate number of words per line. The large writer may fit only half that amount on the same sheet of paper, and when the number of lines is double that or more, the script size would be classified as small.

For a measure of line spacing alone, the judgement is very nearly an aesthetic one. If the lines are so crowded together that lower loops of the line above run into upper loops or even middle zone letters of the line below, the line spacing is too crowded. If lines of script are so far apart that half the height or more of an additional line of writing could fit between existing lines of script, the line spacing is too wide.

What You Are Measuring

You are trying to determine (a) the actual height of lower- case letters (capital letters are not measured when judging script size); (b) whether or not that height remains the same throughout the sample; and (c) whether or not the width of letters and the letter, word, and line spacing is consistent with letter height.

Note: In order to get an accurate measurement of script size, you must also make certain that the writer had enough room in which to express himself naturally. Script size is one indicator which changes radically to fit the space available; many people—especially in this age of government forms—are accustomed to tailoring their writing to the writing space. So, keep in mind that a message squeezed onto a postcard is of no value in determining script size; even lined paper, whether wide or narrow ruled, is also restricting. Baseline measurement is not the only reason that at least your first sample must be written on a full sheet of unlined paper:

FIGURE 2

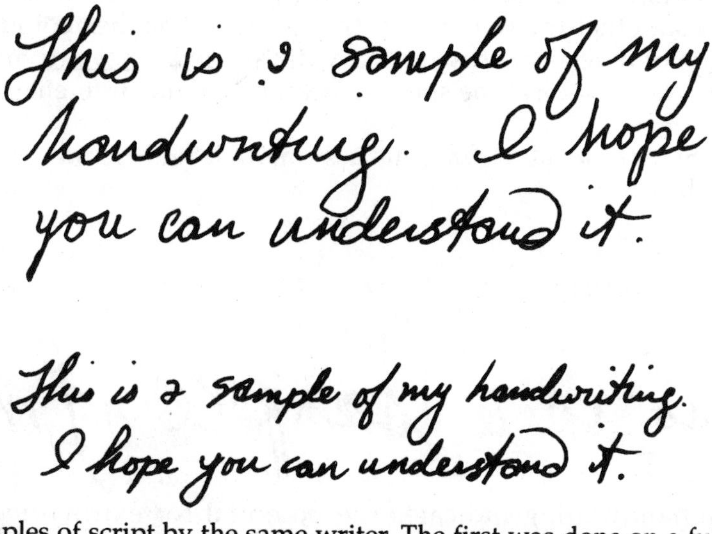

Two samples of script by the same writer. The first was done on a full sheet of paper; the second on a personnel form which allowed limited space for self expression. Sample one is large script and sample two is small—two completely opposite personalities!

The script size tells you, as the graphologist, how much space the writer has allowed himself in which to move: whether he is capable of multiple enthusiasms (large); prefers to concentrate on specifics (small); or is basically conservative but can be adaptable to either end of the spectrum (medium). The size of handwriting is not necessarily a picture of behavior. Like any other indicator by itself, it shows *potential*, but it is a picture of how much the writer wants to include in his life. The larger the script, the more open the writer is to different interests, ideas, and people; the smaller the script, the more he is shutting things out of his life, or limiting his own self-expression.

Organizational Factors

For size, a small, medium *or* large script can be classified as good organization: it takes all kinds to make a world! As long as there is no height variation (absence of stress), if both the letter width and the spacing are consistent with height (absence of conflict), you have a writer whose needs are at peace with what he can do about them.

Extreme size applies either to a script which is too large or too small, and it means the same thing as any other extreme: a writer who is overdoing it. The extremely large script is used by the writer who has too many enthusiasms and can't be pinned down to specifics. The extremely small writer, in contrast, has a tendency to shut everything out of his life except the one thing that does interest him.

Variable size usually indicates a conflict between what the writer wants to be and what he is: and this can range from the person who wants more out of life than he is experiencing to the person who wishes life would let him alone so he can get his work done. Sometimes size variation is a sign of growth or change in the writer's lifestyle; an indicator that his interests and needs are beginning to take a different turn. But even in this case, the variation is still a sign that the writer feels things are not as they could be; the variation is a sign of indecision, discomfort with things as they are, and stress.

Now let's take a look at the specific meanings of the different sizes of script:

A. Overall Size (*Note*: all definitions assume that width and spacing are consistent with height.)

1. *The Large Script*

A large handwriting indicates the potential for extroverted, confident, energetic behavior. The person who writes this way likes to be noticed, and he notices and enjoys variety in his life, and the company of a variety of different people. A large writer tends to be outspoken and gregarious, and will be happiest in professions or activities which include the greatest number of other people, or which demand "something doing": show business or politics, civil and social organizations, big business.

Because the large writer is open to new experiences and finds change stimulating, rather than threatening, he can often put things together in unique and seemingly impossible ways; in a well-organized script, this kind of person makes a good and imaginative manager or coordinator. Large writers generally do not do well in work which requires monotonous repetition, concentrated attention to detail, or lack of personal recognition.

On a personal level, the large writer can often seem boisterous and somewhat overwhelming to other types of people (especially to the small writer!), but he is not necessarily a show-off—he simply needs to know, and go, and see, and do; his exuberance is more often genuine than not, and his flamboyance can simply be called theatrical.

Always check for other signs in the script, however. Very often someone who is shy or has a low self-image will put on a big front to cover up. You already know one of the signs of introversion (left slant); we will be looking at two other signs which could mean that the big behavior is a mask in Chapter 8.

2. *Extremely Large Writing*

When the script is too large, it pictures a writer who is spreading himself too thin; he has so many enthusiasms that he has no time to co-ordinate or make sense of his varied experiences. This is the person who is concerned only with generalities and can't be pinned down to specifics. Jack of all trades and master of none can be interesting to know and handy to have around, but unless there are other positive signs in the script, he is not going to get anything useful accomplished: this writer seems to know something about everything (or wants you to think he does!), but his knowledge is usually shallow. The overlarge script can also be a sign of exaggerated self-confidence or even egotism, and here you have two more traits which spell insecurity! When an overlarge handwriting is combined with other attention-getters, such as this one is (note the circled i-dots), you are dealing with someone who, more than anything else, desperately needs to be noticed.

In short: it doesn't take an experienced graphologist to come to the conclusion that big is more noticeable: the larger the script, the more personal attention the writer needs.

3. *The Medium Script*

I am very interested in more about graphology.

The medium-size writer tends to be conservative, conscientious, and careful; he prefers to strike a balance, to see things run smoothly and without conflicts, and he has a greater concern for appearances and legalities. Of the three script sizes, however, this writer is the most adaptable: he has room for a reasonable variety of interests and experiences, and yet if circumstances prevent him from exploring alternative possibilities, he can cope with day-to-day sameness for however long it is necessary.

The medium writer likes life and moves toward it, appreciating its possibilities and bearing its burdens as they arise. All other things being equal (and again, we are talking about a well-organized script), these writers as a group make the most reliable employees, the best marriage partners and parents, the most supportive neighbors and friends; they are more likely than either the large or the small writer to genuinely care about the effects of their own actions and the feelings of other people. The average-size script is the so-called "average person," who, despite a conventional surface, usually has an inner strength which can be depended upon in a crisis. And however unostentatious and undemanding they may be, these are the people who actually accomplish most of the world's work.

In terms of profession, the medium writer has a greater range of possibilities open to him than either the large or small writer. Here again, the key word is adaptability: he can tolerate the repetition and monotony that is part of any job better than the large writer (and is therefore likely to stay with one job longer), and he can display a versatility which would be uncomfortable and totally out of character for the small writer (and can therefore learn a new job or skill faster). Jobs which call for the practical application of ideas and discoveries, and for cooperation between people, are the best possibilities here; depending on other signs in the script, this can mean anything from advertising or sales work, to public service and social work, to the medical professions, to teaching.

4. *Medium Extreme*

I appreciate your taking the time to answer my inquiry

As with a vertical script, extremes in the medium range of writing are more likely to be found in other factors. In the case of average writing, the one worst extreme to watch for is the writer whose script is too careful. In both the large and the small scripts, a conventional style is a tempering factor; it makes those writers less selfish and more cooperative. But because the medium-size writer tends to be more conventional to begin with, a strictly proper script here means someone who is likely to be too concerned with whether or not he is doing the "right" thing, with strict obedience to laws and social conventions (both his own and other people's), and with "what people will think." Because he is adaptable (and this means able to accommodate himself to other people as well as to changing situations) the medium writer must show the ability to think for himself and to act on his own decisions if he expects to retain his own identity.

5. *The Small Script*

I would like to know what my handwriting

The small writer tends to view life through a microscope rather than a telescope; he usually has very little interest in people and events outside his own particular specialty. This type of person can be analytical, precise, and, in a detached and uninvolved way, very interested in what makes things tick. He can be just as imaginative and creative as the large writer, and just as practical as the medium: this is the "scientists' script," and many of the world's most inventive discoveries have been made by people who write in just this way.

Unlike the other two sizes of script, the small writer is something of an isolationist; he tends to focus all his attention and all his efforts on his own enthusiasm and to shut out distractions—a word which translates as the activities, interests, and social life of other people. He has little or no concern for the larger picture: the work itself is all that matters.

This type of person will do best in a line of work which calls for concentration, patience, investigative ability and a desire for accuracy—such as technical work, research, accounting, statistics—any profession which demands careful and minute measurements and strict attention to details. The small writer would probably not be happy if called upon to supervise someone else's performance, or to engage in such gregarious activities as fund-raising or public relations work (all activities which keep him from doing his own job) and he is highly unlikely to join the company bowling league.

6. *Extremely Small*

I'm interested in learning more about my handwriting; I write this way from the time I was a little

When the writing is too small, it shows someone who is literally boxing himself in, shutting off everyone and everything else. For the normal small writer, his work is an end in itself; but the excessively small script indicates that the writer may be using his work (or hobby, or primary interest) as a means of escape, especially when it is combined with other signs of introversion, such as the left tilt shown in the sample above.

Even in an otherwise well-organized script, the excessively small size can be a danger sign since, like the extreme left tilt, it shows withdrawal: unlike the left tilt, it also means that the writer has found something to substitute for human interaction. In contrast to the very large script, the very tiny writing is an indicator that the writer may be trying to become invisible. Other signs in the script can either temper or increase this potential, but the extremely small writer runs the risk of becoming totally shut off from the rest of the world, both emotionally and intellectually, and this means a risk of becoming narrow-minded, incapable of growth or change, and occasionally something of a fanatic.

In short, the smaller the script, the greater the withdrawal; when it becomes extremely small, it's a way of hiding your head in the sand, or maybe even crawling in a hole and pulling it in after you ("If you can't see me, I'm not there.").

7. *Size Combinations*

Not all scripts, of course, will fall neatly into one category or another. Some may be on the large side of medium; some scripts may fall between small and medium. In borderline samples, as long as size and spacing are consistent, there is no conflict, and no evidence of disorganization. Your analysis should take an average between the characteristics of both sizes involved. For example: the medium-small writer is more adaptable and has less ability to concentrate than the small writer; the medium-large writer has a wider range of interests and is less conservative than the medium writer. And so on.

B. *Size Variation* (inconsistencies in height, width, or spacing)

1. *Height Variation* is judged on the basis of similar parts of letters: ascender to ascender, descender to descender, middle zone to middle zone. Variation between different zones of script (ascender to descender) is a separate indicator, which we will be covering in Chapter 6 (Zones).

Height variation generally shows confusion over goals or interests. This is the writer who is not sure what kind of person he wants to be. Like the variable slant (the writer who can't decide how to react to other people), the variable size means the writer cannot decide how to react to events in his life. And like any other indication of indecision, it's a sign of stress.

2. *Spacing and width variations* are measured in two ways:

a. When the spacing and/or width are inconsistent within themselves (i.e., sometimes wide, sometimes narrow), the meaning is the same as for height variation: confusion over goals, and the writer's inability to decide what kind of lifestyle he wants.

b. When the spacing and/or width are consistent within themselves but inconsistent with the letter height, it shows a *conflict*. There is something the writer wants or feels he needs that his own personality or circumstances prevent him from getting, or perhaps even defining. The variation is still a sign of stress, but it's better defined as frustration.

(1) In general, the wider the letters (in proportion to the script height), the more time the writer has on his hands; he's trying to grow, but he's growing in the wrong direction. Narrow letters indicate that something—usually overwork or too many responsibilities—is cramping his style.

(2) The wider the spacing, the greater the need to "spread out"; this is the person who needs more room, or who feels that life might have something more to offer. Especially if the script size stays the same but the spacing (word and/or line spacing) spreads out, the writer needs more space but doesn't know how to get it. When the spacing closes up too tight, the interpretation is basically the same as for narrow letters; it means that the writer has more work or responsibility than he can handle.

To interpret the meaning of variation in size, you have to combine the meanings of the different sizes of script. For example: wide letters or spacing in an otherwise small script shows an unconscious desire to spread out; it also means a lessening of the ability to concentrate. Someone who starts out large and ends small may want to be involved and enthusiastic, but can't sustain it. A large script with narrow letters or very tight spacing indicates that the writer has taken on more than he can handle; he's got the interests, but not the time or the energy to pursue them.

The script that bounces back and forth shows a writer who is doing the same; concentrating all his energies on a single enthusiasm at one moment, and flying off on a completely unrelated tangent the next. In any of these cases, you are dealing with someone who knows that something very basic is wrong with his life, but who hasn't figured out what it is, or what to do about it.

because it just isn't working

When you see these size variations, you know that the writer has unresolved questions about his lifestyle or chosen field, and that he is in the middle of a conflict between what he is and what he can be, or needs to be, or wants to be. In the case of size variation, the conflict is most often professional: the writer who accidentally or by force of circumstances wound up in the wrong job for his talents or personality. This is true primarily because, for most people, what someone does for a living takes up so much of his time, and has a tremendous impact on the quality and circumstances of his personal lifestyle as well. If, however, a writer whose script shows size variation insists that he loves his job, then you can assume that there is something in his personal lifestyle that is beginning to drive him around the bend.

Either way, this conflict is a very serious one, and can affect everything else in the writer's life. What do you think would be the effect on a wide-ranging, enthusiastic personality who is following a career as an accountant, or the effect of a detail-minded perfectionist who has somehow become the manager of a large corporation? Very few things are more uncomfortable or more self-defeating than being a square peg in a round hole.

Conclusion: *Interpreting Size*

As with baseline, your first step is to match the different size formations with each other before combining them with other indicators. Script height is considered the "stronger" factor: the one which defines the writer's normal or current outlook and needs. Spacing or width variations indicate a conflict between the writer's needs and his actual situation. For example:

1. Small script (concentration, specialization) combined with wide spacing (a need to spread out): "There's got to be more to life than this, and I'm beginning to wonder if what I'm doing is worth the effort."

2. Large script (outgoing, many interests) combined with narrow letters and/or narrow spacing (too much to do in too little time): "I don't want to give up all my interests or ambitions, but I think I may have bitten off more than I can chew."

And a triple-play:

3. Medium script (adaptable, conscientious), combined with narrow letters (too much responsibility) and wide spacing (needs to spread out): "Everybody's leaning on me but I'm not getting anything out of it. When is it *my* turn?"

Your next step is to add your conclusions about size to what you've learned from baseline and slant. As we add more information, of course, the equation can become somewhat bulky. Use your own judgement to determine how size affects other factors in script. For example:

The vertical writer tends to be self-sufficient: the small writer tends to submerge himself in his own special interests. Vertical combined with small presents a picture of greater isolation and much less contact with people and events than either one by itself. Right angle plus small is a modifying factor: at least the writer needs other people, and perhaps sometimes they can drag him away from his desk or out of his shell. If you add a left tilt (shy or uncomfortable around others) to a small script, the resulting combination is comparable to that of a very small script: the writer who is using his work as a substitute for contacts with other people; in fact, he may have withdrawn into his work *because* he doesn't know how to make friends. And in any of these cases, the firmer the baseline (the more the writer believes he knows what he's doing), the more intense the writer's involvement with his primary interest, and the less likely he is to tolerate distractions and/or consider alternative interests. Again, each trait modifies as well as explains the others.

In one way or another, we all draw boundary lines around ourselves, including those things we are able to do or willing to try, and excluding those things in which we have no interest, or which we may actively fear. Script size is a picture of where those boundaries are set. When you are writing up your analysis, keep in mind that in the case of size, you are dealing with the writer's outlook on life: you may feel that the small writer is missing a lot, but he sees himself as concentrating, not self-limiting; the large writer may seem loud and somewhat obvious, but he sees himself as versatile, not spreading himself too thin. The medium writer is versatile, as well as adaptable; and while you may see him as something of a conformist, the ability to make the best of any situation in which you happen to find yourself is certainly a positive trait. What choice someone makes is a matter of preference, and the world needs people who can generalize as well as people who can specialize, and certainly needs people who can make either application work. As a graphologist, your primary concern is not whether the writer is limiting or expanding his range of interest, but whether or not he is in a lifestyle or profession which will enable him to make the most effective use of the abilities and preferences he has.

Principles of the Analysis

Limitation: The size of script indicates how much room the writer needs in order to function and to grow. Large writing shows expansiveness and a need for recognition; small writing shows concentration and precision; medium-size writing shows adaptability and a practical concern for social values.

The question you are trying to answer is: What kind of profession or lifestyle does this writer need in order to develop and use his own individual potentials?

ANALYSIS OUTLINE (continued)

III. SIZE (What kind of environment—professional and/or general lifestyle situation—would suit this writer best?)

    A. Overall size (Primary height measure plus proportional spacing and width)

1. Large (Needs elbow-room, needs variety, likes attention. Managerial potential, co-ordinator; wide range of interests)
2. Extremely Large (Spreads himself too thin; can't concentrate; needs attention)
3. Medium (Adaptable, conservative, reliable. Can make practical use of inventions and discoveries; works well with other people)
4. Medium Extreme (Too conservative; can't innovate; may be afraid to think for himself)
5. Small (Concentration, analytical ability, specialization. Can do research, technical work, etc; dislikes distractions)
6. Extremely Small (Too isolated; can't generalize; evidence of withdrawal)
7. Size Combinations (Borderline measurements):
    (a) Medium to Large (Still adaptable, but needs more variety)
    (b) Small to Medium (Still able to concentrate, but more adaptable)
B. Size Variations (Inconsistencies in height, width, or spacing)
  1. Height Variation (Confusion over needs; can't decide where true interests lie)
  2. Spacing and Width Variation:
    (a) Spacing or width inconsistent by themselves (Confusion over goals; can't define interests)
    (b) Spacing or width inconsistent with height (Conflict between needs and actual situation)
      (1) Letter width variation (Too wide: boredom with current situation. Too narrow: too much to do in too little time)
      (2) Spacing variation (Too wide: needs to spread out, to add more to his life. Too narrow: has more to do than he can handle)

Confused? Relax. Size is a complicated measure to determine only because it has so many facets. Take it one step at a time and you'll work it out.

Doing the Analysis—Size

Let's see what size as a trait indicator adds to our understanding of our four writers, and just how to make sense of all the different facets of this trait measure:

SAMPLE ONE (see page 57)

Size: Height large, with size variation; letter width narrow; spacing tight.
You begin by determining the overall size and defining any contradictions. This is a large script with narrow letter width and tight word and line spacing. That tells us that this writer is someone who is interested in the larger picture and probably needs attention, and that he's bitten off more than he can chew. The smaller size of the d and/or t is not a height variation; these letters are traditionally shorter than other ascenders (it's a schoolform usage). But there is an up-and-down height measurement on other letters as well, which

SAMPLE ONE

This is a sample of the way I normally write. I would like to know what my handwriting tells about me.

SAMPLE TWO

This is a sample of the way I normally write. I would like to know what my handwriting tells about me.

does indicate confusion over goals. What does that mean in relation to what we already know about this writer?

We know that the narrow width and spacing indicates that this writer is trying to crowd as many activities into one day as he can, or maybe too many. Added to the height variation, we can assume that there is something about his profession or lifestyle—or both—that is making him uncomfortable. Given only what we have, a logical if tentative conclusion would be that Writer Number One is working very hard at or for something he doesn't really want. And unless he loosens up, he may never find out whatever it is he does want: the extra work he's taking on is unlikely to give him the time that the large script tells us he needs to explore his own potential and interests. At this point, we still don't know why this writer is driving himself, but based only on the three factors we now have, we can tentatively conclude that he has, at least in some area of his life, taken on more than he can handle, and he's handling it with a rigid self-control.

SAMPLE TWO (see page 57)

Size: Height large with size variation; consistent letter width; some spread between words.

The large writing shows varied interests and outgoing and enthusiastic behavior—and in this case the need for others, as we have already seen, is confirmed by the pronounced right tilt. For this handwriting, we would have to consider the d's and t's as part of our height measurement; they vary up and down just as the other letters. Again, we have confusion over goals, but with the difference here that this writer feels there should be something more to life (word spread, indicating a need to grow). There's also another difference, as shown in the baseline waver: this writer knows something isn't as it should be; the height variation then, as well as being a need for recognition, may be a testing of priorities: an indication that this writer is trying to grow. As with our first writer, however, the variation still indicates stress. Something is stopping this writer from getting where he wants to go, and the strain is taking its toll.

SAMPLE THREE (see page 59)

Size: Medium/toward large. Height reasonably consistent; letter width internally inconsistent; some word spread.

Our disorganized writer is using a basically medium-sized script, but on the large side; the occasional spread between words shows a desire to grow even more, and the variation in letter width indicates a confusion over goals. We might wonder if it is the conservative attitude or lifestyle that is causing the emotional turmoil; we have confirmed our style analysis that he is concerned with appearances, but the fact that the concern takes the form of a mild ostentation would suggest that while this writer wants to be approved of, he'd prefer to do it on his own terms. Add to that the size push against restriction, and we have a writer who will tend to be more restless than most medi-

SAMPLE THREE

This is a sample of the way I normally write—
I would like to know what my handwriting
tells about me.

SAMPLE FOUR

This is a Sample of the way I normally
write. I would like to know what my
handwriting tells about me.

um-size writers, and probably unhappy in a conventional nine-to-five job. While his personal lifestyle would probably remain more or less conventional, this writer would require more personal attention, and more freedom of movement than most medium writers. The possibility exists that whatever it is he wants out of life, he hasn't figured out how to get it, and it's just as likely that he hasn't even figured out what it is.

SAMPLE FOUR (see page 59)

Size: Small/toward medium. Height and letter width reasonably consistent; pronounced word spread.

This handwriting is small-medium, showing someone who is less adaptable and more insulated than a medium script, and less satisfied with a single goal or purpose than than a small script. The wide spacing, again, shows a need to spread out, and this in the handwriting of someone who is experiencing identity problems. What have we added to our understanding of this writer? His life is good, and he is basically satisfied, but he also has the feeling that there might be something that he's missing. It certainly does begin to look as though, in spite of this writer's age, what he's going through is growing pains.

Exercise for Chapter Four

Classify each of your script samples as small, medium, large or borderline; identify any size variations or conflicts.

Answer the question: what is this writer's range of interests? How does this additional information support or alter conclusions you formed earlier?

You are now on your way to becoming a handwriting detective. Let's add some more clues.

TEST YOURSELF

For each of the five script samples given below, determine the size. Specify any size variations or conflicts, and give their meanings. Our answers are in Appendix B.

SAMPLE ONE

Please send information

SAMPLE TWO

Your analysis raised some interesting points, and I am curious now about the process by which

SAMPLE THREE

We had a great time

SAMPLE FOUR

This is a sample of how I normally write.

SAMPLE FIVE

What does my writing show?

5

Determination— The Pressure of Script

How hard are you willing to work for what you want? And how hard are you *able* to work for what you want?

The **pen pressure** of a script sample is a measure of the writer's personal and physical vitality. As a trait indicator, it gives you the writer's level of *drive*: the amount of effort he is capable of putting behind whatever he does.

The *firmness* or *lightness* of pressure tells you how much energy the writer has, and how much of that energy he uses to perform a task (writing); the *evenness* of pressure tells you whether or not he can sustain that particular level of drive.

Definition

Pen pressure is the amount of physical force the writer puts behind his pen as he moves it along the paper; the greater the pressure, the darker (and/or thicker) the penstrokes will be, and the greater the impression they will leave on the page.

Measuring Pressure

In order to get an accurate measure of pressure, you need a sample written with a ball-point pen; this writing instrument can be pressed down on a page with varying degrees of force without damaging it or altering its usefulness. Most people will usually ease up when writing with a fountain pen or fibertip, or even a pencil; partly because the point can be damaged, and, in the case of the fibertip, partly because you can get a broad, dark line without much effort at all. A sample written with a fiber-tip pen can be measured for pressure, but it's harder to gauge; all you have to go by is the width of the strokes. And, unfortunately for this study, a sample reproduced photographically is almost impossible to gauge: to get an accurate measure of pen pressure, you must work from the original of a sample.

Pressure is measured by eye and by feel. Study a sample first to see if the pen strokes are even and consistent. The penstrokes are *even* if they flow smoothly, without sporadic instances of heavier or lighter pressure. The pressure is *consistent* if it remains the same throughout the sample.

Next, check individual penstroke lines for firmness or lightness of pressure. The firmer strokes will be darker and, even with a ballpoint, will show a somewhat thicker line.

Finally, run the tips of your fingers lightly along the underside of the page. You are trying to determine if the pressure of the pen has left its mark on the paper itself (if you can feel the shape of the penstrokes on the other side of the paper).

Firm pen pressure is uniformly dark, with all strokes clearly visible and no fading out around the curves of the letterforms. If you run your finger across the underside of the page, you will feel the indentations made by the pen; if the sample was written on a pad, there may also be a light impression on the page beneath. **Heavy** pressure is very dark (or, if written with a fiber pen, very thick); when written with a ballpoint it can leave a readable impression on the page beneath, and may even leave its mark several pages down; extremely heavy pressure may even tear the page on which it's written.

A **moderate** pressure is clear, and never thicker than the actual width of the penpoint; it may sometimes be visible on the underside of the page on which it is written, but rarely marks the page beneath. **Light** pressure is fine-lined and often leaves no impression even on the page being written on; despite its washed out appearance, all strokes are still clear and readable. **Extremely light** pressure looks faded, and some parts of strokes may be barely visible even from the front of the page.

What You Are Measuring

You are trying to determine (a) the primary force of the pen pressure in general (light, moderate, or firm); and (b) whether or not the pressure remains consistent throughout the sample (whether or not the writer can sustain that level of drive).

Because this text is photographically reproduced, we can't provide samples which will give you all the elements you need to accurately measure pen pressure. The comparison chart in Figure 1 below will at least give you a guide you can use in your studies:

FIGURE 1
Pen Pressure: Light-Dark Comparison

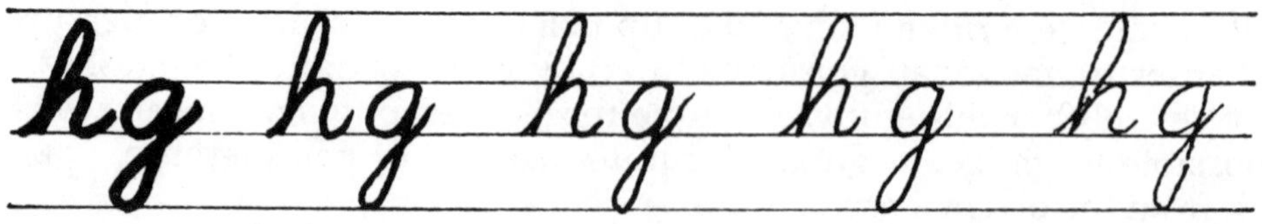

| Heavy | Firm | Moderate | Light | Faded |

When uniform, firm pressure is a sign of energy, power, and force—and also one indication of physical good health, since someone who is ill or in pain will usually be unable to maintain a firm, steady pen pressure. The heavier the pressure, the stronger the emotional intensity of the writer, the more determination he has, and the more of himself he puts into what he does. The lighter the pressure, the more uninvolved and self-effacing the writer, and usually the more personally unambitious as well.

Organizational Factors

There is nothing wrong with being mild-tempered, of course; but firm, even, consistent pen pressure is considered the more positive organizational factor. Consistent pressure, light or dark, shows the writer's mental control *of himself*, because it indicates that the writer knows his own energy level, and does not try to push himself beyond his own capabilities. But at least some firmness is needed for the writer to have control of events as well; if you can't or won't put some energy behind what you do, you are not going to accomplish very much.

Extremes of pressure show extremes in emotional intensity. An extremely heavy pressure—one that literally cuts through the page, or in the case of a fiber pen, breaks or spreads the point—shows someone whose answer to obstacles is brute force. If combined with other negative signs in the script, it can mean a person who will stop at nothing to get what he wants. Extremely light pressure shows someone who would just as soon fade into the woodwork; and, as you can imagine, usually means a person who can be stopped by anything from getting what he wants. Note, however, that light pressure can also be an indication that the writer is tired or ill; this possibility will be confirmed either by other signs in the script, or by a comparison of script samples written at different times by the same writer.

Variable pressure shows someone who cannot maintain his drive, either because he doesn't have enough energy, or because he burns it out in some unrelated emotion. Pen pressure may be slightly darker on downstrokes without being a variation (it is easier to pull the pen toward you); it's also likely to be darker on covered strokes (such as loopless ascenders/the d or t) because the same line is retraced. Pressure can also vary at different times of day, and with conditions of general health or fatigue; so if you have more than one sample of someone's writing, you should not judge variation of pressure with a comparison between them. What you are looking for here is variation in a single sample: pressure which starts either light or dark and ends the opposite, or variations of pressure from light to dark throughout the sample, especially in letters of the same word. Variable pressure is an indicator of frustration, caused by the writer's inability to sustain an effort or finish a task.

These are the types of pen pressure, and what they mean in a sample of handwriting:

A. *Firm Pressure*

This is a sample of my handwriting. I hope you

Firm, even, consistent pressure shows constant drive and sustained determination. It is a sign of energy, vitality, and personal force; and someone who writes this way has the ability to carry though on projects he starts. It is also, at least to a certain extent, an indication of self-assurance; and in terms of leadership qualities, that is a characteristic which carries a lot of weight.

Firm pen pressure is one of the most positive signs in script, since no matter what talents and abilities a writer may have, without determination and the energy to carry through, he is not likely to succeed at what he tries to do. The firmer the pressure, the more forceful the writer; in a well-organized script, this generally means someone who can not only carry his own weight, but who can very often convince others to go along with him as well.

Firm pressure is also a sign of physical good health and vitality, but without the danger signs signs evident in an extreme pressure (below); the drive and determination are present, but not the temper. The writer who uses it is not angry or out to get anyone; he's just determined to get what he wants. He can as easily fight for you as against you, and he can certainly stand up for himself.

B. *Heavy Pressure (Extreme)*

Really, I'm surprised at into that kind of shape.

Since pressure shows the amount of force the writer puts behind what he does, it must be watched carefully; misuse of that force can make the writer a threat to others or to himself.

Pen pressure that is too heavy shows an excess of force. The person who uses unnecessary power to write will also use unnecessary power in other things he does; even in an otherwise well-organized script, excessive pressure is an anger sign; and in a disorganized script it can mean fury, brutality, or viciousness.

Always watch for danger signs. Heavy-pressured script with an extreme right tilt shows an energy which is used up in emotional outbursts. Sudden pressure strokes (as in the slash of a t-bar) are a sign of temper. Words jammed together in a heavy-pressured script may show someone who is literally burning himself out. Remember that the important word is always *control*: a forceful personality has a better chance of getting whatever he wants, but only if he knows what he wants and understands how to go about getting it. The extreme pressure shows unnecessary force, and the potential to lose control of your behavior.

C. *Moderate Pressure*

This is a sample of how I write. I would like to know

A moderately pressured script shows balance, control, and evenness of temper. Such a writer can manage his own affairs, but generally has no desire to manage the affairs of others; his goals are usually well within his reach, and his personal ambition is down-played. All other things being equal, moderate pressure shows calmness, self-control, and a cooperative attitude. Though this type of writer can be depended upon to accomplish his own ends, he lacks the commanding authority, and the desire to control others, usually found in a firmer-pressured script; either because he doesn't want to run things, or doesn't have the self-assurance to believe he can.

Here again, extremes or danger signs must be found in other parts of the script. As with size, extreme conservatism is one; but since the moderate writer does have himself under control, you should also look for signs of hidden stress: emotional turmoil that the writer is simply too well-bred to express.

D. *Light Pressure*

This is a sample of my handwriting. I hope you can read it.

Depending on other signs in the script, light-pressured writing can be a sign of gentleness, or self-effacement, or lack of personal ambition. This writer will tend to be quieter, less forceful, and sometimes less noticeable. As with heavy-pressured script, however, you should check for causes. Pen pressure will be lighter if the writer is tired or ill; this is true even if he normally writes with a firmer pressure. If there are no signs of illness or fatigue, check for signs of sensitivity (Chapter 7), or lack of self-esteem (Chapter 8). A light pressured script is not necessarily a sign of sensitivity, but someone who is sensitive will tend to react to people and events with a light touch, and will write the same way. In a writer who lacks self-confidence, light pressure is an expression of insecurity; the unforceful writing of someone who doesn't want to "push himself" on others. Whatever the cause, light pen pressure is a sign of low energy and vitality; lack of drive and a lessening of personal ambition; and, in a less well-organized script, sometimes even laziness as well.

E. *Faded Pressure (Extreme)*

what you can tell from my

The lighter the pressure, the more uninvolved and self-effacing the writer, and usually the more personally unambitious as well. When you see an extremely light-pressured script, you are looking at a writer who would just as soon not be noticed at all. Just as light pressure is not necessarily a sign of sensitivity, extremely light pressure is not necessarily a sign of laziness: again, it is important to check for signs of possible illness or fatigue. But someone who writes this way is not likely to put a great deal of energy into anything, either because he doesn't care enough, because he's ill, or because he's afraid: of failure, of imposing on people, of being considered pushy.

F. *Variable Pressure*

if you have any ideas on it.

Variable pressure often shows up in the writing of someone who has taken on or been burdened with more than he can handle. It can result in anger, confusion, resentment or unhappiness, or even a lessening of self-esteem (feelings of being a failure), depending on the character of the writer; but it is invariably a sign of frustration: the writer who cannot accomplish what he set out to do.

Pen pressure variation takes a number of different forms:

1. *Fade out* (The sample starts heavier, ends lighter.)

A fade-out shows someone who cannot maintain a given level of drive, either because he underestimates his own energy level, or because he misjudges just how hard the task will be to complete. Put simply, this is someone who tires easily.

2. *Fade in* (The sample starts lighter, ends heavier.)

This variation is less common than a fade-out. It can mean that a normally milder-tempered writer got excited or even angry as he was writing; it can also indicate that the writer has the energy and drive shown in the darker portion of his writing, but was trying to control it or cover it up. In either case, it indicates the potential for a loss of self-control.

3. *Sporadic heavier pressure* (Individual words or phrases within a sample show heavier pressure than the writer's norm: sometimes the heavier pressure may be on single-stroke formations (such as the t-bar). The severity of this indicator depends on how often it appears within a single sample of script.)

Sudden heavy pressure is a sign of anger; sudden heavy pressure pen-strokes are a sign of temper. This is an emotional indicator; it doesn't show a trait, but like baseline bounce or sag it does show what the writer is feeling at the moment of writing.

4. *Internal variation* (The writing shows changes of pen pressure from word to word, or letter to letter, or within single letters, as in our sample, above.)

The greater the internal variation, the more intense the writer's feelings of frustration. Extreme variations from light to dark, especially if in the same word, show severe emotional problems and internal uproar; it is a picture of the writer's inability to carry though on a project, or to reach a goal, and is a sign of wasted emotion and effort. Again, like any variation, it means the writer is under stress and unable to cope.

Conclusion: *Interpreting Pressure*

You add the writer's amount of energy and degree of drive, and his ability to control them both, to what you already know about his character and personality. For example:

Vertical plus small, as we noted earlier, presents a picture of greater isolation than either by itself. Combine that with a light or faded pressure, and you may have a writer who is trying to disappear into himself. He's doing it for his own reasons (vertical), but he is not going to have much impact on his surroundings: should the time ever come when he wants to reach out to other people, he may find that they treat him like the invisible man. The same combination with a firm pressure indicates that the writer has pulled out of the mainstream because he has something important to do, and he may emerge from his solitary laboratory with the scientific discovery of the decade. But take self-sufficiency plus concentration and combine it with a variable pressure, and you may have a writer who is quietly going crazy, either because he is unwilling to lean on someone else or ask advice (vertical), and/or because he is unable to see the larger picture (small). A firm baseline would help this last diagnosis: at least it means that the writer is sure about what he wants to do, even if he can't quite manage to get it to work. But what if the baseline is also erratic? Variable pressure (frustration) and an erratic baseline (self-doubt) adds up to a person who not only can't accomplish anything, but who isn't sure that what he wants to accomplish is worth anything in the first place. It only makes it worse if he is also unwilling or unable to ask for help (vertical), and incapable of accepting the possibility that his answer may lie elsewhere (small).

Even a positive indicator can become a stumbling block when combined with too many negative indicators; in this last case, the small writing may not be a sign of concentration or dedication at all, but simply a symptom of withdrawal, or even fear. It's possible to be afraid to try new things, especially when you can't even manage what you're already working on. Always, as you combine factors, consider the impact of different traits on each other. And look for causes—for reasons the writer is reacting the way he does.

Pen pressure is a measure of how much energy the writer is willing or able to put into making himself effective. And be aware that the inability to make the effort is not always due to laziness. Some people lack physical energy for reasons of health or age; some people deliberately put on the brakes, consciously or unconsciously. In the latter case, there can be many reasons, from an upbringing which tells you that you're not supposed to be "pushy," to an actual fear of success.

Whatever the case, the one factor which can separate the winner from the loser is *drive*: all other things being equal, the harder you try, the better your chances. When you see a firm, steady pressure, you know that the writer has a certain amount of energy and is willing to use it to get the job done; a lack of that energy, or an extreme overuse of it, or the inability to sustain it, is usually a sign that something is wrong.

Principles of the Analysis

DETERMINATION: Pen pressure is a measure of the writer's energy and drive. The firmer the pressure, the more forceful the writer; the lighter the pressure, the less energy he has or is willing to use. Your analysis will reveal whether the writer is in the game or watching from the sidelines.

And, while we are not necessarily espousing the go-getter philosophy, the question you are trying to answer is, quite literally: How much of a mark does this writer want to make on the world?

ANALYSIS OUTLINE (continued)

IV. PRESSURE (How much of an effort is the writer willing or able to make to get what he wants?)
   A. Firm (Energy, vitality, drive)
   B. Heavy (Unnecessary use of force)
   C. Moderate (Balance, control, even temper)
   D. Light (Gentleness, self-effacement, lack of personal ambition)
   E. Faded (Lack of energy, extreme self-effacement, possible illness or laziness if other factors confirm)
   F. Variable (Frustration: inability to sustain energy level)
      1. Fade out (Cannot maintain a given level of drive)
      2. Fade in (Loss of self-control)
      3. Sporadic heavier pressure (Anger or temper)
      4. Internal variation (Intense frustration, due to the writer's inability to function effectively)

Doing the Analysis—Pressure

Each one of the trait indicators, as you have seen, has a variety of possible meanings. No one of them means all those things at the same time! Which interpretation is relevant depends on other factors in the script. Let's see whether we can determine what the intensity of our writers' feelings means in relation to what we already know about them.

SAMPLE ONE (see page 72)

Pressure: Firm and consistent (what appears to be stronger pressure on some of the downstrokes is actually "covered strokes": the pen coming down over the same line that it went up).

We can add constant drive and determination as traits; like the controlled-right tilt, the most positive form of this indicator. But is it a positive factor in this handwriting?

When we consider the crowded word-spacing (too much work or too much responsibility) in a large script (variety of interests, which means even more for this writer to do), and then add the fact that this writer is a hard worker as well (firm pressure), the possibility exists that he may be driving himself into the ground. There's no sign of frustration yet, so he's handling it, but he's definitely feeling the strain. We add to our analysis that this writer knows what he wants out of life, and is willing to work hard and make sacrifices to achieve those ends; with the added notation that he may be pushing himself too hard, too fast, or too far. Writer number one begins to look like the classic picture of a workaholic.

SAMPLE TWO (see page 72)

Pressure: Light, consistent

A light-pressured script shows less energy in use; how do we read that in someone who is enthusiastic and outgoing (combination of size with slant), needs people (pronounced right), and isn't entirely happy about something important that's going on in his life (baseline sag). Since the potential for drive shows up in other parts of script, such as size and angle, it is more likely that the light pressure is self-effacement in this case; it's possible this writer has found he is more likely to get what he wants, with less emotional effort, if he underplays. So we can add that this writer isn't pushy (light pressure); and, though he may be working at his own pace (consistent pressure), his tendency to underplay himself could mean that he's not going to make much of an impression on people and events.

SAMPLE THREE (see page 74)

Pressure: Moderate and consistent

The pen pressure here shows calmness, balance, and controlled reactions to life in general. Yet we know that this writer is experiencing some kind of emotional turmoil, though we don't yet know what or why. Since he is concerned with appearances, as the medium size told us, what we see is a writer who is keeping himself very calm on the surface, while underneath, he is a

SAMPLE ONE

This is a sample of the way I normally write.

I would like to know what my handwriting tells

about me.

SAMPLE TWO

This is a sample of the way I normally

write. I would like to know what my

handwriting tells about me.

bubbling cauldron of self-doubt, indecision, confusion, and unhappiness. Again: none of it is extreme, so he hasn't yet gone off the deep end; also we know this writer has somehow convinced himself that things will work out for the best eventually (baseline upslant). But it is very important that he find his answer—and soon.

SAMPLE FOUR (see page 74)

Pressure: Basically a moderate pressure, but very much on the light side. Occasional heavy pressure strokes on the t-bars and down strokes.

This writer is not self-effacing, but he does have low drive and little ambition, or little desire to work to achieve anything. Since the smaller than medium size shows more limited choices, we can probably assume that despite the desire to spread out, and whatever identity problems may exist, it's doubtful that this writer is going to make much effort to find or work for a solution. That doesn't stop him from being angry when things don't go his way, however (heavier pressure strokes); what we have here is someone who is more likely to sit and stew about his problems, rather than make an effort to resolve them.

Exercise for Chapter Five

Identify the firmness, lightness, or variation of pressure in each sample of script you have collected.

Answer the question: What is the level of vitality or energy in this writer? (I.e., are they likely to be ambitious, mild-tempered, or self-effacing?) Can they sustain that drive?

How does this additional information affect the conclusions you have already formed about this writer?

In the next chapter we will look at the fifth and last of handwriting's major trait indicators.

Note: Because this text can't provide you with original samples, there is no self-test exam for this chapter; for all analysis samples used hereafter, you will be told the script pressure wherever necessary.

SAMPLE THREE

This is a sample of the way I normally write — I would like to know what my handwriting tells about me.

SAMPLE FOUR

This is a sample of the way I normally write. I would like to know what my handwriting tells about me.

6

Orientation—
The Zones of Script

What do you want to be when you grow up? What do you like to do best; what do you like to do least; what would you rather not have to do at all?

The **zones** of script tell you which of life's available experiences the writer wants to include in his life. We are making a distinction here between lifestyle preference (size) and specific needs or goals (zones). Script size indicates how much or how many the writer wants. The zone usage tells you *what* he wants: whether he is likely to be more intellectual (upper zone), more practical (middle zone), or more sensual (lower zone) in his approach to life.

Zone emphasis (greater or lesser size of any zone in comparison to the other two) tells you which kinds of experiences the writer prefers or rejects. The degree of *balance between zones* is a quick measure of the writer's level of maturity.

Definition

There are three zones in script. The *upper zone* includes all ascenders: the upper loops of lower-case letters. The *lower zone* includes all descenders: the lower loops of lower-case letters. And the *middle zone* includes everything that's left: the bottom half of letters with ascenders; the top half of letters with descenders, and all lower-case letters which have neither (such as the a, m, o, etc.). Capital letters are not included in a measurement of zones.

Measuring Zones

Zone emphasis is measured across the lower-case letters since these should, if written as taught, reach into all three zones of script. Each zone also "should" be half the height of the letter (i.e., the height of the middle zone is equal to the length of an ascender on the same letter, or the length of a descender on the same letter):

FIGURE 1
Zone Measurement

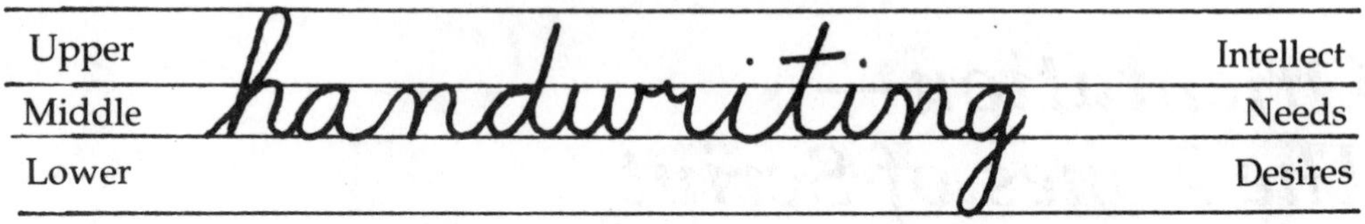

Upper	*handwriting*	Intellect
Middle		Needs
Lower		Desires

You begin your measurement by determining the height (or length) of each zone separately; then you compare the height of each zone to that of the other two. You may find it easier, at least at first, to draw in zone measurement rules; having visible lines to measure between will help you spot both zone emphasis and variations. Draw your rules freehand, the way you did when you drew in the internal baseline (Chapter 2), in this case following the top and bottom boundaries of each zone. Place your measurement rules (1) across (touching) the top of all ascenders; (2) across the top of the middle zone; (3) across the bottom of the middle zone (the internal baseline rule); and (4) across the bottom of descenders:

FIGURE 2
Zone Measurement Rules

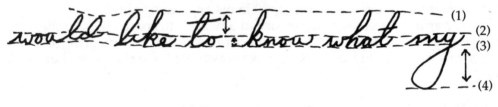

Middle-Zone De-emphasis
(no variation)

A Balanced Script
showing zone variation

What You Are Measuring

Note that while zone analysis uses a height measure, it is *not* a size measure: the actual height (in fractions of inches) of any one zone is not a consideration here. Zone measurement also does not take into account letter width or spacing, and there is no cut-off point for different sizes of script. What you are measuring is *relative height*: you are comparing the size of one part of a letter to the size of another part *of the same letter*. Zone interpretations remain the same no matter what the actual size of the handwriting; and the same zone combinations can occur in any size script.

Zone balance exists when all three zones are roughly equal in size. *Zone emphasis* exists when one zone is measurably larger than either of the others. If one zone is smaller than both of the others, it is called *zone de-emphasis. Zone variation* occurs when (a) there is a change in size within one zone, or (b) there is a change in emphasis between zones, or both.

FIGURE 3
Zone Combinations

Single Zone Emphasis	Balanced	Single Zone De-emphasis

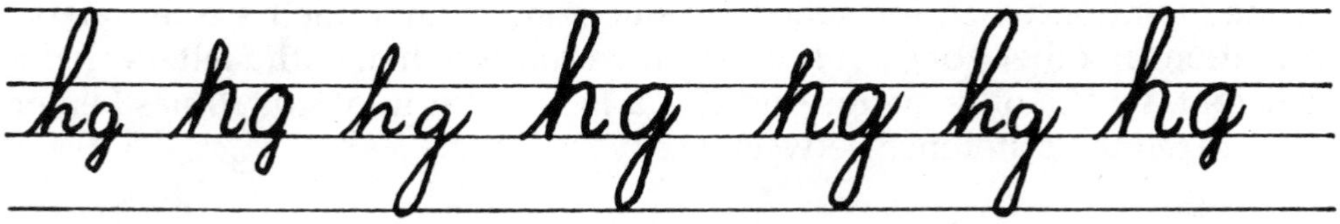

Upper	Middle	Lower		Upper	Middle	Lower

The zones of handwriting reveal dominant interests and emotional reactions in three different, if not necessarily separate, areas of life experience. Briefly: the nature and extent of intellectual curiosity and spiritual reach can be determined by formations in the upper zone; the middle zone is the area which reveals interest in practical and emotional security and social acceptance; and the lower zone shows the desire for physical gratification and material gain.

Organizational Factors

For **Zones,** a well-balanced script (showing fairly equal emphasis between all three zones) is considered good organization; it shows a coordination between the different needs and experiences of living; in short, a sound mind in a healthy body. Emphasis or de-emphasis of any given zone is judged in the same way as script size; it does not necessarily show a lack of mental control, but rather a choice of priorities.

Extremes of zone emphasis are more self-limiting than extremes of size; rather than a choice of interests, it shows an exclusion of some function of the writer's mind, emotions, or body. An extreme exists when one zone is more than twice (extreme emphasis) or less than half (extreme de-emphasis) the size of the other two zones. In Figure 2 above, the first sample shows extreme de-emphasis of the middle zone (half the size of the upper zone; 1/4 the size of the lower zone), and a pronounced to extreme emphasis of the lower zone.

When only one zone is de-emphasized, while either or both of the others are drawn larger, it means a lessening of interest in the area of life which is represented by the de-emphasized zone. When one zone is emphasized at the expense of both of the others, it shows a writer who has literally turned off all activities, interests and experiences except the ones which enter through that particular window on the world.

Variation in zone emphasis can be a sign of either evolving maturity or mental confusion, depending on the age and circumstances of the writer; either way, it does show someone who is having difficulty establishing his priorities. Both these measures must be taken carefully, since often variation in letter size may look like variation in zone emphasis, and vice versa. Naturally, when part of a letter changes its height, the overall size of the letter will also change! The difference is that when measuring a zone, you are measuring horizontally: across *only* the upper zone, *only* the middle zone, or *only* the lower zone. (I.e., the upper zone shows variation if *only* ascenders vary in height.)

Size measure for height is vertical and crosses two zones (upper and middle for letters with ascenders; middle and lower for letters with descenders). It is a zone variation when formations in one zone change their size in relation to formations in other zones. It is a height variation when entire letters change their height, width, or spacing. And it is a fact that it may sometimes be very difficult to tell the difference between the two.

FIGURE 4
A Comparison of Size and Zone Variation

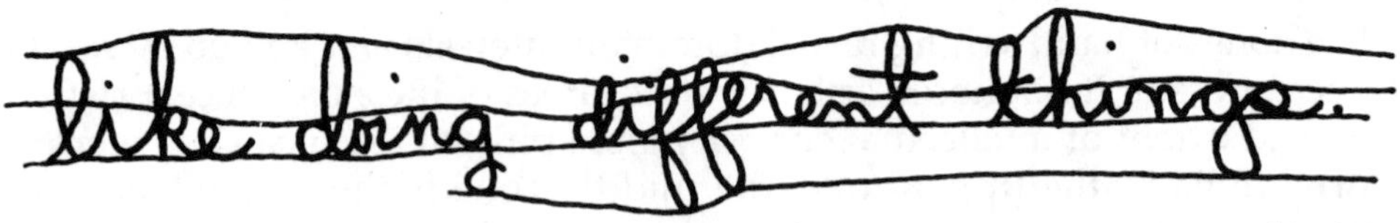

Zone Variation

Size Variation

Sample one is a *zone variation*. Note that the problem is in the upper and lower zones; in fact, it is an emphasis shift between the two. The middle zone is fairly constant, and the actual size of the letters, overall, is also fairly constant. This writer is testing his priorities. The script is large, so he likes lots to do; he just hasn't decided what he likes to do best.

Sample two is a *size variation*. And, yes, there is a zone variation here, too, primarily in the middle zone. But the actual height of the letters, as well as the width and spacing, also change. It's a size variation because that's where the conflict lies: the probable cause of the conflict is in the zone which shows the most stress. This writer is evidently having a lot of trouble in the social area of his life, and it may very well be the reason he can't decide whether he needs more room (word spread), or has too much responsibility (narrow and variable width).

For zones, measure carefully, and compare the parts of the letter to itself, not to any other letter in the sample.

Now that we've got you totally confused, we'll tell you what each of the zones mean. Let's take it from the top:

A. The Upper Zone

The upper zone of handwriting is the realm of the mind. The shape, size, and reach of letterforms in the upper zone show the nature and the extent of intellectual curiosity, spiritual strivings, imagination, and creativity. Note that this is not necessarily a measure of how intelligent the writer is, but of how (and if) his intelligence is being used. The taller the upper zone strokes (in relation to the middle and lower zones), the higher the mental reach, the more the writer wants to understand his world. The shorter the upper zone strokes, the less interest the writer has in personal/intellectual self-development; in fact, the less he even thinks at all.

1. *Upper Zone Emphasis*

A handwriting which stays predominantly in the upper zone shows someone to whom mental development is more important than anything else life has to offer. Such a writer will tend to neglect both social and physical needs in favor of intellectual or spiritual exploration; and very often, the learning is an end in itself. Depending on other signs in the script, this can be the handwriting of the scholar; it can also be the handwriting of the person who intellectualizes all events—who has to find a reason for everything that happens to him. And, if there are other negative signs in the script, it can be the writing of the person who is escaping from the problems of social and physical demands and decisions by retreating into the world of thought and dreams.

2. *Upper Zone De-emphasis*

In contrast, when the script shows very short extensions into the upper zone, it means that the writer has very little interest in his own intellectual development (or spiritual reach). Again, we equate intellectual development with personal development; it's not just a matter of wanting to know facts, but of the ability to explore ideas, the desire to find out what you can be as a person. The writer who avoids learning or thinking is less likely to be able to grow and change.

B. The Middle Zone

The middle zone shows the socialization of the writer. This is the area of practical involvement in the world, and of essential needs; from survival requirements (food-warmth-shelter) to basic emotional fulfillment (feelings of security and the need for social acceptance). Formations in the middle zone show the writer's interest and involvement in the day-to-day activities of home, work, and play. The larger the middle zone letters in relation to ascenders and descenders, the more important social involvement and social mores are to the writer—both his own, and those of other people. When the middle zone is de-emphasized, it shows a writer who is less concerned with these basic practical considerations, and usually less interested in or trying to shut out the concerns, demands, and opinions of other people.

1. *Middle Zone Emphasis*

I am Aquarius with Virgo rising

A handwriting which stays predominantly in the middle zone shows someone who has very few needs or drives outside of family life. This is the person for whom earning a living and raising a family comprise the whole of existence, with the emphasis on *his* job and *his* family. It can also indicate someone to whom social mores and customs are vitally important and not to be changed, or to whom social acceptance means more than any other kind of personal achievement. Middle zone emphasis (especially when combined with very rounded formations, as in the sample above) is characteristic of the handwriting of children. The young child is primarily concerned with emotional security and the approval of authority (in the form of parents and teachers and other significant adults). Upper and lower zone extensions are among the first signs of an evolving independence of thought and action in a growing child. In an adult's script, the type of writing shown in our sample is an unquestionable sign of mental, emotional, and even physical immaturity.

2. *Middle Zone De-Emphasis*

would like to know what my

When the middle zone is very much smaller than either the upper or lower zones, it means the writer has shut these basic needs out of his life. There are any number of reasons for this particular attitude. Sometimes, the writer really doesn't need social involvement, or is so interested in his own intellectual and/or physical development that he hasn't got time for it. Many times, middle-zone de-emphasis is the writer's means of defending himself against "significant others" who demand too much of his essential self; a reaction against other people who wanted to decide what he should be when he grew up. But in shutting them out of his life, he shuts off this part of his life as well.

C. The Lower Zone

Lower zone formations show the nature and extent of the writer's physical needs and desires: sexual requirements, physical appetites (food, drink, or drugs), and physical drives (sports or exercise). It also indicates the importance of any goals which supplement, provide, or substitute for physical needs, such as financial goals or other material acquisitions. The longer the lower zone extensions, the more naturally sensual the writer (i.e., the more physically sensual he would be if social mores did not interfere), and the greater his need for physical stimulation, or, in cases where the physical drive has been discouraged and therefore sublimated, for something to replace it. Shortened extensions in the lower zone show a lack of need for physical stimulation or activity, or a disinterest in material gain.

1. *Lower Zone Emphasis*

A handwriting which concentrates in the lower zone shows an extremely physical and usually sensual nature; the writer to whom physical gratification is the prime goal of life. The drive can result in sexual promiscuity, exaggerated body-building, overindulgence in food or drink, or greed for luxury and material acquisitions, depending on how the writer expresses his needs. But whichever the expressed goal, what you have essentially is someone who thinks with his glands.

2. *Lower Zone De-Emphasis*

Shortened lower-zone extensions are used by the writer who ignores his body as long as its general physical health does not interfere with whatever else he wants to do. It is not merely a lack of physical drives, but a disinterest in the physical aspect of self. This person is not likely to join a health club, for example: not because he's lazy, but because he genuinely doesn't care about his body's appearance; as long as everything works well enough that his body doesn't bother him, he doesn't bother with his body. Lower zone de-emphasis indicates a lessening of interest in physical comfort, or physical stimulation, and very often a low sexual drive.

D. Zone Combinations

De-emphasis of only one zone is less limiting than de-emphasis of two, but it still means that something is being excluded from the writer's life. When one of the emphasized zones is slightly larger or more pronounced than the other, which is usually the case, it may also mean that the abilities acquired by developing the lesser of the two emphasized zones are being used to acquire the drives of the greater.

1. *Upper-Lower Emphasis* (with middle de-emphasis resulting)

De-emphasis of the middle zone with upper and lower zones stressed shows a combination of intelligence and physical drives, and little interest in or avoidance of family and social life. If the lower zone is the larger of the two, you are looking at someone who uses his head to get what his body wants: in most cases, it indicates a writer who is very success- or money-conscious. If the upper zone is the larger of the two, then personal development is this writer's definition of success, and physical or material acquisitions are a means of getting it (it's hard to be intellectually independent when you are financially dependent).

2. *Upper-Middle Emphasis* (with lower de-emphasis implied)

De-emphasis of the lower zone with upper and middle zones stressed shows a writer who does his thinking and scheming to further his social aspirations, and who has very little interest in physical activity and probably a low sexual drive. If the upper zone is the larger of the two, the writer tends to use his accomplishments to impress his peers; he needs the people who make up his world to think highly of him. If the middle zone is the larger, then his abilities and accomplishments are being used for the benefit or advancement of his significant others; he cares more about his family and community than he does about his own personal needs.

3. *Middle-Lower Emphasis* (with upper de-emphasis)

how I form my writing.

De-emphasis of the upper zone with middle and lower zones stressed shows social aspirations combined with physical drives, and little or no intellectual curiosity or originality of thought or action. Here, too, success is likely to be measured (by the writer) in terms of social approval or recognition. If the lower zone is stressed, the writer is likely to use his physical attributes or material possessions as a means of impressing others; he is very likely to be concerned with how he looks, the way he dresses, or what he has. When the middle zone is the larger, the writer is likely to judge his success by the comfort of his family or community or by what he can provide for them.

E. Zone Variation

like doing different things.

Variation in zone emphasis can be either a positive or negative sign, depending on the age or circumstances of the writer. If the variation is not too extreme, what it shows is a writer who is testing the effects of different priorities. Especially in a young person, like the writer of our sample, this is a natural part of growing up. But however natural it is, never forget that it is called, very accurately, "growing pains"; and though it may be a positive indicator here (a sign that the child is beginning the attempt to decide what he wants to be), it is still very uncomfortable for the person going through it. Even in a writer who is older, zone variation can be a sign of transition, if the writer's life has recently undergone or is undergoing a radical change: it is not unusual to see it in the handwriting of someone recently divorced, or recently retired.

As with anything else, it's a matter of degree: usually a variation in zone emphasis is gradual, a growing up or growing down of different parts of the script. But when the variation is extreme, and especially if it continues over a long period of time, it means the writer is someone who doesn't know what he wants out of life, or what type of pursuits will serve best serve his interests. And of all stress signs in script, this one shows the greatest amount of confusion.

F.   Zone Balance

When all three zones are roughly equal in size (and our last sample is just that, despite the variation), it means that the writer prefers a well-rounded existence: a balance between intellectual development, social involvement, and physical drives. All other things being equal, this is the writer who is not afraid, or unwilling, to use his mind to its full capacity; who is able to fulfill his role in society, whatever that role may be; and who is capable of acknowledging and satisfying his normal physical needs. Like the large size script, a balanced handwriting (of whatever size) is used by someone who likes a certain variety of experiences; in this case, however, it is not so much a matter of wanting more out of life, but rather a willingness and/or ability to at least try the different kinds of experiences life has to offer. As we noted above, the balanced script is graphology's indicator of a well-rounded personality: a sound mind in a healthy body.

Conclusion: *Interpreting Zones*

The three zones of script can almost be considered as three separate trait indicators, since even penstroke formations take on a slightly different meaning in each different zone. How the writer feels about each different area of his life will be shown by the way he shapes letters or parts of letters in a given zone (Chapter 7: Penstroke Formations). Whether or if one area of his life matters more than another will be shown by the relative sizes of the different zones.

Zone analysis by itself is handled as a single trait indicator. You begin by determining the zone usage: the physical appearance and size of each zone in relation to the other two. If there is an imbalance, be certain to specify which zones are emphasized or de-emphasized, if any two are the same, or if all three are different (do you have a clear middle-zone de-emphasis with upper and lower balance, or is it a middle-zone de-emphasis with lower zone concentration: the lower zone measurably larger than the upper zone? It does make a difference!). Once you have identified the zone usage, that is the interpretation you will combine with the other four trait indicators you have already identified in your sample.

For example: the tendency toward personal isolation shown in a small, vertical script is tempered by balanced zones. It still means that the writer tends to shut out distractions, and also to shut out personal involvement with others. But the zone balance indicates that his field of interest is automatically wider than the smallness of the script would indicate by itself, because he retains a healthy interest in all areas of life. (He does not depend on other people, but he still includes them in his life: the middle zone shows he does have a family and/or social life.) It alters the meaning of the vertical script, too: it means he feels he can go it alone if he has to, and not that he prefers to.

A large script shows a need for a variety of experiences, for more personal space. If that is combined with a strong upper-zone emphasis, with the middle and lower zones small to non-existent, the writer's variety is confined to intellectual pursuits. He may have a wide-ranging mind which pursues knowledge in any form and from any source, but he can't or won't do anything else. In this case, the zone imbalance adds a conflict to the script: a discrepancy between a lifestyle preference for many things to do (large size) and a set of goals which deliberately limits what the writer will do (upper-zone emphasis).

When you see zone emphasis in a handwriting, you are looking at a writer who has not only made a choice about what he will do, but what he won't. When the emphasis or de-emphasis is slight, it merely indicates a preference; usually, however, when the emphasis is extreme, you will find other negative signs in the script as well, either as cause of the emphasis, or as effect. Life has a way of intruding on even the most self-contained individual; and it is also, unfortunately, very often possible for someone to have made the wrong choice *for himself*—or the right choice for the wrong reasons. As a graphologist, it is your task to help your subjects understand both the choice they have made and its implications. In the final analysis, the first step in getting what you want is knowing exactly what it is.

Principles of the Analysis

ORIENTATION: Zone usage tells you what in his life really matters to the writer. Your analysis will reveal the writer's priorities: the choices he has made or rejected.

The question you are trying to answer is: Does this writer prefer a well-rounded existence (balanced); is he more interested in or influenced by intellectual (upper), social (middle), or physical (lower) drives or involvement; or is he going through growing pains (varied)?

ANALYSIS OUTLINE (continued)

V. Zones (What does the writer want out of life?)
  A. Upper Zone (Intellectual and spiritual interests; personal growth and development)
  B. Middle Zone (Social needs or involvement: family and community; needs for basic feelings of security)
  C. Lower Zone (Physical or material needs and drives)
  D. Zone Emphasis (Concentration on the larger zone(s): exclusion of the smaller zone(s).)
    1. Single-zone emphasis (Indicates a preference for the activities of the largest zone)
    2. Single-zone de-emphasis (Indicates a distaste for or avoidance of the activities of the smallest zone)
    3. Zone Combinations (One activity excluded; a second activity being used to acquire the benefits of the third)
  E. Zone Variation (Growing pains: difficulty in or inability to decide what really matters)
  F. Zone Balance (Well-rounded personality)

Doing the Analysis—Zones

At this point in our analysis, we know what our writers think about others, what they think about life, how much energy they have invested in carrying out their intentions, and of course, how much control they have over themselves and their impulses. Now let's see just what it is in their lives that our writers consider most important—or easiest to live without.

SAMPLE ONE (see page 87)

Zones: Upper-lower combination, with lower zone stressed.

Tight control and little leeway; this writer works hard, even though he does seem to have the strength to do it, and is willing to make sacrifices. Question: what is he sacrificing?

It would seem that what he's sacrificing is normal social contacts: the middle-zone de-emphasis is not extreme, but it comes very close. The controlled-right tilt tells us that he likes people but doesn't need them; the middle zone tells us that most of the time he doesn't want them either. This writer is not someone who is likely to ask advice or take it; and the trait combination suggests that he's not likely to lean on others either, even in need.

What does he want? The zone emphasis stresses upper and lower; the lower zone is larger, so what this writer is working so hard for is physical or material goals. And he is pushing himself very hard: this writer *has to* succeed; and, again the combination of traits we have so far would suggest that he probably reads success as financial gain and/or professional status.

This writer is also someone who *has to* believe he knows all the answers (rigid baseline), but he doesn't: the slight size variation shows a certain amount of confusion over goals, and the narrow width and spacing indicate that he may have bitten off more than he can chew. In any other handwriting, that minor variation would be considered "within acceptable limits"; people don't write with machine-like precision after all, do they? But this one does, so any variation is significant. Note that all the size variation is actually a zone variation, and all confined to the upper zone. Combined with the fact that he is a hard worker with consistent drive and determination (pressure), we know that this writer is driving himself, physically and emotionally, toward some end which he has not even clarified in his own mind.

Now the question we need to answer is *why*?

SAMPLE TWO (see page 87)

Zones: Middle-zone de-emphasis; upper zone stressed.

Enthusiastic, outgoing, needs other people but doesn't push either his ambitions or himself on those others and, like writer number one, suppressing a part of his life.

Again, this is a handwriting in which personal (upper) and physical (lower) drives take precedence over emotional security needs (middle), but with a dif-

SAMPLE ONE

This is a sample of the way I normally write.

I would like to know what my handwriting tells

about me.

SAMPLE TWO

This is a sample of the way I normally

write. I would like to know what my

handwriting tells about me.

ference. In this case, the upper zone is emphasized, indicating that the writer has a greater interest in intellectual or spiritual development. The upper zone variation indicates that he may not know exactly what it is he's looking for (which confirms our baseline interpretation). But notice that most of the size variation takes place in the middle zone. Despite the fact that this writer has de-emphasized this part of his life, that is where most of the stress and indecision is happening. Maybe that's why the de-emphasis tends to the extreme.

But it is still a contradiction. Unlike writer number one, this writer needs other people (pronounced-right), but he is downplaying their influence in his life (middle zone de-emphasis and variation); and since he's obviously under stress, the choice was a difficult one to make. Why did he make it?

This writer is someone who wants to find out what he can be. The middle-zone problems would indicate that significant others in his life are probably telling him that he's wasting his time; if that is the case, then what we have is someone who is being forced to make his own guidelines, despite whatever he was raised to be. The possibility exists that most of this writer's problems are being caused by other people: and since, in spite of his need for others, he is shutting them out of his life, the possibility also exists that he knows it.

SAMPLE THREE (see page 89)

Zones: Balanced, but variable.

Generally friendly, basically conventional, somewhat more restless than most people, and subconsciously looking for ways to spread out, and proba-bly, in this case, to grow. The baseline variation indicates a lack of clear objec-tives, and certainly self-doubts and/or serious questions about goals. The moderate pressure, as we have learned, is not so much calmness and balance as it is this writer's way of keeping a tight rein on himself.

We add zone balance, so writer number three has established a kind of equilibrium: he is interested in and willing to explore all the possibilities life has to offer. The variation of size and variation of emphasis spreads across all three zones, however; sometimes a greater reach into intellectual exploration, sometimes a greater need for physical satisfaction, and sometimes either sup-pression or acknowledgement of the importance of social demands.

We can still judge this writer as restless, but we now have at least a clue as to why: he does not know what he wants to be when he grows up.

SAMPLE FOUR (see page 89)

Zones: Lower zone emphasis; upper zone de-emphasis.

Fairly adaptable but likely to make more specific or more limited choices; lack of concentration and attention to detail and some desire to spread out; low drive or low physical energy; and a basic satisfaction with life as it is. Well, what is that life?

In this case, the middle zone is secondary but still stressed, showing the importance and acceptance of socially acceptable goals; the lower zone is

SAMPLE THREE

This is a sample of the way I normally write. I would like to know what my handwriting tells about me.

SAMPLE FOUR

This is a sample of the way I normally write. I would like to know what my handwriting tells about me.

largest, which confirms that this writer likes his comfort. The occasional swing into the upper zone (but from the middle zone!) shows that this writer thinks he may find some answer to whatever restlessness he feels in spiritual or mental development, but the de-emphasis of the upper zone indicates that no great effort is really being made in this direction. That could temper at least one earlier conclusion: it's possible that the style changes may not be an identity search at all, but more likely a way of being different without putting too much thought or effort into it.

This writer values physical or material goals, but is not willing (pressure) or able (upper zone de-emphasis) to put much effort into achieving them for himself. Well, we have a trait: it's called *laziness*; certainly intellectual, if not physical as well. And we could wonder if the restlessness and identity problems might be a reaction to the possibility that whoever has been providing for this writer is no longer as willing to make the effort either.

Exercise for Chapter Six

Identify the zone emphasis in each sample of script you have collected. Answer the question: Is this writer more concerned with intellectual, social, or physical goals; or leading a fairly balanced life? How does this additional information affect the conclusions you have already formed about this writer?

Summation: What we have so far is an outline of character and personality traits as simple, and as incomplete, as stick figure drawings. Now we begin to add color and form to our personality sketches: to find out how our writers feel, and why they act the way they do. The next section takes us into letter forms—the A-B-C of handwriting.

TEST YOURSELF

For each of the five script samples given below, measure and compare the zone usage. Specify what you believe each writer wants most out of life. Our answers are in Appendix B.

SAMPLE ONE

This is a sample of how I

SAMPLE TWO

what you can tell from my

SAMPLE THREE

I would like more informatin about

SAMPLE FOUR

way I normally form my handwriting).

SAMPLE FIVE

send me information about your

Review 1

What have we established so far?

1. We know whether or not the writer is in charge of his own life, or if someone or something else is calling the shots (organization).

2. We know whether or not the writer is experiencing self-doubts or has questions about the way he is living his life; and if so, how severe they are (baseline).

3. If he is going though emotional highs and lows, we know whether those doubts exist because he is looking for guidelines (disorganized), or because he is fighting guidelines other people or events are trying to rule for him (organized). If he's emotionally stable, we know whether it's because he's keeping himself on too tight a leash (rigid organization), because he's given up something he feels he can't have (conflicting indicators), or because he has simply found exactly what he wants (may it happen to us all!)

4. We know if he is an original, or at least a flexible thinker (unique formations, organized)—which is to say, if he can change his plans to meet changing circumstances—or if he's simply confused in some way (unique formations, disorganized).

5. We know how he feels about other people and we know whether or not the writer's decisions and feelings about self will be influenced by what he perceives as other people's reactions, and if so, how much (angle).

6. We know what kind of lifestyle situation and/or professional environment would be most productive for the writer, and we know whether or not he knows what it is, and if he is pursuing it (size).

7. We know whether or not the writer is willing—or able—to work for what he wants, and if not, why not (pressure). And finally;

8. We know what he wants, whether or not he knows what he wants, and whether or not he's getting it (zone emphasis).

If at this point you cannot tell at least this much from any sample of handwriting, then before you continue with the next analysis section, you should review any points you've missed. This study is cumulative, and the information in the following chapters will influence and be influenced by what you already know about organization and the major trait indicators.

7

Behavior Patterns— Shapes in the Alphabet

If the tilt of your writing shows that you like other people and want their company, why don't you have any friends? If your pen pressure proves that you're a hard worker, why can't you get anything done? And if your baseline indicates that you know you're going about everything the wrong way, how did you manage to become such an outstanding success?

The **penstroke formations** that make up letters and words tell you how the writer thinks and feels; they provide specific information about his habits, characteristics, talents and potentials. Most important, they reveal underlying, and often unconscious, motivation: they tell you how the writer functions, and what is likely to interfere with, or matter more than, his ability to function.

This chapter covers only penstroke formations used in the lower-case English script alphabet. The chapters that follow explain penstroke interpretation for capitals, script form, and identity words.

Definition

A penstroke formation is any shape, identifiable or not, formed on a writing surface using a writing instrument. Doodles are penstrokes; so are any shapes scribbled or drawn by preliterate children.

In the study of handwriting analysis, we confine ourselves to the penstrokes used to form letters and words in a cursive (script) alphabet, and any penstrokes added to script writing. The basic penstroke formations which make up or are included in the cursive alphabet fall into three general categories: *letterform* (the basic shape of the letter itself); the *necessary accessories* (such as i-dots and t-bars); and the *unnecessary accessories* (penstrokes added to the basic letterform).

Measuring Penstrokes

In order to measure the penstroke formations used in writing, you need to

FIGURE 1
American Schoolform Cursive

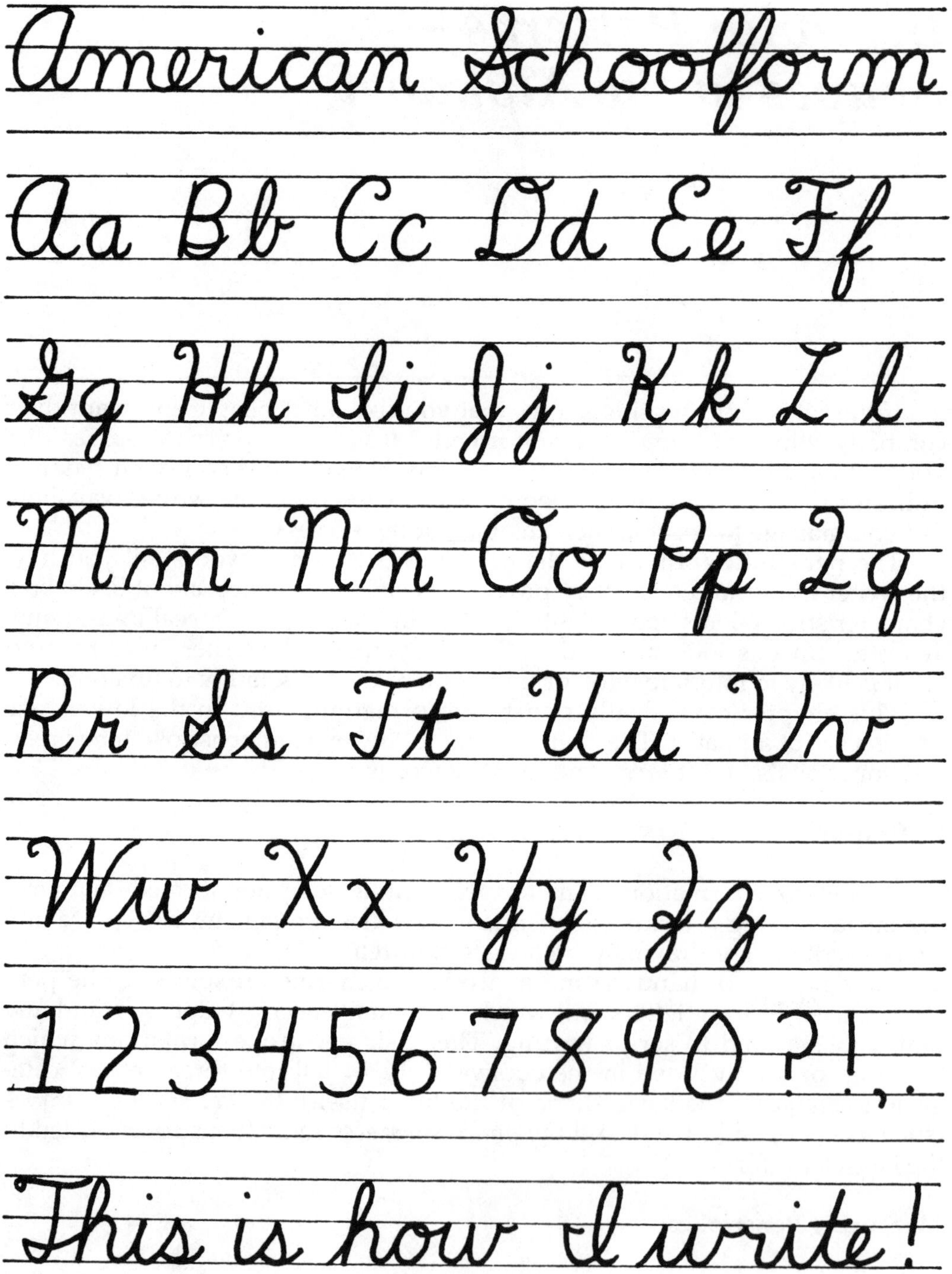

American Schoolform

Aa Bb Cc Dd Ee Ff

Gg Hh Ii Jj Kk Ll

Mm Nn Oo Pp Qq

Rr Ss Tt Uu Vv

Ww Xx Yy Zz

1 2 3 4 5 6 7 8 9 0 ? ! , .

This is how I write!

know something about the cursive alphabet; and since we also need a standard against which to measure individuality of style, the alphabet we will use is the one you probably learned when you first began to write: American Schoolform. The chart on page 96 gives you all the upper- and lower-case cursive letters as they are taught in the primary grades, and also shows how connectors are used to form these letters into words.

If a writer is using penstrokes to form letters and words in an English script alphabet, there are 26 shapes he can choose from (or 52, if you distinguish between lowercase and capital letters). But there are an infinite number of penstroke formations that different writers can make of these basic letter-shapes and their accessories.

It would be impossible to record every conceivable variation of each of the script letters of the alphabet. And it would be a waste of your time to try to memorize long lists of oddly-shaped letter forms, or to search through a graphological dictionary looking for every letter variation you run across in a sample of script. Because one thing is certain: somewhere along the line, some writer is going to come up with a penstroke combination no one has ever seen or used before, and whose meaning is not analyzed in any sourcebook ever written about graphology.

Fortunately, it's not necessary to compile or learn a dictionary listing of several thousand variant configurations. Letter formations can be grouped into a limited number of categories, and all formations in a given category have the same basic meaning no matter how you use them, and no matter what school system you learned to write in. Further, all letter formations are combinations of penstrokes, and *a specific penstroke shape has a specific meaning, which does not change no matter what other penstrokes it may be combined with*. To measure letter form and shape you analyze the individual penstrokes that form it—you break a letter down into its component parts and then combine your interpretation of those parts to determine its overall meaning. It is not difficult to do. If you learn the meanings of the basic script letterform penstrokes thoroughly (and there are not that many of them), you will be able to deduce the meaning of some unusual combination you have never seen before or may never see again.

In the following sections we will break down the cursive alphabet into similar formations, and see how additions to or changes in the basic form provide information about the nature of the writer who uses them.

What You Are Measuring

You are trying to determine how the writer uses penstrokes to form letters, and which penstrokes he uses or leaves out. *Note*: The penstroke interpretations given in this and the following chapters apply equally to lettershapes and penstrokes used in American Schoolform style.

Organizational Factors

In cursive writing, good organization for **Penstroke Formations** consists of letterforms which are clear, simple, and make the script easier to read and/or faster to write. Clarity of form indicates a similar clarity of thought. And, except for someone whose job it is to make script look beautiful—such as a professional calligrapher—the fewer the complications in the script, the less likely the writer is to complicate his own life with non-essentials.

Complications in script, as we noted in Chapter One, are any unnecessary strokes or additions to the letterform. They show mental confusion translated into action: the person who cannot get anything done because he is too involved with non-essentials. All the "unnecessary accessories" are included in this category, whether they are simply formed, or intricately complex.

As with the major trait indicators, any **extreme** means the writer is over-reacting in some way; how he is overreacting will be determined by the pen-stroke formation involved. Changes to the basic letterform may indicate either pronounced or extreme traits, depending on their usage; ornamentation is in and of itself an extreme complication.

The occasional use of a penstroke formation different from the writer's normal style is not considered a penstroke variation. *Habit*, or consistent usage, is the graphologist's guide to basic character traits. Every penstroke can be interpreted, but a single penstroke, used only once in a sample, is not evidence of an essential trait in the writer's makeup. To be significant, the same type of formation must reappear throughout the script; even if it is not used all the time, it does indicate a basic need or characteristic. Consistent usage can be either a positive or negative organizational indicator, depending on the penstroke formation(s) used.

Now, let's review our A-B-Cs. We'll begin by breaking down the letter forms by class.

A. Letter Form

Letter forms fall into two general categories: closed and open formations, and looped and loopless formations. They do not change their category no matter how they are written. If a closed formation, for example, is not completed by the writer, it does not become an open formation; it is a closed formation left open.

The lower-case a is a closed formation: so also is the middle zone of the d, and the upper half of the middle zone on the k. The cup of the b, and letters like u and w, are open formations; the m and n, and the middle zone of the h, are inverted cups and also fall into this category.

Loops are normally found on ascenders and descenders; the only middle-zone formation with a loop is the e. There are only two letters with ascenders but without loops: the d and t use a covered downstroke. Some letters use both formations; for example, the b is both open and looped, and the g is both closed and looped; the d is closed and loopless. Please refer to Figure 1 to help you identify similar letters.

1. Closed and Open Letters: Reticence and Receptivity
A closed formation is formed like a circle; the pen must return to the beginning point to complete the closure (and then leave from there to form another part of the letter or the connector). An open, or cup, formation has an

entrance which can "face," or be open at, the top (b or u), side (the c), or bottom (m, n, h). Open and closed formations tell you how the writer responds to ideas or information, and how willing he is to share his own thoughts.

Closed letters show reserve; the writer who does not say everything he happens to think, or take at face value everything you happen to say. It does not show an inability to communicate; it indicates the ability to keep your own counsel. The writer who uses it is someone who knows when to keep his mouth shut, and when to take what you say with a grain of salt.

On the other hand, a writer who **locks closed** a letter which should be open (in the direction of communication!) is not about to tell you anything, no matter what the situation, or even how tempting the provocation (see also: cup formations, below).

Open letters mean a more open person; and the writer who opens up his middle zone letters where they should be closed will tend to be more chatty, more likely to discuss his feelings, and more receptive to other people's ideas. This is a sign of carelessness only if confirmed by other signs in the script (as missing i-dots and t-bars); and even in that case, it still refers to careless chatter. Watch this formation closely, however: when it runs through the entire middle zone, you may have someone who can't keep a secret; and especially if it is pronounced (more open), it can indicate gullibility as well.

Notice that the g and the q use identical strokes in the middle zone; and open/closed formations have the same meaning here. The formation of the d is also similar, but the opening is toward the top (upper zone), so the writer's interest is more likely to be ideas than opinions.

When a letter is open only as much as it is supposed to be, it shows receptivity. The middle zone **cup** (open at the *top*; note that even the schoolform c keeps a tight lid on) is used by the writer who is open to ideas, and probably willing to talk about them. There is no carelessness or lack of thought involved here; the traditional form shows someone not open-mouthed, just open-minded.

If the opening is **very wide,** however, it's a confirmation of gullibility; this writer will literally swallow anything he's told. The wide cup may or may not be combined with openings on closed letters; talkativeness and gullibility are not the same traits!

The cup that is **very narrow** or **tightly closed** shows more than just caution or reserve; someone who writes this way is suspicious of others, and probably narrow-minded as well. This is the person who "wouldn't give you the time of day."

Look for confirmation in other letter forms. The v and the w use identical letter strokes, and the u is also a similar formation. Notice especially that the tightly closed cup alters the shape of the letter in such a way that it can be mistaken for something else; and this is a picture of the way such a writer communicates—when and if he communicates.

We'll be talking about knots and ties a little later on, but: If the tightly-closed cup shows closed-mouthed suspicion, what do you think it means if that cup is not only tightly closed, but tied firmly with a knot?

Interpreting similar formations category: If a cup closed where it should be open means suspicion and narrow-mindedness, what do you think it means if a writer closes up the bottom of his m or n? Remember, you are dealing with an inverted cup, so it faces the lower zone, which expresses physical drives rather than intellectual ideas. The meaning of the closure is the same, only its orientation has varied. What is it, then, that the writer is suspicious of, or narrow-minded about?

A letter open where it should be closed is either a pronounced or extreme trait (depending on how wide the opening and/or how often it occurs in the script); the same is true of a cup formation which is narrowed (pronounced), or locked closed (extreme). When a cup is very wide it is a pronounced trait; if combined with openings on closed letters, it becomes an extreme.

The orientation changes in each zone of script: in the upper zone, these formations show the writer's response to ideas; in the middle zone his attitude toward social contacts; and in the lower zone an open or closed mind regarding physical drives. The combination of open and closed letters in script style is not a contradiction: you can be willing to talk and not willing to listen, or vice versa.

2. *Loops: Sense and Sensitivity*

The loop is a fold or doubling of the penstroke which forms a closed oval or eye-shaped formation. A covering stroke is one in which the downstroke retraces the upstroke; this is the traditional (Schoolbook) loopless formation. Loopless formations can be formed with a covering stroke, or with a single (printed) stroke.

Loops indicate feeling: they show whether or not the writer is emotionally involved with what he is doing, and how much feeling is involved. The interpretation of loop formations differs slightly in the different zones, but in general, wide loops show great feeling; the narrow loop shows a more self-contained and practical attitude; and the single printed stroke, replacing the loop, is a sign of a direct, to-the-point approach. The printed stroke can also be divided into three categories: blunt endings (a blunt nature), the club ending (brutality), and the sharp ending (anger or viciousness). Let's see what happens when we attach the loops to letter forms:

$$beg$$

Loops placed where they are "supposed to" be, at about the correct width (and they vary slightly even in Schoolbook), show that the feeling is there, but its expression is conservative (controlled).

b l   h h

Very fat, wide loops in the **upper zone** show a writer whose judgements are more likely to be based on feelings than on facts. If the loop is taller than it is wide (see bottom left), the interest is likely to be spiritual—or, at least, in some intellectual area which satisfies an emotional need. If the loop is wider than it is tall (bottom right), it is a sign of social aspirations; the writer who is looking for recognition, praise, or acceptance as a result of his intellectual achievements.

e g

The same width in the **middle zone** shows the writer's need to include other people—as many as possible—in his world. In the **lower zone**, it shows a writer who tends to overindulge in the pursuit of sensual or erotic fulfillment; sex, food-drink-drugs, or the physical comforts money can buy.

b k

Narrow loops in the **upper zone**, especially with pointed tops, show a more critical (i.e., discerning) intelligence; a writer with sharper insights and less emotional fogging, whose judgements are normally based on data. In this case, a very tall loop suggests someone who is interested in the data for what it means or how it can be used, rather than in how it can increase his social standing.

e g

The **narrow or closed loop** in the **middle zone** shows secrecy, caution, or skepticism—again, a colder, or data-based reaction, but in this case toward people rather than facts or information. This writer may find it difficult to like or trust people. Check this formation for verification in hidden loops (below). The narrow loop in the **lower zone** can also show an unemotional (and in some cases uninvolved) approach, but in this case it relates to physical drives.

b f

The writer who **eliminates upper zone loops** has very little time for nonsense and very little patience with stalling tactics. In a fast handwriting, mixed with other printed forms, you have a writer who is trying to save time without scribbling illegibly. This is someone whose mind is racing too fast for his pen, yet who still wants to be clearly understood. Mixed with intuitive breaks (see Connectors/Script Form, Chapter 8) and other signs of intellectual imagination, the simplified form shows a creative and original mind. The type of creativity is most likely to be practical rather than decorative, however; and whether this writer is an artist, scientist, or business executive, he is someone who wants to have accomplished something as a result of his time and effort.

The **middle zone** "e" formed with a **covered downstroke** (to look like a dotless i) can also show quickness of thought if confirmed by other signs. If not, it shows concealment (again; a letter form which looks like some other letter), impatience, or a desire to shut others out.

On the other hand, when the **lower case e is filled in**, it is a sure sign of sensuality, and of a very specific nature: the writer who uses it has not chosen something to substitute for physical stimulation, he needs physical stimulation.

Watch the printed form carefully in the **lower zone**. The elimination of loops where loops should be shows someone who wants to eliminate non-essentials, but keep in mind that these "non-essentials" include such things as feeling, sensitivity, or even imagination. The single, printed downstroke is both a space and a time saver, and the writer who uses it is likely to have a very practical, direct approach. The lower zone shows physical drives; and lack of loops here shows a practical, direct, and unemotional approach toward physical functions or needs. All other things being equal, the blunt ending (as on the g) simply shows a blunt nature (the person who tells it like it is; blunt endings are one of the indicators for honesty in a well-organized script, and for lack of diplomacy if the script is disorganized). But stress or rage signs are also common in the lower zone: a heavy-pressured, club-like ending (the j) shows unnecessary force or brutality; sharp terminals (the y) are indications of anger or viciousness.

Extra loops (where the traditional form does not call for them) indicate that there is something the writer is sensitive about; if they are very wide, the writer is hyper-sensitive. "Sensitive" in this case means thin-skinned: any slight, real or imagined, is going to hurt, even if the writer is aware that he is overreacting, or that no slight was intended.

When extra loops are closed inside the middle zone of a letter, they become **hidden loops**; and they mean there is something our sensitive writer is secretive about as well. The deeper the loop, the more the writer is hiding. When the hidden loops extend more than halfway down the height of the letter (bottom left), and especially if there is a deep double looping (bottom right), you could be dealing with a downright liar. In middle zone formations (which tell you how the writer deals with significant others), this type of lying is very often a defense mechanism; the writer is hiding behind a mask. Again, extra loops mean that the writer is sensitive about something.

Small, tight loops formed at the *top* of the middle zone are a sign of diplomacy; again, concealment of the writer's true feelings (though in this case, more on the order of a white lie). When they are added onto letters which ordinarily do not call for them, you have a writer who is likely to be sensitive about other people's feelings. Recall that the orientation of the loop here is toward the upper zone: what the writer is concealing is what he sees as facts.

On the other hand, as hidden loops are a sign of secrecy, the **lack of loops** is usually a sign of honesty (or, as we discussed above, bluntness). The writer who uses the covered downstroke (where it belongs) may be quiet, but he doesn't necessarily have anything to hide.

Combine your stroke meanings category: If a letter shows a diplomatic loop, or deep hidden loops, but is opened where it should be closed, what can you deduce from these two conflicting signs? Secrecy combined with openness? We know we have a writer who is likely to be talkative, but the chances are also good that he's not telling you what he really thinks or feels. The trait is called insincerity.

Always, but especially with these feeling signs, look for odd or unique formations, which can show anything from originality, to affectation, to guilt. For example:

Upper zone loops are supposed to start at the baseline when they begin a word. The writer who **starts loops in the upper zone** is forcing a separation between mind and matter; what goes on in his head is private, and the "real" world of day-to-day contacts and obligations is not permitted to intrude. Again, this is an original formation, and if gracefully formed, it shows a writer who can and does deliberately use his creativity and/or imagination as a means of escape when he wants or needs it. Question: what do you think it would mean in a disorganized script? Remember: it's an escape from the reality of day-to-day contacts with others in a writer who lacks control.

Because physical drives are often overlaid with guilt, **lower zone loops** can be very revealing. Watch, for example, to see if the loops are **completed** (returned to the baseline). If they are not, then whatever the sensual requirement of the writer it is unsatisfied or unfulfilled. This is probably the most common variation from schoolform you will find in script.

Peculiarly formed or **twisted** return loops (bottom left and center) are signs of guilt. They are generally found in the handwriting of anyone who has been taught that his sex drive, whatever its orientation, is something evil or dirty but who, because he is physically normal, has those urges anyway. Keep in mind, however, that *loops are feeling signs*. They show not what the writer is, but how he feels about what he is. Twisted or eccentric lower zone loops tell you the writer feels guilty—but they do not necessarily mean that the writer has actually done anything to feel guilty about.

The **flourished loop** (bottom right), gracefully formed, is a form of ostentation, which in the lower zone usually means love of money or material things. But this particular formation can also show selfishness, introversion, bigotry or clannishness, or guilt. Remember your major trait indicators: it's a swing back to the left (into self), and tied with a knot (see below).

Check the chart. Any letters formed by similar penstrokes have similar meanings.

The wider the loop, the more extreme the emotional involvement, especially if the loops are repeated throughout the script, and the more difficult it is for the writer to make reasoned judgements in those areas; to separate his feelings from the situation. The narrower the loop, the less the writer is guided or controlled by his feelings.

Extra loops indicate an additional sensitivity: somewhere in the writer's psyche, there is a wound that has been rubbed raw. How much it hurts is shown by the width of the loop, and also by how frequently the formation occurs. Hidden loops indicate that feelings are being hidden (it's a loop plus a closure): at the top of a letter (upper zone) showing the ability to keep a secret (emotional reaction to facts); in the middle zone showing the writer's need to keep his own secrets (emotional reaction to others); and in the lower zone, indicating feelings of guilt (emotional reaction to physical drives).

B. The Necessary Accessories

The necessary accessories are penstrokes which are formed separately from the letter but belong to it, and which are necessary to ensure clarity of meaning in writing. Letterform accessories fall into two categories; dots (as, the i-dot and j- dot), and bars (the t-bar and the cross of the x).

Letter dots and bars are standard formations in the lower-case alphabet, but they are considered accessories to script because they are not made with a single, continuous penstroke as part of the letter, nor is the word ordinarily interrupted at the letter to form them. You have to remember to go back and put them in. I-dots and t-bars are the most commonly used script accessories, and they are very revealing: where (and if) they are placed, in relation to the letter stem, and how they are shaped, can give you some valuable insights into the nature of the writer.

1. I-dots:

Correctly formed, the dot is just that; a dot—a single point mark of the writing instrument against the writing surface.

In Schoolform, the dot of the i (and the j) is placed in line with the stem, and at a distance from it that puts it about halfway into the upper zone; it is an extension of the letterform. Note that "in line with the stem" means that the dot follows the slant of the letter: if the script leans right, the dot would not be considered right of stem (and if the script leans left it would not be left of stem) as long as it follows the line of the letter. Dots placed in the Schoolform manner show precision as an attitude and, to a certain extent, good eye-hand coordination.

High, flyaway dots show imagination, a reach into the upper zone from the middle zone. If the dot stays pretty much in line with the stem, the writer retains control over his dreams and fantasies; dots to the far right show an imagination which may be impractical but is at least optimistic; and dots to the left are formed by the writer who always imagines the worst. Dots thrown just anywhere (not in the general vicinity of the letter) show a writer who is aware of how he should be doing something, but who tends to be careless.

Dots close to the stem show attention to detail and/or the ability to concentrate: it is small writing (size). If the dot slides to the left, the writer has a tendency to be over-cautious.

The **absence of dots** is a definite sign of carelessness; the writer who just can't be bothered with petty details. Check to see if he's also missing t-bars or punctuation.

The dot that's no longer a dot falls under the heading of original formations, and it can be very revealing. The **circled i-dot**, as we have already shown, is a contrived form, and its user is willing to expend extra time and effort to be noticed. When the dot becomes a **dash**, it usually means a writer who's in a hurry; and if that dash is high off the stem, the hurry is enthusiasm and drive. The **inverted-v** form shows a more critical person, though in this case the criticism means finding fault. For both the latter formations, note the pressure. If it's heavy, and especially if the dot is heavier than other parts of the script, you're looking at a sign of anger.

2. T-Bars

The bar of the t (and the x) is a single stroke which divides the letter stem in half. On the stem of the t it is normally formed from left to right; on the x, it is a slanted downstroke from top right to bottom left.

In Schoolform, the **t-bar** is placed about halfway up the stem and equally balanced on both sides of it. The balance is important. One trait the t-bar most definitely reveals is the nature of the writer's planning ability.

-t, t-

The penstroke forming the t-bar is a movement from self to others; from planning to completion. If it **stops short of the stem**, you have a writer who doesn't finish what he starts, either because of poor planning ability, or because he's a procrastinator. If the bar **starts after the stem** then you are dealing with an impulsive nature; the writer who talks (or acts) before he stops to think.

t̄, t́ t̖, t́

Some t-bar formations confirm i-dot usages. When the bar is **high on the stem**, it shows a reach into the upper zone, in this case usually meaning idealism. It is the Schoolform t-bar which shows concentration: a bar that is very **low on the stem** has a baseline interpretation; depression or feelings of inferiority. The **upslant** t-bar can be interpreted like the baseline bounce; it means something is going well for the writer. If it repeats throughout the script, it indicates a basic optimism. The **downslant** t-bar tells you that the writer is not pleased with something; if this runs through the script, then the writer feels nothing is ever going to work out the way he wants it to. If the downslant t-bar shows a pointed or slash ending, it indicates a critical, argumentative nature.

t̃, t̃

Wavy horizontals, especially if graceful, indicate that the writer has a sense of humor. If overdone, or combined with other negative indicators, it means the writer tends to be frivolous.

t, t tbar

T-bar endings confirm the single-stroke lower-zone terminals when they show bluntness (left), sharp temper (middle), or a heavy-handed attitude (club-shaped ending). They also add a meaning of their own: if the t-bar is very long (capping the other letters in the word), the writer is someone who likes to be in charge. In a well-organized script, managerial tendencies are not necessarily a problem and can be a plus; in a disorganized script, this formation just means someone who is bossy and likes to run things without necessarily knowing how.

$$\overline{\mathcal{L}} , \mathcal{L}$$

If the t-bar **misses the stem**, or is **missing altogether**, what do you have? You guessed it: carelessness and lack of attention to details. Check to see if the writer remembers to go back and cross his x whenever he has occasion to use it. When the t-bar is there, but **floating above the stem**, you also have a dreamer; his head, like his t-bar, is in the clouds.

$$\mathcal{A} , \mathcal{A}$$

Watch for unusual formations. The t-bar that is formed with a stroke up from the stem can indicate that the writer is in a hurry, but it must also be considered as a knot or tie, and is therefore a sign of stubbornness ("Whaddya mean I have to lift my pen off the page to do this?"). Where a variety of forms are used for the bar in the same sample, and especially if the change in form depends on where the letter t falls in a word, you have a versatile writer—one who can change his actions to meet the circumstances. In a disorganized script, the versatile becomes unpredictable: the writer who does not logically plan how he's going to do anything. Always look for confirmation in other signs.

Dots and bars are interpreted as penstrokes by shape and form. The interpretations of these two types of penstrokes apply to any similar penstrokes, such as those used in punctuation, or added in some fashion to the basic letterform. As part of the letterform, they also indicate specific functional traits: carelessness (if missing); attention to detail (if present); and planning ability (if complete).

C. The Unnecessary Accessories

As far as Schoolbook is concerned, we've covered all the formations in the lower-case alphabet: open and closed letters, looped and loopless letters, i-dots and t-bars. Pre-strokes and end-strokes are connectors only: a penstroke whose purpose is to join the letters of a word, and in such a way that it facilitates the smooth flow of script. When used as connectors, they are not extra strokes. Knots and ties properly belong exclusively to the uppercase alphabet, and when they are used as they are intended to be used, they are also connectors. When these strokes are used in some other manner, as they so often are, they become an *unnecessary accessory* to script: an extra effort made by the writer which, for whatever reason, *impedes* the smooth flow of script. As with anything else, there is a variety of forms these strokes can take. For purposes of study, we divide them into three categories: pre-strokes and end-strokes; knots and ties; and ornamentation.

1. *Pre-Strokes and End-Strokes—Insecurity*

In general, the pre-stroke (an extra penstroke on the beginning of a word) gives the writer a chance to think before he begins writing; the endstroke (a tail added to the letterform) provides the same pause for reflection before the next word. Let's attach them to letters and see what happens:

a, r, a

The **prop-stroke** (left and center) shows a writer who needs assurances—connections with others around him—that tell him what he is doing is all right with them. It's a sign of insecurity: the writer who uses it needs to take extra time to think about how he's going to word what he wants to say. The **tail-prop** (right) has a similar meaning; this writer is carefully considering what he's going to say next. In both cases, they show hesitation, a stall for more time, and they are similar to the "ah," "uh," "er" used by a nervous speaker.

Combine your stroke meaning category. If the prestroke shows insecurity, and deep hidden loops (especially if formed by the prestroke) show a liar, the two together tell you the reason for the untruthfulness: worry, and perhaps fear, about what others would think if they only knew whatever the writer is hiding.

a

Any unconventional form shows someone who wants to be different. As with the circled i-dot, this writer is copying something he has seen someplace else as a way of calling attention to his own uniqueness. But note this particular sign of uniqueness is formed with a prop stroke. Why do you think this writer is showing off? Does he only need attention—or reassurance?

c, b, t

This formation is certainly a pre-stroke, but definitely not a connector. Note the cup formation (receptivity): the **upturned hook**, like a beckoning finger, shows an acquisitive nature. It can be a very healthy trait: the person who knows the value of material things and likes to own them; it is one of a group of traits which combine to indicate ambition. But if it's overdone (if it runs through the entire script), it shows possessiveness or greed. Look for the same formation on t-bars and capital letters (and if it is possessiveness, you will also find signs of jealousy). And yes, however healthy, acquisitiveness falls into the realm of insecurity even in a well-organized script; the writer who values himself by how much of value he owns.

$$\mathcal{t}, \mathcal{t}$$

The **downturned hook** also implies a grabbing-onto, but it has proven to be a more negative sign. Like the v-formation i-dots, it shows a critical nature, but it is also an anger sign, and it shows someone who has a very low boiling point for competition or disputes over "territoriality." The writer who uses it can be vindictive or hostile, and there is a very great likelihood that opposition, real or imagined, will be met with retaliation. If found in a well-organized script, the writer probably recognizes it as a negative trait and keeps it well under control; if it runs though a disorganized script, then it is a definite danger signal which can predict the possibility of viciousness or violence. Insecurity again, but on the offense; directed at anyone or anything that makes the writer feel less than adequate.

$$\mathcal{h}, \mathcal{r}, c$$

The **upswing endstroke** belongs there; and like other rounded formations it shows a cooperative, easy-going, generally genial attitude. When it's extended (longer than Schoolform), it has a variety of meanings, depending on its form. It can be a reach into the upper zone (the h), an unconscious desire for more, or even just some, intellectual stimulation; if very pronounced (the r), it shows a writer who is trying to call attention to himself (but note that when he's doing it, he's putting up a block between himself and communication). When it stays in the middle zone, it's more of a peace-making gesture; the writer who wants to prevent arguments and stay out of trouble.

$$\mathcal{a}, \mathcal{b}, g$$

The **covering backstroke**, swinging toward the left, is also a defensive gesture, but much stronger, similar to someone holding up his arms to ward off a blow. No matter what else the script shows—including a strong right tilt—anyone who uses this forced swing back to the left is afraid he is going to get hurt. Look for similar signs of introversion or unconscious fears in the upper and lower zones.

2. *Knots and Ties—Stubborn Tenacity*

Knots and ties are small, tightly formed loop-style formations added on to the basic letterform. Like any added loops they indicate that feeling is being added to a situation; like other unnecessary accessories, they are a way to slow down communication. The combination results in a writer with a little less "give."

Knots and ties show stubbornness, tenacity, inflexibility; the writer who likes to tie things up into neat little packages and then hang onto them. Again, tenacity can certainly be a useful trait, but its positive or negative character depends on extremes. There is a difference between someone who sticks to his guns and someone who is simply pigheaded. *All ties which are not used as connectors are strokes back into self*; and knots can just as easily mean someone who is going around in circles as someone who knows what he wants.

What does it mean when an open letter is not only locked closed but tied with a knot? That tight little loop added onto the open cup can mean a writer who is simply careful about what he says (diplomatic loop), but when it reaches back to tie the letter form closed, you can add stubbornness and suspicion of others; and an absolute unwillingness to listen. (Remember forms that look like other forms? This writer is not being up front with you.)

Consider the necessary strokes in the letter forms before making your judgements of knots or ties. The return stroke of the f or q *must* swing inward in order to complete the loop. If it occasionally swings back a bit too far, you may just have a writer who's in a hurry—though he does hurry with a certain flourish!—and can't take the time to be more precise. If it's repeated, or it if becomes a knot, you can consider it a sign of tenacity; but again, consider the implications in terms of the letter form. There *is no* middle zone formation on the f, and it is certainly faster and more efficient to use the connector that belongs with it. What would you say about a writer who not only adds a middle zone (social pressures) where there isn't any, but swings it to the left? It's certainly possible that this writer is having some problems reconciling his intellectual and/or physical drives with what he or others think he "should be" doing. And since the knot does show stubbornness, who do you think is winning this argument over priorities?

Extra knots (and yes, they are *all* extra strokes, but even extremes have their extremes), the formations that are even more in opposition to the pattern of the letterform, are unnecessary complications—and they show a writer who gets involved in just that. Where they are decorative, graceful, or show planning (the s), it can be a sign of artistic ability or appreciation. When they just appear haphazardly, or are ungraceful or crude, you have a writer who tends to get tied up in non-essential details. (Remember the printed down-stroke? This is his opposite number.)

Combine your stroke meanings category: If the t-bar that stops short of the stem shows a writer who never finishes what he starts, and if you find the aimless curliques (as in the small 'a' above) scattered throughout that same script, how would you expect that writer to function, given an independent project and no one to tell him he'd better get cracking on it? The trait is called procrastination.

3. Ornamentation and Original Formations

Ornamentation describes any decoration added to the script. It can take the form of exaggeration of normal penstrokes such as loops or necessary accessories, the addition and elaboration of extra penstrokes, or a specific let-terform variation. (For example, where single letters from another cursive style are inserted into the script *by a writer who learned to write in this country* they are, like the circled i-dot, a bid for attention. The most commonly used formation in this case is the Greek or Spencerian 'e': an uppercase E used as a lowercase letter.) And, as we have mentioned, there is no limit to the variety of forms writers can invent.

The interpretation of ornamentation and original formations is a matter of type and degree. Where the added or altered penstroke makes writing faster or easier (such as the single-stroke t), it is an indication of ingenuity; the writer who is able to find ways to shorten a time-consuming job, and not afraid to try out original methods. When decorations are added onto a script that is grace-ful and/or elegant, the writer is demonstrating a certain aesthetic sense; it may not necessarily mean that he has artistic ability, but it does indicate that he has a sense of the beautiful and wants his handwriting to reflect it. Where the additions are added to a crude script, or where they are distracting in themselves or make the writing hard to read, they show confusion, insecurity, and an inappropriate means of attention-getting:

Sometimes I think that

In the final analysis, extra strokes always mean that the writer's mind is on something other than what he's doing, and if those extra strokes are ornamen-tation, they tell you the writer needs to be noticed.

Conclusion: *Interpreting Penstrokes*

If someone whose script leans right likes other people and wants their company, why doesn't he have any friends? Check the letterform. Open and closed formations in general show how the writer communicates (or listens!), which certainly explains how he's going to get along with others, no matter what he wants. Looping can explain interpersonal problems: deep double looping inside middle zone formations means the writer can't let others know how he really feels. Or, maybe he's hypersensitive (looped d's and/or t's), or on the defensive (backswing return); if so, it's difficult for him to let others get too close, no matter how much he needs them. The reasons are endless, and a left tilt is not the only indicator that tells you the writer is afraid of being hurt.

If firm, consistent pressure indicates a writer who works hard to achieve his goals, how do you explain the fact that he can't ever seem to get anything done? Well, he could be a procrastinator (t-bar short of stem; added knots or decorations), or a daydreamer (t-bar floating above stem), or just plain careless (missing i-dots and t-bars), and that means all the effort he puts into what he does is going for nothing. And if an erratic baseline means the writer believes he can't do anything right, how did he manage to become such an outstanding success? Do the i-dots show imagination and enthusiasm? Do the t-bars indicate a versatile mind, and do other original formations indicate that this writer thinks differently from most people? The person who hears a different drummer may be original, creative, inventive, even a genius—but the fact remains that he has no guidelines: no way of judging whether or not he's heading in the right direction. He doesn't even have a standard against which to evaluate his own success. The erratic baseline is always a negative indicator, for obvious reasons, but you would be surprised at how often it is found in the handwriting of innovative people. The penstroke formations add shape and form to your portrait of the writer: they give you the underlying reasons for what he is, and why he can (or can't) be what he wants to be.

Principles of the Analysis

BEHAVIOR PATTERNS: The penstroke formations tell you why a person performs a task the way he does. Your analysis will reveal the writer's underlying motivations: the reasons that make him the kind of person he is.

The questions you are trying to answer are these: How, how well, and how much does the writer communicate or listen (closed and open formations); is he practical or emotional (loops); and in either case, can he keep his temper (slashing strokes, etc.). Does he take the time to do a job properly, or is something else more important (necessary accessories); is his mind on something other than what he's doing, and if so, what (unnecessary accessories)?

ANALYSIS OUTLINE (continued)

VI. LOWER-CASE ALPHABET PENSTROKES (What motivates this writer: How does he think, feel, and react to events in his life?)
    A. Letter Form (How does this writer communicate, and/or deal with events in his life?)
        1. Closed formations (Does he keep his own counsel, or like to talk?)

2. Open formations (Is he receptive to ideas and willing to listen to opinions, or is he narrow- or close-minded?)

3. Looped and loopless formations (Is he basically emotional, or basically practical?)

   a) Hidden loops (Does he have something to hide?)

   b) Extra loops (Is he extra sensitive?)

B. The Necessary Accessories (How does he do his job?)

   1. I-dots (Concentration, imagination, or carelessness)

   2. T-bars (Carry-through, temper, dominance, or carelessness)

C. The Unnecessary Accessories (What is likely to matter more than, or interfere with, his ability to function?)

   1. Pre-strokes and End-strokes (Insecurity, acquisitiveness, temper)

   2. Knots and Ties (Stubbornness, tenacity, inflexibility)

   3. Ornamentation (Complications and need for attention)

Doing the Analysis—Formations in the lower-case alphabet

How do our four writers feel—and react to those feelings?

SAMPLE ONE (see page 117)

PENSTROKES:

1. No openings on closed formations. Narrow openings on cup formations due to script jamming (i.e., openings consistent with letter width); most cups tend to be wider.

2. Loops are narrow and some are pointed; loops eliminated on some letters; no loops added. Some e's filled in.

3. I-dots close to stem and precise. T-bars level and precise, but occasionally higher on the stem.

4. No unnecessary penstrokes added to the script.

What do the penstrokes tell us? This writer keeps his own counsel (confirmed by the controlled-right, de-emphasized middle zone; he doesn't share what he feels), on the other hand, since there are no hidden or extra loops, he's not hiding anything. This very clear, simple script is one indicator of a basic honesty; if this writer does tell you something, you can expect it to be the truth. This is confirmed by the blunt endings on t-bars; he keeps his counsel, but he calls them as he sees them. The wider cup formations indicate that he is very receptive to ideas, so he is also someone who likes to learn.

Loops are narrow and sometimes pointed, so he is practical, and this means that the ideas he's interested in are ideas that work. You can expect someone who writes this way to be a reader, but primarily of non-fiction or information texts; he's probably very little interested in fiction. The lower zone loops also show practicality, so we were probably correct in assuming that his drive is toward financial or professional success, but there is an interesting contradiction here. The filled-in e's tell us that this writer is extremely physically sensual. Some of that sensuality could be satisfied by owning nice things, but this writer is not acquisitive; if in fact that lower zone drive is toward job success, then he's not only given up his social life, he's given up his sexual needs as well. Narrow loops mean a writer who thinks with his head rather than his emotions, but we could wonder if in this case they also mean that his feelings, like everything else, are tightly under control.

I-dots are precise and close to stem; this is unusual in a large script and it is usually a tempering factor: it means that in spite of wide-ranging interests, the writer is capable of the type of concentration and attention to detail usually found in a small script. The combination is a good managerial quality; the ability to see the larger picture and pay attention to necessary details at the same time. The t-bar balance is harder to judge. They're shorter on the right where they might run into another letter; that's just the kind of neatness that could be expected in this clear, precise style. They are longer on the right side wherever there is room, which could be further evidence of practicality (the getting done part is more important than the getting started part), and some evidence, again, of a managerial nature or experience (the t-bar is not capping lower zone letters, but it does have a longer reach). The only time they are balanced is when they are high on the stem, which means that whatever this writer's hopes or dreams, he plans them carefully. But the t-bar variation might also be a confirmation of the upper zone variation: the confusion over goals is evidently (and quite logically) having an effect on this writer's ability to plan. If you don't know exactly where you want to go, it is difficult to figure out how to get there.

Even so, it's encouraging in this kind of style to find evidence of idealism (t-bar higher on the stem) and optimism (upslant). It's also very healthy, considering the pressures this writer is under. It means that somewhere deep within him he believes things *should be* better, and also that perhaps, someday, they *will be* better as well.

SAMPLE TWO (see page 117)

PENSTROKES:
   1. No openings on closed formations. Cups consistent with letter width.
   2. Loops are wide; they tend to be pointed in the upper and middle zone and rounded in the lower zone. Loops added to d and t are very wide. No hidden loops.
   3. Most i-dots are high but fairly in line with the stem. T-bars upslant throughout, and dominate the middle zone (i.e., longer on the right). Position on stem normally centered. Note occasional "claw" ending on some longer t-bars.
   4. Added strokes: defensive backstrokes, end-stroke lifts.
   What stands out most in this handwriting are the loops; this writer is emotional, hypersensitive, and definitely on the defensive (backstrokes). He's also got some bottled-up anger to deal with. The down-turned hook (or claw) is usually found on the beginning of the t-bar; here it's on the end of an extended t-bar. What happens when we combine our stroke meanings? The extended bar shows a need to dominate or give orders; combined with the controlled anger as an afterthought, it becomes more of an "I'll show you" reaction. This

SAMPLE ONE

This is a sample of the way I normally write.
I would like to know what my handwriting tells
about me.

SAMPLE TWO

This is a sample of the way I normally
write. I would like to know what my
handwriting tells about me.

writer is telling people: "I'm the boss here: don't get in my way."

Again, we have someone who is basically honest but not very communicative (closed formations; no hidden loops); he's imaginative (high dots), and the imagination is practical (in line with the stem). He is emotionally involved in all areas of his life (wide loops), and is hypersensitive to hurts and slights (loops on d's and t's). Note that these loops usually show up first on the d; if found on both the d and t, and throughout the script, as it is here, the sensitivity is extreme. This writer also feels defensive (backstrokes), and this results in a domineering attitude and a well-controlled but nonetheless present anger.

Loops are pointed in the upper zone, so despite the feeling involved, this writer can be practical in this area; despite his need for others, he can also be practical in his reactions to them (pointed tops in the middle zone). Lower zone loops are wide and rounded, showing great warmth and feeling in this area; this writer is sensual too, but recognizes and expresses it physically in some way.

Great feeling, warmth, need for others—combined with anger, defensiveness, hypersensitivity, and a domineering attitude. It confirms our earlier analysis: other people are important to this writer but they are giving him a lot of negative feedback, and his reaction is both defensive and angry. Since other people are making him feel this way, it does make sense, in spite of his need for them (pronounced right), to shut them out of his life as much as possible (de-emphasized middle zone).

SAMPLE THREE (see page 120)

PENSTROKES:

1. Some openings on closed formations. Cups consistent with letter width, and varying with that width.

2. Script is basically loopless in the upper zone; where present, they start in the upper zone. Loop added to small and right-most tending d's. Lower zone loops incomplete. Hidden loops only on opened closed formations, or added as knots to the edge of cup formations.

3. Most i-dots are Schoolform height, with a tendency to slide to the left; where there is a t-bar, they float above it. T-bar terminals are long (capping the middle zone), but start just barely back of stem. Position on stem normally centered; endings blunt.

4. Added strokes: middle zone knots, defensive backstrokes.

So this writer is willing to talk, but he's not willing to tell you what he really thinks or feels. He's hiding something, and it's possible that whatever he's hiding is also what is making him defensive and sensitive.

He is also forcing a separation between himself and the "real world" (upper zone loops that start in the upper zone), and it may not be simply his own private means of escape, because despite a very practical intelligence (loopless upper zone), he is weak on planning ability as well (t-bars). As far as his intellectual life is concerned, he prefers practical facts to emotion and fiction. But as far as his day-to-day practices are concerned, he prefers fantasy to reality. And the fact that he tends to be stubborn as well (knots) is not in this script a positive indicator.

What we had up to this point is someone who doesn't know what he wants to be when he grows up, and who is going through emotional stress because of it. What we have now is a possible reason why: someone who may have the facts, or even prefer them (loopless ascenders), but who can't use them. Poor planning ability, preference for his own fantasy world, and a basic stubbornness, combined with the fact that he's got something to hide that he's probably sensitive about. It's still a graceful and attractive script style (he puts on a good front), but its writer is not likely to respond to counseling, and may never find what he needs unless he learns to straighten out his own act. It may be that, despite the stress of the growing pains, he's also not quite ready to grow up.

SAMPLE FOUR (see page 120)

PENSTROKES:

1. Rare small openings on closed formations; most carefully closed. Cup openings wider toward the upper zone; narrower toward the lower zone. Note that the "Greek" e puts an extra cup opening toward the middle zone.

2. Loops are present throughout but not too wide for this size script; loops added to the d. Lower zone loops are incomplete. Most loops are rounded. Diplomatic loops appear on the o's; only one hidden loop on another letter.

3. Some i-dots missing; some left of stem, one high and to the right. T-bars show different lengths and tend to be low on the stem; endings blunt.

4. Added strokes: middle zone knots, defensive backstrokes, terminal lifts. Also note insertion of capital letters into the middle zone: capital S and capital/Greek style E on "SamplE"; capital B in "aBout."

Here we also have someone who doesn't say everything he thinks, but in this case probably because he's been taught to be careful of other people's feelings (diplomatic loops). He's a good listener, though, even if somewhat less willing to listen to, or perhaps slightly narrow-minded about, discussions about physical/material drives.

Feeling is present, but not a controlling factor in this script; he cares about what happens in his life, but the only area in which he ever gets carried away is in physical/material drives (wider lower zone loops)—in which area he isn't getting as much as he needs. This type of conflict is also a very common one, and it's based on a kind of shyness. If you were raised to believe that people just don't talk about "such things" (and "such things" remember, can be *either* money or sex!), then it is difficult to express your own needs, and correspondingly difficult to fulfill them.

This writer needs attention and recognition (capital letter inserts), but probably can't admit it (raised endstrokes that turn into defensive backstrokes). He's sensitive to slights (looped d), on the defensive, tends to imagine the worst (left i-dots), and is not entirely happy (low t-bars). He also tends to be somewhat careless (missing i-dots, dots placed anywhere), so in spite of his need for recognition and the fact that his life is not going as well as it appears on the surface, he's not really making an effort to get things right. Something is beginning to go very wrong in this writer's life, and all signs indicate that he is not capable of setting things straight.

SAMPLE THREE

This is a sample of the way I normally write —
I would like to know what my handwriting
tells about me.

SAMPLE FOUR

This is a sample of the way I normally
write. I would like to know what my
handwriting tells about me.

Exercise for Chapter Seven

Identify and describe the penstroke formations in the lower-case alphabet for each sample of handwriting you have collected. Answer the questions: How does this writer communicate, how does he feel, how does he perform a task, and what kind of person does he seem to be under his mask? How does this additional information affect the conclusions you have already formed about this writer?

It's not as complicated as it sounds. The basic letterforms and accessories are open and closed formations, looped and loopless formations, dots and bars. Most other formations found in script, including knots, ties and ornamentation, are variations on these basic forms. Of course, you don't have it all yet. We still have to talk about capitals, connectors and script form. But the penstroke meanings do not change, no matter what context you find them in. Learn the meanings of the formations themselves, and you can combine these basic meanings to interpret any formation you find in script.

TEST YOURSELF

For each sample shown below, two different penstroke formations are indicated by the arrows. Describe what each formation means, and then combine their meanings to name the trait which *best* fits each writer. Our answers are in Appendix B.

SAMPLE ONE

I have been doing research for eight months now — I

SAMPLE TWO

now tell me what you think about someone like that

SAMPLE THREE

I knew what I should do — I should tell him so, but

SAMPLE FOUR

can you let me know as soon as possible just what

8

Confidence and Attitudes— Capitals and Script Form

Do you feel competent? When you have a job to do, are you sure of yourself, a little shaky about your know-how, or convinced you're going to mess it up? How do you arrive at conclusions? Do you accept what you're told, recognize alternatives, or find your own answers? And how do you work with others? Do you cooperate with them, expect them to cooperate with you, or lack the word cooperate in your vocabulary?

Capital letters give you a measure of the writer's *confidence* in his ability; they tell you whether or not he believes he's good at what he does. The writer's use of **connectors** tells you how he *reasons*: literally, logically, or by intuitive leaps. And **script form** gives you a measure of the writer's *attitudes*; the amount of care he takes in presenting his work to others, and therefore a measure of just how much he values other people's opinions of his thinking or behavior.

This chapter picks up where Chapter 7 left off. You've seen how penstrokes are used to form letters. We continue with the way those letters are joined into words and sentences. Capitals tell you whether the writer feels he can do a good job; script form tells you how he actually does it.

Definition

Capital letters comprise what is very nearly a second alphabet. They are not only generally larger than lower-case letterforms, but also, with very few exceptions, the letter itself has an entirely different configuration. The English language, unlike many other languages, encourages a generous use of capitals; they are used to begin sentences, to emphasize proper nouns (names of people, places, and things), and, of course, for the pronoun I. The key word here is *emphasis*. Students of written English are taught that when you capitalize something, you are telling your reader that it is important. A capital letter is by definition, then, a letterform used to identify something that matters.

Connectors are penstrokes whose function is to join individual letters into words in cursive writing, and in such a way that it facilitates the smooth flow of script. The general form of script refers to the overall shape of letters *and* their connectors: rounded, angular, or scrawled. Taken together, these three factors make up a *handwriting pattern*: the manner in which a writer uses letterform penstrokes to form words and sentences.

Measuring Words and Sentences

There are two measurements for capital letters. You begin with a size comparison between capitals and lowercase letters. Capitals are measured across two zones (upper and middle), and then compared in actual height to the script size. Capital letters should dominate the handwriting: they are consistent with script size if they are at least as tall as letters with ascenders or slightly taller (up to 1 1/2 times the overall size of the script); they should also be at least twice the size of middle zone formations (the size of two middle-zone letters sitting on top of each other).

For your second measurement, you compare the relative height of *all* capitals *to each other*. It is important to note where and if a change in size occurs. As with any other measurement, a slight variation can occur without constituting an inconsistency; what you are looking for is a measurable change in the size of capital letters in different parts of the sample.

For connectors, the primary measurement is a determination of whether or not they are present, and when and if printed insertions (single letters using the printed letter rather than the script formation) are used. Script form is measured by eye: are the penstrokes used to form letters and connectors mostly rounded, mostly angular, mostly scrawled, or some combination?

What You Are Measuring

You are trying to determine the size of capitals in relation to lowercase letters, and in relation to each other; whether or not the writer uses connectors to form words, and the overall shape of all penstrokes used in writing the sample.

Organizational Factors

For **Capitals**, good organization consists of letterforms which are consistent with script size or slightly taller; this usage indicates that the writer has confidence in his abilities. For **script form** a measurement of good organization is the same as for letterform: a script style which is clear, simple and easy to write (indicating again, clarity of thought and lack of complications). The use or absence of **Connectors** is not an organizational indicator.

Extreme capitals are measured as extreme size: too large or too small. Capitals on either extreme indicate feelings of insecurity. When they are extremely large, the insecurity is expressed as egotism; when they are extremely small, it is a lack of confidence. For script form, the meanings of extremes will depend on the type of formation used.

Variation exists when capitals change size within a sample; this measurement does not compare capitals and lower-case letters. Where capital height varies, it indicates that the writer cannot maintain a given level of confidence;

his assessment of his own abilities alters in different situations or under different circumstances. For script form, variation would describe a handwriting in which different styles of cursive are combined (Note that it does *not* describe a handwriting which mixes printing and cursive); the most common variation is a mixture of rounded and angular forms. **Form variation** indicates that the writer's life is going through changes, and would be interpreted in much the same way as zone variation.

As with letterform, **habit** (consistent usage) is also a factor in determining good organization. And again, whether the trait is positive or negative will depend on the usage involved.

Let's start our study of sentences at the beginning: with capital letters.

A. Capital Letters—and Confidence

Handwriting is both a form of speech and a physical skill, and it can be compared to both. When you're sure you know what you're talking about, you begin speaking loud and clear. When you're sure you know what you're doing, you begin doing it loud and clear. Capital letters begin a sentence, begin a thought, begin an action when they begin a sample of handwriting; and if the writer has confidence in his ability to perform, those capitals will come in loud and clear.

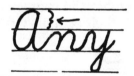

When **capital letters are consistent with script size** or slightly taller, then you are dealing with a writer who feels confident in his ability to handle a task or assignment. If the capitals retain their confident appearance throughout the script, it indicates a generalized feeling of competence; the writer who is aware that he can handle familiar situations well, and probably deal with or easily learn new or unusual ones when they occur.

Do not judge this trait indicator only by the initial capital, however. It is important to be aware of any size change in capitals throughout the entire sample. The relative size of capitals may vary with subject matter, and this is not a negative factor; it simply shows a writer who is more sure of himself in one area than he is in another. Every rule has its exceptions, so when you see capitals that are normally a specific height but abruptly change size at a given point in the sample, you should check the subject matter to find out how and why the writer's confidence has slipped:

There are other reasons for height variation in capitals, however. If the writer is putting on a bold front but does not really feel confident, then only the initial capital may look self-assured; other capitals in the sample will all be smaller. If the writer is someone who starts out with a flourish, but cannot sustain confidence, the size of the capitals will gradually dwindle throughout the script.

If the initial capital is smaller than internal formations, it generally indicates that the writer has a tendency to underplay; he knows he can handle things, but for whatever reason, he doesn't let other people know. When capitals vary in height sporadically (sometimes larger, sometimes smaller, and with no connection to subject matter), you would interpret it as you do pressure variation: this writer lacks confidence but is trying to bolster himself, and he is definitely under stress.

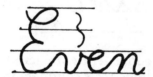

Small capitals that barely top the middle zone show a lack of confidence. This is especially true if upper zone formations top the capitals. When you see these shrunken capitals, you know the writer is not sure he can do the job properly, or even at all. (Remember the characteristics of the handwriting of children? Most youngsters form their capitals very small.)

Too much of a good thing can be just as bad as too little, however, and sometimes worse. **Over-large, over-flourished capitals** are a sign of pretentiousness or egotism—and egotism is yet another subdivision of the trait we call insecurity. The writer who feels the need to put on this extra-bold front is in fact suffering from a lack of real confidence and low self-esteem.

The writer who **eliminates capitals** altogether, even on the pronoun I, is also demonstrating a kind of insecurity, but not necessarily a lack of confidence in ability (though it may be a lack of belief in self). Like the circled i-dot, this form is something the writer has probably seen elsewhere and copied (ever hear of e.e. cummings?), and it tells you the same thing: the writer needs attention, and doesn't feel that being himself is going to get it for him:

mary had a little lamb, it's fleece
as snow. every where that mary

In this case, however, the reason for the insecurity is a much more damaging one: many people who write this way have had their egos severely bruised by someone who matters (usually a parent). The writer needs attention from that someone because without it he feels that nothing he does, however well he does it, is worth very much.

What if the writer simply neglects to capitalize a proper noun? In some cases, you can assume that he didn't know the word had to be capitalized—but not if it is someone's name. Remember that you give importance to a word by capitalizing it, whether or not it's a proper noun, and especially if the word falls in the middle of a sentence. The refusal to capitalize is a deliberate insult, conscious or otherwise; the writer's way of telling you that in his opinion this person has no value whatsoever. Do you think you can name the trait demonstrated by someone whose only way to feel important is by belittling someone else? Note that a similar interpretation would apply if the only place a capital diminishes in size is when it begins someone else's name; if it diminishes on the writer's own name, you're dealing with an identity problem (Chapter 9).

The study of letterform includes extra strokes as well as size. Many Schoolform capitals start with an extra little decoration on the front of the letter; and Schoolform or not, it is still an extra stroke and a non-essential. In this case, the intention is to enhance the letter. What do you make of the original formation in this sample? (One hint: it's a prestroke.) Graphology calls it the **wind-up formation**, in the sense of a pitcher getting ready to throw a ball. Let's use it as an example of how you figure out the meaning of a formation you've never seen before.

First: pre-strokes give the writer a chance to nerve himself up before committing himself. The windup is a much longer hesitation before charging into a *capital* (before starting a job!), and just incidentally also decorates the capital. What does decoration mean? Decoration, or ornamentation, is a way of calling attention to yourself, and also of making yourself look better than you are—or feel you are. What does that give us?

In an actual sample of script, of course, part of your interpretation would have to based on how large the capital is in relation to lowercase letters. But with just the information we have, we'd say this writer *needs* to look good, but is afraid to get started because he's not sure he can look as good as he needs to. Graphology calls it a wind-up stroke, but a better picture might be of an insecure swimmer posturing for several minutes on the high diving board before he works up the nerve to jump into the water.

Confidence in your ability and confidence in yourself, as you will learn in the next chapter (Identity Words) are not the same thing. *Capital letters are an indicator of the writer's confidence in his ability to perform a task.* You can be afraid of your own shadow but still recognize the fact that when you're given a job, you can deliver the goods! When capital letters are a healthy size and lack decoration, they tell you that the writer knows he has ability, at least in the area shown by the confident capitals.

B. Word Breaks and Printed Forms—Thought Patterns

Connectors form letters into words. Their purpose is not clarity of meaning, as with the necessary accessories: in fact, a printed message is easier to read than almost any script style. Their purpose is speed and convenience for the writer: joining letters into connected words is an easier and faster way to write than forming each separate letter individually. The script alphabet is designed to accept connectors, and to that end it is different in form from the printed version of the alphabet. So then, what would be the purpose of using the script form, but leaving out the connectors?

Well, sometimes you can't help it; the word might be too long, you might be interrupted in the middle of what you're doing, or you may not remember how the connector is formed. When a single word is broken up into separate segments, either because of a missing connector or the insertion of a printed form, it is *never* by itself a sign of disorganization. Word breaks show intuitive thought, imagination, and creativity even more clearly than high-flying i-dots or extensions into the upper zone.

The writer who joins every letter in a word, no matter how long the word, is someone who has a very literal mind:

handwriting

antidisestablishmentarianism

Schoolform teaches that every letter in a word is "supposed to" be connected in script, but there are times when it makes sense, or simply makes it easier, to lift the pen off the paper so that you can move your hand to a new position. In a well-organized script, all letters connected indicate that the writer is capable of following plans and blueprints—or orders—with precision and accuracy. But he is not likely to be able to read between the lines, possibly in job performance, and especially in the input he gets from other people.

The writer who can split a longer word at a logical point is a little bit more flexible and somewhat more imaginative; just because authority gave him a job to do doesn't mean that the procedure they ordained is necessarily the best one, and he can make adjustments when necessary:

hand'writing

When you see word breaks even in very short words, the writer is showing you that very often the pattern of his thought is interrupted by intuitive flashes. Something he's doing or something he's saying reminds him of or gives him an idea for something else, and the break-in is reflected in the missing connectors:

see spot run

Many creative people in all fields write in this fashion, but watch for signs of disorganization too. If the writing is disjointed in other ways, you could just as easily be dealing with a scatterbrain.

Printed insertions, as we have already discussed, are a means of simplifying script (*if* the printed letter is, in fact, simpler). It's a practical solution for someone who's in a hurry and still wants his message clearly understood. And practical is the word: you analyze the printed letter as you would any simplified letterform (Chapter 6: Loopless formations), and the word breaks, where they occur, as we've just described:

handwriting

Printing in place of script, however, while still very practical and precise, is certainly not as fast. Its primary purpose is always *clarity of message*; the neater the printing, the more important it is for the writer to make sure his message is understood. When printing is used for labeling, for example, it shows efficiency; or if it's used by someone whose handwriting is normally illegible, the extra effort shows consideration—and to a very great degree, because a person who normally scrawls, as you will see, tends to be normally hurried or impatient:

handwriting?

Printing also, however, conceals the writer's true self—at least, from the graphologist. While you may be able to deduce some information on the basis of major trait indicators from a printed sample, you can't be certain of what you see, because printing is normally more careful than script, and all the indicators may be different from what they would be if the sample were written. And, of course, you can't get at underlying motivation (letterform, etc.) from a printed sample at all. A sample for analysis does not require clarity, it requires naturalness, so if—after you have instructed your subject to *write* his sample and told him you can't analyze print—you still get a printed sample instead of script, that person is being evasive.

C. Script Form—Attitudes

The form of script (letter shape plus connectors) gives you a picture of the writer's attitude toward his finished product (whether he's doing the work to please others or please himself). Again, there are many variations possible on the general form of script, but reduced to essential differences, we are only dealing with three basic styles: rounded, angular, and scrawled.

1. *Round Writing*

One way to get a feel for the kind of person who uses a particular style of script is to make the formations yourself. Try these penmanship exercises:

mmm uuu eeeee ooooo

It takes patience, but more than that, it takes an eye for appearances to form these strokes evenly and correctly. Rounded forms mean a cooperative attitude, even temper, affability, and the desire to please. And you will notice, as you collect more samples, that whenever a writer *is* trying to impress his reader with these traits, at least visually, he will revert to a rounded style if he can, no matter what his own writing normally looks like. (Note that if the roundhand he chooses is Schoolform, he's also telling you that he is "obedient"; that he's willing to do the job exactly as authority decrees.)

FIGURE 1
Samples of Roundhand Styles

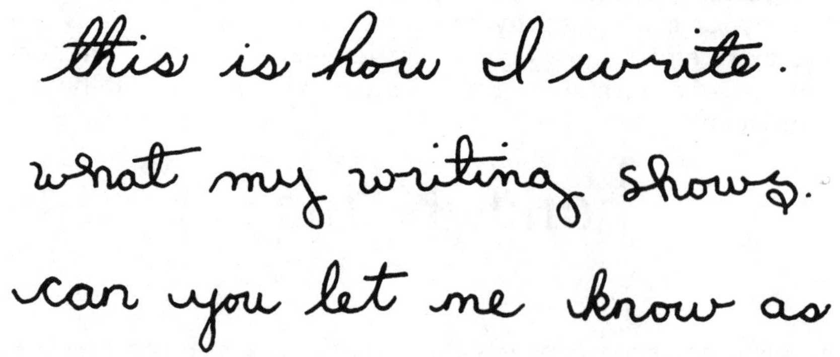

this is how I write.

what my writing shows.

can you let me know as

Despite the care and artistic effort involved, rounded forms, especially when they are are your natural style, are easier to write. The letters flow into each other neatly and gracefully, the pen stays on the paper and moves in a smooth, restful, uninvolved pattern, and the finished result is pleasing to the eye. Schoolform, for example, is a very simple, graceful roundhand. It's a clear script without a lot of complicated penstrokes that might confuse the six-year-old child who is just learning his letters. And the adult writer who uses roundhand is someone who prefers just that—no complications. Do not expect the writer who uses a rounded form to be a quick or original thinker, unduly ambitious, or a particularly hard worker; while he may like comfort, owning expensive things and impressing others, and often has the ability to achieve his ends, he will be just as content to ride along on someone else's efforts if he can. As with any other style, variation in the script indicators must be taken into account, but in general, roundhand writers are people who firmly believe that following the rules and cooperating with others will get them what they want.

2. *Angular Writing*

And angular script is not as graceful as the roundhand, or as easy on the nerves, but it is quicker to write:

Angular writers are less concerned with what people might think than they are with getting the job done—and getting it done in their own way and according to their own rules. They tend to be more impatient, and less willing to put up with other people's foibles—especially when it takes the form of interference.

FIGURE 2
Samples of Angular Script

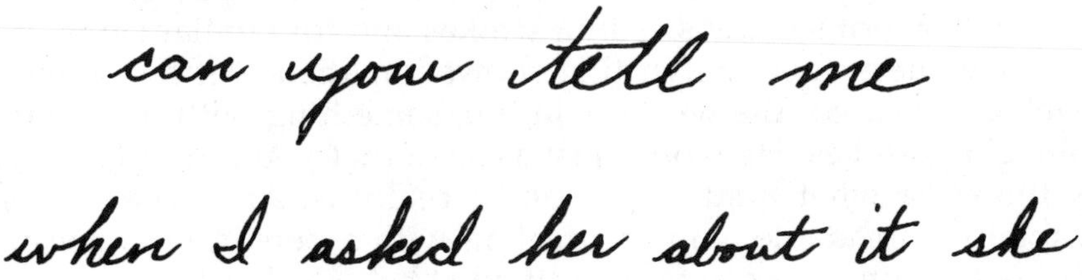

An angular script is one in which letter forms that call for curves are formed instead so that they come to either a blunt or a sharp point (i.e., instead of round strokes, the handwriting is made up of angles). Angularity in a school child's handwriting is one of the earliest signs of growing independence of thought; the angular formations usually show up first on the m and the n. Adults who use this form of script are telling you that they have strong opinions, original ideas, quick minds, and a critical nature (in *both* the discerning and the fault-finding sense). They also have ambitions which they have defined for themselves and want to achieve though their own efforts and in their own way. Angular writers can (and will) make decisions and carry them out, and they are more likely to be successful at what they choose to do—as long as it's on their own terms. In a well-organized script, angular writing shows force and determination even where the pressure is lighter; but keep in mind that those same signs of independence and internal strength can also be much more dangerous in a script filled with negative indicators. A roundhand writer who is unhappy is unlikely to take it out on someone else, but the sharp formations of anger, rarely if ever found in rounded writing, can be present even in the most controlled angular script. Angular writers do not like taking orders from others, and they are usually indifferent to social pressures. The gentleness, patience, and desire to please found in roundhand is lacking in the angular script, but dependence on others is also lacking. If the angular writer chooses you for a friend, it's because he likes you, not because he needs you. If he decides you're his enemy, you'd better be on your guard.

These same criteria, as you have already seen, apply to individual letter-forms as well as the script as a whole. Rounded forms show a more affectionate, easy-going, mild-tempered outlook; sharp or angular formations show impatience, quick thinking, or temper.

3. *The Scrawl*

This is a fast writing style too; in fact, it is so fast as to often be completely illegible, and lacking identifiable formations as well:

This script form can be very difficult to judge; you must depend on almost any other indicator than the form itself. It is certainly original, independent, and about as far from Schoolform as it is possible to get. If it's legible, contains simplified forms, and shows other signs of good organization, then you are dealing with a very quick, probably versatile, and certainly nonconformist mind. If the letter forms show slashing strokes and/or similar signs of haste, anger, or carelessness, then the writing shows impatience. If the script is tangled as well as scrawled, the writer is hiding something with his (seemingly) fast, semi-legible strokes. He would just as soon that you didn't find out how he really thinks or what kind of person he really is. And when the scrawl becomes totally unreadable, you are dealing with a person who doesn't care whether or not anyone else can figure out what he's all about.

FIGURE 3
Samples of Scrawl Style

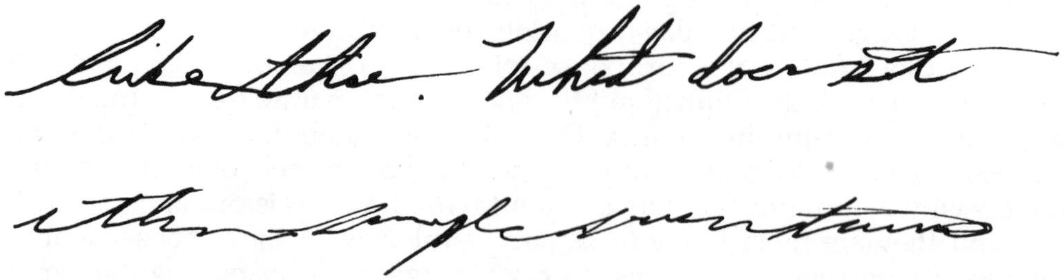

The hasty scrawl is often used by someone who is writing a quick note to himself; and if you've ever done so, you will remember that you sometimes find you can't read what you yourself have written! When this is the writer's natural style, you have someone who is more concerned with getting the words on paper than with whether or not he communicates well; or, in the case of behavior other than writing, more concerned with getting the job done in the fastest way possible whether or not it's usable by someone else. When an illegible scrawl shows up in a communication intended for someone else's eyes, it can also be a sign of careless indifference, a lack of interest in communicating or being understood, or, because of the concealment, even guilt. And it has one more meaning as well, especially if the message is an important one; an attitude on the part of the writer that he's important enough that you have to take whatever he dishes out ("This is good enough for you; if you can't figure it out, it's your problem, and I can't be bothered making it any clearer.")

The scrawl is not all negative, of course. The "I don't have time for this nonsense" attitude can be a simple statement of fact, if the writer is genuinely a very busy person. Even the neatest and most presentable script can degenerate into a scrawl at the tail-end of hours of writing. But the basic interpretation of the scrawl is that the writer, for whatever reason, is not concerned with your opinion of what he does or says, and not even particularly concerned with whether or not he is understood.

Most scripts contain elements of more than one of these styles. For a general judgement of the writer's nature, go by the dominant form. But as we discussed in the section on penstrokes and letter shapes, the meanings of even sporadic roundforms, angular forms, or scrawled forms can apply to individual letters, or to separate parts (zones) of the script.

Conclusion: *Interpreting Words and Sentences*

You have three trait indicators to consider: capitals, connectors, and script form. All three give you a different perspective on the writer's *functional ability*: the way he is likely to perform a task. In doing the analysis, you work with each script indicator individually, combining them one at a time with analysis interpretations you already have. For example:

Suppose a script with a strong right tilt and a slightly emphasized middle zone. You know that you are dealing with someone who needs other people, and is primarily concerned with social values. If this script shows large capitals, then the writer believes in his own ability and is therefore not as vulnerable to criticism from his very significant others. But what if the capitals barely top the middle zone? If all letters are connected, it's possible that the reason he has no confidence in his ability is because he believes other people when they tell him he's no good. If in addition to the small caps the script is very round as well, it can mean that whatever the writer does, he can't manage to please—or, it could mean that he has given up competence as his way of pleasing others ("Other people will like me better if I am not better than they are.").

Roundhand formations in a large or small script are usually a tempering factor: it means that these writers, who tend to be more self-oriented, are at least concerned with what other people think of them. But what if a medium script shows a very rounded style? The writer is already someone who tends to be more concerned with social mores; the cooperative, get-along-at-all-costs roundhand in this size is one more factor that makes the medium an extreme: everything this writer does is intended to please.

How do you combine rounded formations with a de-emphasized middle zone? You interpret it in terms of the script. The writer is neglecting the family-community-security part of his life, but he still needs approval, and he is willing to make an extra effort to ensure that people will think well of him, even if he does have few close relationships.

Combine your trait indicators. You begin by describing the actual mechanics of how each trait indicator is used (pronounced-right, open a, flourished capital, etc.—give it a name), and then you define what that particular formation means in its "pure" form (unaffected by any other trait). The rest of your analysis is a judgement call: how does this trait indicator affect the meaning of other trait indicators in the same sample?

Don't be afraid to depend on your own judgements. You know what the trait indicators mean: plain common sense will tell you what they mean when you put them together. When in doubt, reason it out. There's only one real rule in doing an analysis: if it doesn't make good sense, it's probably wrong.

Principles of the Analysis

ATTITUDES: The sentence formations give you the writer's level of confidence and reasoning ability, as well as his attitude toward the people who make up his world, and will be judging his work. Your analysis will reveal whether or not the writer feels competent, whether or not he can see beyond the facts he's given, and how much of himself he is willing to give—or give up.

The questions you are trying to answer are these: Does this writer have confidence in his ability to perform a task (capitals); is he literal, logical, or intuitive in his approach to work and relationships (connectors); and is he basically cooperative (rounded), independent (angular), or indifferent (scrawled) in his dealings with other people?

ANALYSIS OUTLINE (continued)

VII. SENTENCE FORMATION (What are the writer's general attitudes and intentions?)
   A. Capitals (Does the writer feel competent/have confidence in his abilities?)
   B. Connectors (Does he reason literally, logically, or intuitively?)
   C. Script Form (What is his attitude toward other people?)
      1. Rounded (Cooperative, patient, wants to please)
      2. Angular (Independent, critical, quick thinking)
      3. Scrawled (Indifferent, uncooperative, impatient)

Doing the Analysis—Words and Sentences

The only internal capitals in these samples is the pronoun I. You've been told that this formation is interpreted differently from other trait indicators, and we will examine just how differently in the next chapter. For now, don't attempt to interpret the pronoun I as a letterform, just measure its relative height as a capital letter: a measure of the writer's confidence in his ability to do a job. And let's see what capitals, connectors, and script form add to our understanding of these writers.

SAMPLE ONE (see page 136)

CAPITALS:
Height: Variable. Initial cap smaller than ascenders; internal cap (very) decreased in size; second sentence cap tallest in sample.
Idiosyncracies: Prestroke on the T is a simplified abbreviation of Schoolform; connector to next letter angular but graceful.
CONNECTORS: No word breaks
SCRIPT FORM: Angular

The taller h-loop after a T (in Th words) is common to many handwriting samples, and generally results from a flourish of the connector whenever these two letters are joined; in any case, it is an "allowable" variation. But if you measure across the upper zone in this sample, you will see that many ascenders are still taller than that initial cap. The second sentence cap is taller, but it tops ascenders only where the upper zone itself varies in size; the internal capital (in the middle of the first sentence) is very much smaller in size than the rest of the script. All you know about the pronoun I is that it somehow reflects self-image; but at this point we would have to say that despite the large script and the driving determination, this writer has some serious doubts about just how good he is.

All letters are connected, so this writer tends to be somewhat literal; combined with slightly wider cup formations, it means that he does have a tendency to take things at face value without reading—or being able to read —between the lines. The angular script shows critical judgement and independent opinions in all three zones, which is a tempering factor. This writer is someone who makes up his own mind, and prefers to do things his own way. Note, however, that especially in the middle zone, wherever there is room the formations are more rounded; so whatever impatience this writer might display, it is likely to be a result of the jamming. But he does tend to be cooperative in significant social situations: this writer's family has a definite influence on how he will behave.

Angularity in a (too) well-organized script with a firm pressure indicates an aggressive ambition. Despite the de-emphasis in the middle zone, the slightly more rounded formations there, plus the tendency to believe what he's taught or told, would indicate that this writer is much more susceptible to opinion than the overall style would suggest. We know that in some way he lacks self-confidence (smaller internal I), so we might ask, at this point, if the large writing is in fact indicative of varied interests, or if this writer writes large simply to be noticed. He's under lot of pressure and it's very possible,

SAMPLE ONE

This is a sample of the way I normally write.

I would like to know what my handwriting tells

about me.

SAMPLE TWO

This is a sample of the way I normally

write. I would like to know what my

handwriting tells about me.

given the variation of form in the middle zone, that like writer number two, the pressure comes from significant others, and from his own need to feel worthwhile.

SAMPLE TWO *(see page 136)*

CAPITALS:
   Height: Variable. Initial cap is the largest; internal cap (slightly) decreased in size; second sentence cap slightly taller than ascenders.
   Idiosyncracies: Initial cap shows decorative prestroke (simple, but decorative!); the connector is not used to join it to the next letter in the word.
CONNECTORS: Occasional word breaks; breaks located at word syllables.
SCRIPT FORM: Angular, with some rounded formations.

This writer gets going with much more of a flourish, but despite his need to show others he's got the right stuff, he's not as confident as he appears. This is not so much a case of diminishing capitals as it is a case of a large (and to a certain extent flourished) initial capital, so this writer is someone who needs to let you know up front that he's the man for the job. Note that the internal capital is the smallest, so this writer also has some doubts, if not as serious as our first writer, about his level of self-worth.

Word breaks are at logical points and usually in longer words, so writer number two is capable of changing the rules when they don't work right, and has a little bit more ability to see where the original job guidelines might be wrong. Since the script is well-organized despite the baseline bounce, that factor, plus the high-placed i-dots, would indicate that this writer has the ability to be original, and perhaps creative.

In this script, the middle zone is angular, showing independence and a critical nature in social areas; this writer has at least some argument, if not downright rebellious reactions, with social pressures and expectations. Upper and lower zone loops are very wide but pointed, showing great feeling but, because of the angularity, a practical imagination and critical judgement. The script as a whole, however, gives the impression of a roundhand style, despite the angular formations. The impression is nearly correct. If you look closely, you can see that there is a mixture of angularity and roundhand forms, so this is a handwriting that is going through changes. Despite the emotional involvement in all areas of his life, this writer is learning to be more independent, more critical, and less cooperative than either his upbringing or basic character (pronounced right) would normally allow.

Our first two writers have much in common. This handwriting shows a similar kind of professional ability and lifestyle preferences as our first sample, but in a writer who is more attuned to his emotions, less likely to push to get noticed (light pressure), but with a greater need to be noticed (larger and flourished initial capital), and who probably comes from a different background.

SAMPLE THREE (see page 139)

CAPITALS:
   Height: Consistent with script size. Second sentence cap slightly taller.
   Idiosyncracies: Decorative prestroke; graceful connector.
CONNECTORS: Word breaks throughout script; printed insertions used. Breaks exist in shorter words as well as longer ones.
SCRIPT FORM: Angular.

Writer number three does have confidence in his abilities, even if he does underplay himself. He may not know yet what he wants to be, but he's sure that whatever it is he'll be able to handle it—and that's a healthy sign for this script.

Word breaks are wherever and whenever; our writer is intuitive but the script is disorganized, so he tends to be a bit disorganized in his thinking as well. The script is angular but very graceful and attractive, which is unusual in an angular style (normally unconcerned with appearances). Writer number three has a definite eye for appearances and a pronounced artistic sense and that, combined with the intuitive word breaks, high-flying i-dots, and graceful, original formations definitely makes this person creative. The disorganization exists because he doesn't know what field to enter, and it is probably this writer's creative impulses that are making him restless. Let's see if we can at least partially solve his problem with a description of a work environment that might suit him.

We have an angular formation showing independence of thought, and revealing a creativity that takes the time to concentrate on beauty of style. We see original approaches both in doing a job and in dealing with people. This is someone who would work best if left alone—he should not be asked to give or take orders or direction—and who would most likely do best in some field that requires both artistic or imaginative outlets and the opportunity to communicate it to others. We can't tell just from the handwriting if this writer is in fact a creative artist, but he certainly belongs in some field connected with the arts.

SAMPLE FOUR (see page 139)

CAPITALS:
   Height: Initial cap barely tops the middle zone. Capitals grow larger throughout the sample; internal cap consistent with script size; second sentence cap slightly taller.
   Idiosyncracies: None on non-pronoun capital.
CONNECTORS: Word breaks sporadic; breaks exist in shorter words as well as longer ones.
SCRIPT FORM: Rounded.

SAMPLE THREE

This is a sample of the way I normally write—
I would like to know what my handwriting
tells about me.

SAMPLE FOUR

This is a sample of the way I normally
write. I would like to know what my
handwriting tells about me.

Here again we have a writer who is underplaying (not letting others know just how sure of himself he really is), but with a difference. The initial cap shows a total lack of aptitude confidence. The first thing you learn about this writer is that he feels he can't do anything well. But internal caps are consistent with or taller than script size, showing a healthy amount of confidence. You know that the pronoun I will be interpreted differently than other capitals, but even so you might begin to wonder at this point just what this writer is really saying. It's unusual for someone to feel sure of himself when he feels he can't do anything well; does this writer actually feel incompetent professionally, or is the "lack of ability" a mask? The small initial capital could mean that he hasn't learned to do anything well, but it doesn't mean he really believes he can't.

Most letters are connected, with sporadic word breaks; this writer can reason intuitively but usually tends to take things at face value. The script is very round, very open, very sensitive; and, as we have already determined, largely contented. This writer has made a comfortable place for himself by simply going along with the expectations of others. But remember, there are unconscious fears (the defensive backstrokes) and peacemaking gestures, and that, plus the style variations and the occasional reaches into the upper zone would suggest the possibility that this writer suspects that at any moment something can go wrong, and that he had better be ready to cope with it. In fact, something is already wrong. Remember the baseline sag?

We have someone here who has made a career out of going along with other people. He may not always find it entirely satisfactory (note the incompleted loops in the lower zone) but he is willing to do almost anything to appease the authority whose rule over his life he has accepted—even if it means occasionally being afraid, occasionally being unhappy, and in general letting others think he's not much good at whatever he does.

Exercise for Chapter Eight

For each sample you have collected, measure and describe the capitals and use of connectors, and rate each sample as basically round, angular or scrawled. Check for original or unusual formations, and see what formations, standard or not, are repeated.

Answer the questions: Does this writer have confidence in his ability? How does he think and reason? Is he cooperative, independent, or indifferent? Is he confident?

How does this additional information affect the conclusions you have already formed about this writer?

In the next chapter we will be discussing self-image—and another exception to a rule: one single letter in the alphabet which reveals more about the writer as a person than all other formations combined. But a discussion of identity words also includes signatures, so before we reveal the identities of our volunteer writers, go back over the four samples we've been analyzing and see if you can decide which two are men and which two are women.

TEST YOURSELF

For each sample shown below, compare the size of capitals to script size and note any unusual formations. Describe the use of connectors, and determine the general form of the script. Give your analysis of *only* these three factors. Our answers are in Appendix B.

SAMPLE ONE

This is how I form my handwriting

SAMPLE TWO

More than anything I like

SAMPLE THREE

This is a sample of my writing.

SAMPLE FOUR

I am aquarius with Virgo rising

SAMPLE FIVE

amy Ttine margo there

9

Self-Image—
The Identity Words

How do you feel about yourself? Do you approve of yourself as a person; do you respect the person you are? If you were someone else, knowing what you know about you, would you trust you; would you choose you for a friend? Do you consider yourself to be a worthwhile human being?

How you value yourself as a person will influence everything else you do. In script, the **identity words** are the indicators which most clearly show what the writer thinks of himself (internal self-image: the pronoun I); how he wants others to see him (projected self-image: the signature); and how he rates himself in relation to other people (relative self-image: you-me formations).

Definition

The identity words are pronouns and names which refer specifically to the writer of a sample of script. They include the pronoun I, the signature (or any other use the writer makes of his own name), and "me" formations (any words which refer back to the writer, as; me, myself, my, mine, etc.). A measurement of the "me" formations also includes "you" formations: names or pronouns which refer to someone the writer is addressing in his sample, or talking about.

Measuring Identity Words

Identity words are often emphasized differently from the rest of the handwriting. The same interpretations that apply to formations in the text of a sample apply to formations in these words, but, as in different zones of script, they take on a slightly different meaning because of their frame of reference. In order to accurately evaluate their significance, you must analyze these words separately, and then compare your analysis of identity words to your analysis of the remainder of the text.

The *pronoun I* is analyzed as both a letterform and as a capital. Pay special attention to the penstroke formations that make up this letter: complications, sensitive loops, any and all penstrokes which are part of the letterform, are indicators of how the writer defines his identity. As a letterform, the pronoun I is a picture of the writer's *self-image*.

The pronoun I is always capitalized in English (or should be), and wherever it falls in the sample, this capital should be consistent with script size or slightly taller *even if other capitals are not*; it is a healthy sign if the pronoun I is slightly taller even than consistent capitals. As a capital, this letterform gives you a measure of the writer's feelings of *self-worth*. It tells you how much he values himself as a person.

The *signature* is analyzed as an emphasized word formation (i.e., as a capitalized word). Each capital in the signature should be considered separately; you compare height and form usage on each name to determine which, if any, of the writer's names are more important to him. You also analyze the trait indicators and penstroke formations that make up the words themselves, and then compare the style of the signature to the style of the text, to see if there is any significant variation in usage. The signature is the writer's *projected self-image*. Be aware, when you are analyzing this formation, that the writer is also aware this is the "me" others will see.

Me formations are generally analyzed by comparing them to *you formations*. For the most part, all you need be concerned with here is the relative size of these two types of words: does the writer draw himself larger or smaller in comparison to other people in his life? If either me-formations or you-formations are emphasized or decorated in some other way, the type(s) of penstrokes used should, of course, be analyzed as well. The writer's *comparative self-image* tells you how he rates himself in relation to others: better than, lesser than, or equal to.

What You Are Measuring

You are trying to determine: the capital height and penstroke usage of the pronoun I in relation to the rest of the script; the style of the signature in comparison to the style of the script, and the relative heights of capitals used in the signature; and the relative size of words which refer to the writer, and words the writer uses to refer to someone else.

Organizational Factors

For IDENTITY WORDS, good organization consists of formations in which any capitals are consistent with or slightly larger than script size, and in which the penstroke usage avoids complication, decoration, and variation. Confident capitals indicate a healthy self-image; clarity and consistency of style indicate a clear self-image (they show that the writer understands who and what he is).

Extremes, **variation**, and **complications** for identity words are analyzed as for the major trait indicators and the penstroke formations, with the understanding that any interpretations apply specifically and solely to the writer's attitude toward himself. Any negative indicators in these formations are considered to be more damaging to the writer than negative indicators in any other parts of the script.

We will begin our study of identity words with the formation most writers recognize as an identity word: the signature.

A. Signature: The Me I Want You To See

Your signature is your mask: a picture of yourself as you want the world to perceive you. Most people are *consciously* aware that their signature is a projection of self—it is, after all, your name! It is also the symbol of your identity that other people see most often. Many people will design their signature accordingly; choosing a style that they like, that "suits" them, or that they feel looks impressive. This is one of the reasons that you cannot base an analysis on the signature alone. While it is the writer's way of saying "this is me," the signature is very often not a true picture of personality; rather, it is a picture of the personality the writer hopes he is projecting.

(In the same respect, you should not do an analysis without the signature. The text of a handwriting sample tells you what kind of person the writer is; the signature tells you the way he wants to be seen—and very often, the way he wants to *be*.)

What kind of person the writer actually is will, of course, influence how successfully he can project either a similar or totally different image of himself, and what that projected image will be. But as you analyze this script form, you should keep in mind that the writer is aware that his signature is an identity word: the picture of himself that he presents to the outside world.

1. *No Variation*: The What You See is What You Get Signature

This is a sample of my hand writing. I would like to know what it tells about me.

Mark L

The text and signature can vary slightly and still be called a match; most people do sign their names more often than they handwrite something else, which means that the signature is likely to be more fluent (practiced). If you compare the major trait indicators and the penstroke formations and get an approximate style/form match, you can judge the signature to be an honest reflection of self.

When the signature is similar to or exactly matches the style of the text, you are looking at a person who is not afraid to expose his true nature to the examination of others. And (unless, of course, the style of the handwriting says otherwise), this is usually a writer who has little or no pretenses.

That does not necessarily mean that a writer whose signature is (markedly) different is either pretentious or basically dishonest, of course—but it does mean that for some reason he is showing you a face different from his own.

The type of differences that exist in style and form between signature and text will give you clues to the reason.

2. *Trait Variation*: The You Don't Know Me At All Signature
Use both the major trait indicators and the penstroke formations in making your comparison. For example:
(a) *Slant variation*

This is how I normally write; I would like to know — what my writing shows.

Pauline W

If the text is left-slanting and the signature slants right, the writer wants to appear more outgoing and sociable than he really is. Depending on just how much introversion the text shows, this can be a tremendous effort: the person who, despite shyness, fear, or even dislike of others, is doing his best to relate, if only on the surface.

What if the text shows a writer who is outgoing, gregarious, interested in others, or even depending on others, and the signature slants back left to indicate that the writer is introverted, shy, unassuming, or even cold? Then you are dealing with the person who is "much friendlier than he looks"—the writer who is covering up his genuine warmth and friendliness by projecting reserve.

(b) *Size Variation*
A signature noticeably larger than the text shows someone who is drawing himself larger than life; to project the image of the kind of person who would write with a large, bold script (and, as we have already discussed, you do not have to know anything about handwriting analysis to automatically arrive at the conclusion that bigger is more impressive!). The large signature is telling other people that he wants to be noticed—or, at least, to be more noticeable:

This is a sample of my handwriting.
I hope you can understand it.

Thomas A

But just as there are people who overplay themselves, there are also those who underplay.

When the signature is noticeably smaller than the script, you have a writer who does not need or does not want personal recognition; he would prefer to work behind the scenes. You can double that if the writer signs his first name only with initials—but work carefully. If the script and/or the signature show introversion, then the abbreviation or elimination of the name may mean the writer feels he has no real identity at all.

This is also true if capitals on the signature, or on any other use of the writer's name, are smaller than script size, and especially if they are smaller than other capitals. Remember: capitalization tells your reader you think a given word is important; the writer who diminishes or eliminates capitals on his own name is telling you that he believes he doesn't matter.

Other major trait variations can be compared in the same way. If, for example, the signature is darker pressured than the text, you have a person who is trying to appear more forceful than he has the energy to sustain; if it's lighter pressured, he may be trying to come across as less "pushy."

(c) *Style or Form Variation*

The actual penstroke formations used in the signature do not usually vary radically from those in the text, but they can—and when they do, the personality mask is that much greater a disguise.

This "I would like to be friendly but I'm afraid of being hurt" style of text, combined with the large, flourished signature, shows a writer who under no circumstances is going to let you know that you can or if you do hurt him. Analyze the text and the signature separately, then compare them, keeping in mind that the text, as both a sustained effort and a generally more impersonal topic, tells you what kind of person the writer is, while the signature shows you what he is trying to *appear* to be.

The signature difference, especially if pronounced, is a defense mechanism however it is used. The writer is trying to present a picture of himself that he feels will be more acceptable to others, or that will help him get along better in his environment. But whatever the reason for the personality mask, its general intention is, in effect, to keep you from finding out what he really is, and therefore tampering with that hidden reality. The way someone signs his name usually reflects the way he will behave, especially with strangers; and when behavior is very different from the kind of person you actually are, it generally means that you are afraid the kind of person you actually are may not be acceptable to others.

Very often, in comparing text and signature, it will seem as though you're dealing with two totally different personalities. If you look closely, however, you will find similar formations even in a very different text and signature. It is possible to disguise your true nature: actually changing it is a different matter. In a variant text to signature, where the formations *do* match is where you are most likely to find the reason(s) for the mask—or the real "self" of the writer.

3. SIGNATURE FORMATIONS: Personality Styles

The writer who does design his signature in some way is likely to turn it into what he, at least, considers a work of art. When the writer decorates his signature, it's usually an attempt to establish a special identity: and you can figure out what the writer considers special by analyzing the script formations. Again; there are many kinds of signature types. We will take only a few of the more common variations here:

(a) *Ruffles and Flourishes*: The Great I Am Signature

You know what over-sized capitals, excessive ornamentation, and similar usages mean in text script. They mean the same thing in the signature—doubled.

The writer who uses these ruffles and flourishes is trying to be noticed: but he is also trying to make himself feel important, and/or to impress you with just how important he is.

When the flourishes turn the signature into an unreadable scrawl, and especially if the writer adds underlines, circling, and other unnecessary and attention-getting strokes, you have a significant sign of egotism. This is the writer who is telling you that he is someone *so* important that you should be able to recognize him even if you can't read what he has written.

The *type* of flourish can also be interpreted, as a penstroke formation:

Remember the covering backstroke? It's a defensive gesture in the signature as well as the text, and if it is used to circle the name, the writer is not just showing off, he's trying to shield himself in some way.

Zone extensions should also be considered. Extensions into the lower zone show physical or material drives, and this includes underlining (traditionally taught as yet another means of emphasizing something!). The underline can be anything from a single, forceful stroke that shows a determination to get attention, to the horizontal dollar sign which means money matters, very much, to the writer.

(b) *Illegible Scrawls*: The What Do You Want From Me Now Signature

An illegible signature is not a sign of egotism if the writer really *is* someone important—or extremely busy. Anyone who is overworked and overburdened is going to use shortcuts to make his life easier, and someone who has to sign his name to a seemingly endless number of documents is eventually going to develop a style of least resistance. The very simplified scrawl (illegible but lacking time-consuming flourishes) shows the hurry and impatience of someone who is short of time and probably under pressure—and often, someone who is genuinely important enough that he doesn't have to care whether you recognize him or not. Check for signs of demands on the writer in the text as well (overcrowding is one).

Use your own judgement category: An illegible handwriting shows non-conformity, haste, impatience, and/or indifference to the opinions of others.

Question: what if the writer's text style is a scrawl, but the signature is carefully executed with Schoolform neatness? The surface personality being presented for examination is cooperative, amicable, conforming, obedient—and requires an extra effort on the part of a person who really doesn't give a damn what you think. Or does he? There is more to analysis of handwriting than a statement of general form, but a cooperative mask on an uncooperative individual is at least one indication of insincerity—and probably based on the writer's lack of courage in his convictions.

General Note

You know that handwriting changes. The signature changes even more. The text style of script alters with moods, with growing maturity, with general conditions of health, etc. *The signature will change every time it is written.* The variations will be slight, and they will have little to do with the writer's feelings or attitudes: the changes exist, again, because people do not write with machine-like precision; and because the signature is so practiced that most writers don't pay attention to what they're writing once they have their signature styles down pat.

If ever you find two signatures which are absolutely identical—so much the same that you can lay one of them down over the other and get an exact point-to-point match—then you know, without any question, that at least one of them is a forgery.

B. The Personal Pronoun I: The Me I Live With

Self-image—what you think of yourself, and what you want to be able to think of yourself—has a greater influence on your behavior and reactions than any other aspect of your character and personality.

Do not confuse self-respect with egotism. In fact, in a very real sense these two characteristics are direct opposites. And do not confuse humility with self-humiliation. A healthy self-image is vital to survival; a belief in yourself, and respect for yourself as a person, gives you the strength you need to cope with whatever happens to you. And what the writer truly thinks of himself is shown in a single letter of the alphabet: the personal pronoun I.

As with the signature, you analyze the style and form of the I according to the same rules that you use for the rest of the script. But your interpretations in this case apply specifically to the writer's picture of and feelings about himself:

1. *The I as a Capital Letter:* Self-Confidence

The pronoun I measures self-confidence in the same way that other capitals measure confidence in ability, and the two are not necessarily the same. It is possible to be sure of your facts and be unsure of yourself! Check the relative size of the I throughout the script, and give greater weight to the formation in the middle of a sentence than you do to the one which starts a sentence or a sample of handwriting:

I told him that I would

When the initial pronoun shows confidence and one in the middle of a sentence contradicts it, the writer may be trying to convince you—or himself—that he has self-confidence, but he is actually diffident and unsure of himself. This is the person who "comes on strong"; who seems self-assured to those who know him but who, inside, feels less than adequate.

Use your own judgement category: A reverse of this relationship is rare, but how would you judge a small initial I with larger, bolder ones in mid-sentence? Hint: What is the significance of a large script with a small signature?

The personal pronoun can (and even should) be slightly larger than other capitals without being a sign of exaggerated self-confidence; also, while both larger size and flourishes do have the same meaning, you can allow a little more leeway before calling it excessive. Remember: *anything that helps the writer to cope is a positive trait*, and an evaluation of yourself as a worthwhile human being is, in the long run, the only defense you have against the problems life will inevitably throw at you. Never fault someone for self-assurance. In a society which preaches against it, it's a hard-won prize!

2. *The I as Identity*: Self-Image

Very often the capital I will slant in a different direction, or be a different size and/or pressure than the rest of the script. In this case, you judge it according to the same rules that apply to differences in signature, keeping in mind that rather than a conscious projection of self, the ego-I reveals the writer's true feelings about himself: feelings about which he may not even be aware. A left-slanting I in a right-slanting script shows someone who has been badly hurt, in most cases by someone he cared about very much, and is now afraid of being hurt again. He may still be genuinely friendly and outgoing, but he is holding his essential self back (you can't hurt him badly again if he doesn't let you get close enough). The I which leans further to the right than the rest of the script shows a greater dependence for ego-support on others than an extreme right tilt by itself. The vertical I, in a script that tilts either way, is a very healthy sign. Remember that vertical writing shows someone who is self-contained; the vertical pronoun is used by a writer who can take a good deal of battering before it will affect his self-image.

Whatever traits may show up in other formations, when they show up in the I, their meaning is stronger. However the pronoun I is formed, it shows how—and if—the writer manages to cope.

3. *The I as a Letter Form*: Self-Expression

Penstrokes used to form the I are also interpreted in terms of self. Let's look at some examples of how the personal nature of this letter affects the interpretation of its form:

The traditional (Schoolform) style encourages a certain amount of self-containment and reserve. Note that the cup, while it is slightly open, faces left and is covered. The loop is on the right (the side of communication), but any way you write it, the I starts with a stroke toward the left and ends with a stroke right. The Schoolform I shows a writer who can open up about himself, but who doesn't do it before he checks with his feelings first.

It also shows something else. The cup formation swings left and is sharply angular. This type of formation indicates a tendency on the part of the writer to be self-critical (and, on letters like the capital S where it's a knot, to be stubborn about it as well). Check *all* penstrokes: this usage tells you that the writer is likely to blame himself if things go wrong.

Wide loops mean greater feeling; the wider the I loop, the more self-involved the writer. How much he actually opens up depends on closures or knot-and-tie formations, of course, but the wide upper loop shows a writer who just loves to talk about himself, or hear you talk (in positive terms, of course!) about him. Plenty of personal attention will keep this writer happy.

You interpret the narrow loop in terms of self-containment rather than lack of feeling. This writer requires, and usually prefers, less personal attention, and is less likely to bend your ear about his problems, experiences or beliefs. What he feels he feels, and what he knows he knows, and he doesn't need your confirmation or approval to tell him it's all right. Check for verification or conflicting signs in the slant, pressure, and size, of course.

Loops that stay in the upper zone equal separation from social involvement; this type of formation means independence, especially if the letter is vertical. See where the tail of the loop ends; if it goes right, the writer is still interested in others, and if it swings up, especially if that swing raises the height of the letter, he's likely to be more idealistic (i.e., a personal approach to ideas). If he keeps the cup stroke (which is usually so closed as to be barely visible on this type of formation), he would rather that you didn't pry into his personal affairs.

$$\mathscr{L}, \mathscr{L}\ am$$

Loops can be turned inward, too. The I that is nothing but a double knot—very small, hunched over, and closed in—shows insecurity and lack of self-belief. Small capitals show low confidence, remember; closures show something hidden away; loops indicate that what is hidden away is feeling. The I in this curled up "fetal position" tells you the writer is literally tied up in knots; he feels defensive, probably fearful, and has little or no self-confidence at all. Especially when the entire letter stays in the middle zone, your interpretation should be that the writer believes he is incapable of fending for himself.

If the "fetal" I is consistent with script size, the writer is still tied up in knots, but in a different way. The addition of height to this formation indicates self-confidence present, but the stubbornness (knots) and self-involvement (double loops) means the writer feels that the person he is is the person he "should be." This type of writer is very unlikely, or will find it very difficult, to change himself to meet changing circumstances. Despite the confident height, it is the self-involvement in his own feelings that takes precedence, and he will tend to want to play it safe, to keep things at status quo if he can.

$$/$$

What happens when we eliminate the loops altogether? Simplified formations show less self-involvement; the more straightforward the form, the more mind rules over emotion. The single, unadorned downstroke, especially if it is heavy-presssured and either vertical or only slightly to the right, shows a very stable self-image. This is the writer who has learned not to take things personally; who is much less likely to be hurt by slights or insults even if they are intentional, and much more likely to be able to assert himself without the need to undermine someone else's self-image in the process.

Watch this formation carefully, however, and check it carefully against the rest of the script. If the text style shows that the writer *is* sensitive, or has been hurt, or is in any way afraid of more hurt, the single-stroke "numero uno" pronoun can indicate that the writer has simply stopped feeling anything, as a defense against more pain. It still means that he is less vulnerable and that he has taught himself self-assurance in spite of any ego bruising he's received in the past. But it also means that he's accomplished it by cutting off his ability to feel as much, or even anything at all.

$$I, I, I$$

The printed form of a letter is used for clarity, but is also a way of hiding your real feelings. The printed form of the I requires accessory strokes (like the i-dot and t-bar, which are not part of the letter stroke). So despite the simplified form, the writer who uses it is paying a little more attention to himself, and certainly wants to be clearly identifiable.

You can also judge the shape of the accessory stroke as you judge the t-bar (blunt, pointed, etc.), but note that the writer is putting both a ceiling and a floor on the range of his activities. This writer is deliberately limiting his range of self-expression; and the more precise the formation, the greater the rigidity.

$$I^e, \quad \text{(script I)}, \quad \text{(script I)}$$

Pay special attention to odd or unusual formations in the pronoun I. Interpret the meaning of a peculiarly shaped letter in terms of left or right strokes, knots and ties, and so on. But remember that it takes more time to contrive and execute some unique form, and the more contrived, the more time the writer is spending trying to figure out just how to express himself (or, in terms of the pronoun I, to define himself). A complex letterform does not necessarily mean a complex personality; what it shows is someone who is confused about just what his real identity is.

Large, bold, vertical or slightly right pronoun I formations show a healthy self-image and confidence in your own value as a person. The simpler the better: the fewer loops, knots, or left- (or even right-) tending strokes—in short, the fewer self-bolstering complications—the more likely it is that the writer has a clear picture of who and what he is, and therefore the more likely it is that he will be able to retain his self-image intact, in spite of this ego-battering world we live in.

C. You-Me Formations: The Way I Value Others

You-me formations are not a major indicator in the analysis. You may not find them in all samples, or they may not be emphasized in any way. Pronouns may not always reflect comparative self-image even if the writer feels a difference in status: as with the signature, writers are more aware that it is proper names which have identity significance. The writer is making a comparison only if similar you-me formations show a difference in form; measure this indicator proper name to proper name, pronoun to pronoun. A difference in emphasis may be found on all you-me formations, or only on pronouns, or (as in our sample), only on proper names:

I like winter better than summer— you can always find a way to get warm! Mark says he doesn't care, as long as he's on vacation any season is fine with him.

Marianne Johnson

For the record, the "Mark" referred to in this sample is the writer's husband. You know that a large initial capital and a smaller internal capital means the inability to sustain confidence; without confirmation, we might have to assume that this is the writer's problem, especially since other pronouns (he, he's, him) are not diminished in size. However, we have our confirmation in the signature: note the larger capital on her name and the smaller one on the last name, which is his. (Do you have any ideas about what this lady thinks of her husband, her marriage, and her status as a wife?)

When words like you, his, her, or the proper name of the person being addressed or written about are noticeably larger or more elaborate than the me, my, mine and especially the I, then the writer is saying that he considers those (specific) others more important than himself. Watch for contradictory signs in the script, of course; if the handwriting shows egotism, the build-up on the you-formations is probably insincere.

Words which refer to self can be a little larger than the rest of the text, or larger than any you formations, without necessarily meaning a superiority complex. But when a you-formation is noticeably smaller than the rest of the text, then as far as the writer is concerned, he doesn't think much of that person at all.

Conclusion: *Interpreting Identity Words*

You begin by analyzing the identity words separately; then you compare your findings to your analysis of the rest of the text.

Identity words constitute a separate part of script, and despite the fact that in general no single penstroke, letterform, or word is significant in and of itself, these formations *are* more important than anything else in the sample. Whatever approach to handwriting analysis you eventually develop, you should keep an eye on identity words throughout the course of your analysis interpretations: what the writer thinks of himself is both cause and result of everything else you find in his script.

So: suppose a left-leaning, wide-looped script with defensive backstrokes and hidden loops. You know that such a writer is afraid of being hurt. But if the pronoun I is tall and strong, you also know that the writer has the ego-strength to deal with whatever is being dumped on him. It still hurts; but it won't defeat him. You can also assume that the reason he's afraid of being hurt is because he has been hurt. His shyness and withdrawal are not lack of self-assurance, but the result of abuse.

Suppose an open, clear script showing affection, consideration for others, and a basic honesty. Add to it a signature which is scrawled, or left-leaning, or complicated, or in some way very different from the text style. If the writer is hiding something, is he still honest? No reason why not: the concealment of self in the signature could also be a defense mechanism. A writer with this basic nature could be very vulnerable, unless he makes certain he knows you very well before he reveals what kind of person he really is.

Suppose a script that shows a diminished pronoun I but also diminished you-formations (in comparison to me-formations). You can interpret that almost the same as you would if the pronoun I were large and elaborated: the writer feels less than adequate, and therefore also feels the need to downgrade someone—everyone—else.

Words which refer to self are a reflection of the writer's self-image as he perceives it, self-image as it is, and self-image as he wishes it could be.

Use your common sense category: Whenever a writer signs his name, he is thinking about himself. Whenever he uses the pronoun I, or even words like my, me, or mine, he is thinking about himself. He many not be aware, on a conscious level, of how much he respects or dislikes the person who walks around inside his shoes. But that person *is* the most important person in his life; and what he thinks about himself, and how he expresses what he thinks, reveals the single most important influence on his character, personality, and behavior.

Real security comes from within: in the final analysis, the only opinion that really matters is your own.

Principles of the Analysis

SELF-IMAGE: The identity words tell you how the writer feels about himself as a person, and about himself in relation to other people. Your analysis will reveal whether or not the writer believes he is a worthwhile human being.

The questions you are trying to answer are these: Does this writer have confidence in himself, and a clear sense of his own identity (pronoun I); how does this writer need other people to perceive him (signature); and how does he rate himself in comparison to the people who make up his world (you-me formations)?

ANALYSIS OUTLINE (continued)

VIII. IDENTITY WORDS (What is this writer's opinion of himself?)
    A. Signature (How does he need to be seen by others?)
    B. The Pronoun I (How does he see himself?)
    C. You-Me Formations (How does he rate himself in relation to other people?)

Doing the Analysis: Identity Words

The signatures we are now including with our samples for analysis are *not* the writers' real names (you already know too much about them!). They were designed by a graphic artist to match the style and form of these writers' actual signatures as they appeared on the original samples. The reason for this minor subterfuge is simply because it is important for you to see the entire signature, but our subjects, while willing to cooperate, would just as soon retain at least some degree of anonymity. None of the writers, by the way, are related. (Note also that you-me formations cannot be judged in these samples; they were written according to a different sample specification than the one recommended in the Preface.)

Along with the signatures, we'll fill in some background information for you, too.

SAMPLE ONE (see page 158)

Subject is male, age 27, recently promoted to manager-trainee for a national sales organization, married with two young children.

IDENTITY WORDS:
Signature: Similar in style to script; slightly stronger right tilt. Capital on first name smaller than on second.
Pronoun I: Closed (covered) cup at base with a sharp (self-critical) return; narrow ascender loop ends in the upper zone. Used as an initial capital, the pronoun is consistent with script size: internal I very diminished in size.
You-Me Formations: No differences.
We'll take the signature first. It is not very different from the text, but it does have a more pronounced right tilt, so despite the fact that he is holding himself in check, when you meet this man you are likely to find him friendly and warm. Note, however, the smaller capital on his own name (the first name), and the unusually (for him) strong left swing, with a very critical left side point, in the capital S. Stubbornness, defensiveness, and a self-critical attitude, all on a name which, for a man, is likely to be his family name. He rates himself less than his antecedents; this type of form usually indicates that the paternal image is very powerful—in fact, overpowering, and in this handwriting, very critical as well.

Now let's find out why he's driving himself. Certainly he appears outgoing and self-confident when you meet him—note that the I which begins a sentence matches the size and tilt of the signature—but what does he really think of himself? Look at the pronoun I in the middle of the first sentence of the sample. A self-contained upper loop with a (self-?) critical pointed top which nonetheless reaches toward other people; a locked-tight bottom cup which keeps himself to himself but nonetheless leads from people; and the condensed size—the smallest upper zone formation in this handwriting—showing a lack of real self-confidence and self-belief. Our Mr. Smith is pushing himself because he has to prove himself, and his low self-esteem is a result of both his

This is a sample of the way I normally write.

I would like to know what my handwriting tells

about me.

John Smith

need for others, no matter how suppressed, and what he thinks other people think of him.

This feeling of inadequacy goes back a lot further than any current pressures. Somewhere along the line, someone stepped on this writer's ego, and did a very thorough job of it. Considering the fact that he rates his father's name greater than his own, who do you think was important enough to have that kind of impact on this man's life? This writer does not believe he is a worthwhile person, and everything he does, or tries to do, is an attempt to prove himself worthy—whether or not he is aware of it.

What advice would you give to John Smith? He has to slow down, if for no other purpose than to take a look at what he has accomplished so that he can feel better about himself. Despite his basic physical strength (firm, even pressure) and fairly young age, this writer is a prime candidate for a nervous breakdown, ulcer, or heart attack. What he needs, more than anything else, is to re-evaluate his own sense of purpose; and to decide that what *he* wants should be what matters most. Until and unless John Smith develops a greater respect for himself, nothing he does will ever make him feel successful.

Question: *Is* this an example of good organization?

SAMPLE TWO (see page 160)

Subject is female, age 30, worked her way up to department store buyer, also for a large company, is unmarried, and lives apart from her natal family.

IDENTITY WORDS:
Signature: Similar in style to script; formations tend to be more rounded. Capital on first name smaller than on second.
Pronoun I: Basically Schoolform: covered cup at base with sharp left return; narrower than Schoolform ascender loop; upswing on the final stroke. Internal pronoun slightly smaller than script size.
You-Me Formations: No differences.

Jane's signature shows the same thing that John's does, with the more rounded, more cooperative form, though in her case, the outgoing tilt is her own. Whatever else she is suppressing, it's not the truth about what kind of person she is—that's out in the open. She is simply more courteous when dealing with strangers.

Since Jane never married, her last name is a family name, too, and she evidently has the same kind of problem when measuring herself against whatever the family expectations might have been. The critical return is lacking, however (on the S), so whatever degree of inadequacy she feels in this context, either the type of negative input was different, or she reacted in a different way. The result was the same as for John Smith, though. This woman has been judged lacking in some way by her family and, consciously or unconsciously, she has internalized that judgement.

She's less sure of herself than she is of her ability (initial I, second sentence, smaller than initial capital); she is also less sure of herself than she allows other people to see (smaller internal I as compared to initial I). Both her

This is a sample of the way I normally write. I would like to know what my handwriting tells about me.

Jane Smith

pronoun I's are otherwise the same: self-contained (narrower than schoolform and than most of her other loops), a little bit defensive (terminal upswing), *but* generally confident. They also, however, show a very pronounced left-swinging critical return, so it is likely that, even though she ignores criticism from her family, she's a very harsh judge of herself.

Fortunately, that hasn't undermined her self-confidence. This is a lady who knows what she's worth, and who knows what she can do and is determined to do it. And in this case, the self-critical tendency could be a plus: she doesn't allow anyone else to judge her, but she is capable of seeing her own faults. She does have occasional self-doubts about whether she's doing the "right thing" (baseline waver), and she may be willing to pour oil on the waters when necessary (peacemaking gestures). But while she doesn't push herself, either internally or at other people (light pressure), she's not going to give up what she knows she can do to satisfy someone else's preferences or expectations of her.

Ms Jane Smith doesn't need your advice. She's already getting enough of the wrong kind, and coping with it very well.

Question: What kind of person do you think she would be like to work for?

SAMPLE THREE (see page 162)

Subject is male, age 32, changes his place of employment regularly but does well on the job; currently night manager of a motor inn which is part of a larger chain. He is unmarried, and lives apart from his natal family.

IDENTITY WORDS:
Signature: Twice as large as the script; flourished, but with the same basic grace of style. Note that terminal flourish is a defensive and backswinging upstroke.
Pronoun I: Ascender loopless, top cap; bottom curl replaces the cup and forms an incomplete (open) loop.
You-Me Formations: No differences.

Notice the larger size, and attention-getting (if defensive) terminal flourish on Mr. Brown's signature. This style is basically the same as the handwriting, so he still wants to be appreciated; but he also wants to be noticed. Whatever he is currently doing with his life, it is not getting him enough recognition.

What kind of recognition does he want or need? There is no loop at all in the I, and while it is slightly less dominant in the middle of a sentence, it's still fairly sturdy, so he's not involved in ego-building. Notice how it's formed, though. Instead of starting at the bottom, it starts at the top, with a stroke toward the right and upward, and it ends with the beginnings of a connecting loop that could join it to middle-zone letters. This is a man who does not need ego-stroking (loopless ascender on the I), but he probably does need praise. And he would probably be happiest if the praise showed appreciation of what he has accomplished.

But as the rest of the script has already told us, he is still searching for something to do with his intelligence, talents and abilities. He is idealistic

SAMPLE THREE

This is a sample of the way I normally write—
I would like to know what my handwriting
tells about me.

Thomas Brown

enough (upper stroke in the I) to believe it exists if he can only find it; and he is practical enough (simple formations in the upper zone), or perhaps cautious enough (curled formation in the bottom of the mid-sentence I) to believe that he should not start his "real life" (a stable job or a family of his own) until he has found it.

What advice would you give Mr. Thomas Brown? This is a situation in which you, the people expert, need the advice and assistance of another kind of expert: an employment counselor. Mr. Brown knows that he is looking for something, and pretty much what he is looking for: something that will use his talents and gain him personal recognition which to him is more important than money. But he doesn't know which of his abilities will serve him, or how to find such a life-work. And unless *you* have job counseling background, you also cannot help him find it. Tell him what abilities and proclivities you've found in his script, and recommend that he go for employment testing and counseling.

Question: Is his self-image secure enough to hold him together until he finds what he's looking for?

SAMPLE FOUR (see page 164)

Subject is female, age 35, married immediately out of high school, three children (the oldest is 15).

IDENTITY WORDS:
Signature: Identical in style to script. The smaller T in the Th formation is an acceptable variation; otherwise, capitals are size-consistent.
Pronoun I: Double-loop/closed knot formation ("fetal I"); consistent with script size.
You-Me Formations: Me-formations tend to be larger than script; no you-formations. Note, however, that in the signature the writer does not use her own first name.

This is just the way this lady signs her name—*Mrs.* Thomas Brown—and it took quite a bit of correspondence before we found out what her own first name was. This writer has merged her identity in her husband's and obviously, given the shape of the pronoun I, she believes that's the way things should be. Her "self confidence" is based on the fact that she has no self-identity at all.

She knows she should be more self-sufficient, or at least less dependent (note the taller I in the beginning of the sentence, and the fact that her own I is at least vertical), and she is making the effort. But she also feels that there is not much she can do well (small capitals) except run her house and cooperate with others (dominant and rounded middle zone). We only know that something is going wrong because of the baseline sag and the defensive backstrokes; the two together tell us that something may be threatening her security.

We do not have a long enough sample of writing to accurately determine what, specifically, is happening; but we can tentatively assume that she may be having marital problems, and since her marriage is her whole life, that's more than enough reason for her fears.

SAMPLE FOUR

This is a Sample of the way I normally write. I would like to know what my handwriting tells about me.

Mrs Thomas (Brown)

What advice would you give Mrs. Thomas Brown? In the case of anyone who is having ego problems, for whatever reason, the best advice you can give them is to find something they can do well, or to help them recognize something they already do well. In the case of someone who has no marketable skills, you should suggest that they develop one—if they'll listen, and this lady probably won't.

The point is that Mrs. Brown's marriage could go on at its current comfortable pace for the rest of her life; but knowing that she could take care of herself if she had to, whether or not she may want to, would make her happier about herself and therefore better able to cope. No matter how right for them someone's chosen lifestyle may be—and Mrs. Brown has made the right choice for herself in choosing marriage—the lack of a concrete self-image is a danger signal. Whenever someone depends on something or someone else for self-fulfillment, the possibility also exists that they may lose that ego prop.

Question: What do you think would happen to Mrs. Brown if she lost her husband through death or divorce?

Exercise for Chapter Eight

1. For each sample of handwriting you have collected, analyze the signature *only*, then compare your analysis of the signature with conclusions you have formed about the text.

Answer the question: How does this writer's projected personality agree or differ with his inner nature?

2. Determine what the pronoun I's in your samples tell you about the writers' self-image.

Answer the question: How does this self-image explain some of the other conclusions you have arrived at in the course of your analysis?

3. Compare you-me formations, and determine how the writer rates himself in relation to *you* (as friend, acquaintance, or even authority figure: remember, the sample was written for analysis).

Answer the question: how does this writer rate himself in relation to (possibly significant) others?

In our final chapter for this section of the text, we'll put all these pieces back together. You'll see one way—if not necessarily the only way—to do a complete step-by-step character and personality analysis.

TEST YOURSELF

For each of the samples shown below, based on your analysis of identity words *only* describe the writer's level of assurance or self-image in a word or phrase. Our answers are in Appendix B.

SAMPLE ONE

Dear Sir
I want to see about
Your Ael

Miss Jane W

SAMPLE TWO

This is my handwriting.
I hope you can read it.

Lawrence H grl

SAMPLE THREE

this is a sample of my handwriting. I hope
you can understand it.

Ando h. j.

SAMPLE FOUR

I would also appreciate More information
about graphology.

Allen B

Review 2

Before we review, let's add one more trait indicator to the analysis.

If you have collected samples according to the instructions given in the Preface, most of them are "laboratory specimens": written according to your specifications, and for your study purposes. In a "natural" sample the writer uses his own specifications: he makes his own choice of text, paper, and writing instrument.

In a natural sample, you may not have all the indicators you need for a thorough analysis (especially if the sample is very short); some of the indicators you do have may not be as clearly defined. But you do know that the writer's general style will be less constrained when he is not aware that what he writes is going to be analyzed. Further, a natural sample gives you some additional clues to the writer's own preferences and needs.

Sentences into Paragraphs: Presentation

Presentation is the overall visual impact of a handwriting sample. It is a minor organizational indicator; i.e., it must be interpreted in light of what the internal organization shows, and if it is not possible to make a judgement of presentation, the analysis can be completed without it.

Sample presentation is measured by eye, and considers two factors: **margins** (the width and variation of margins, and the placement of the text as a body of copy on the page), and **materials** (the type of paper and writing instrument being used).

The personality quirks indicated by overall presentation can be determined, to some extent, from almost any sample; but in order to be certain these characteristics are in fact natural *to that writer*, you need to see several samples showing the same usages. Only if the writer shows specific usages most of the time (habit!) can you assume that they do in fact reflect his characteristic attitudes and traits.

Presentation is significant because the writer is more likely to be aware that he will be judged by how his sample *looks* than by the way he forms his letters. Here's what he's telling you when he sets up his pages:

A. MARGINS: The placement of the writing on the page.

To check margin usage, you need at least one full page of writing; a sample that runs two or more pages will give you a more accurate measure. There are three factors to examine: margin balance, margin placement, and margin width.

1. **Margin balance** shows *planning ability*.

In (English) writing, planning starts at the left and carry-through ends at the right; if the two widths are very different, then the writer's behavior (right) does not reflect his original intention (left).

Planning also starts at the top of the page and ends at the bottom. Variation in top and bottom margins often depends on the length of the message, so this same judgement only applies if that message is long enough to fill at least one full page. But: the writer should have some idea of how much he has to say before he begins his message, so if a very short note is squeezed up at the top of a page or a very long letter starts too far down to fit, it's still evidence of poor planning.

2. **Placement** on the page shows *attitudes*.

Margins which precisely frame a page show a certain formality. Business letters, formal invitations, and other messages where visual appearance is important, pay special attention to marginal precision. And the writer who also ordinarily pays great attention to this distracting detail is either very concerned about appearances, or very proper in his relationships with others.

If the margins seem to have no logical format at all, then along with possible evidence of poor planning, you judge the presentation as you would judge a scrawl; a writer who is primarily concerned with getting his message down on paper, and has little or no interest in how it looks to someone else.

3. **Margin widths** show feelings about *relationships*.

The more writing you put on a page, the more you have to tell someone. Wide margins show reserve: on the left, a holding back of self, and on the right, a holding back of expression. Narrow margins show a greater need to communicate or associate with others. Margin width can also show "thrift" or "extravagance." If the writing is generally careless, for example, wide margins are just a waste of paper. When the script shows jamming, then narrow margins show thrift (or stinginess), i.e., saving time, space, and materials, and/or making the most use of the time-space-materials available. But overriding this, the need for others is still the primary interpretation of margin width.

In judging marginal usage, you combine these interpretations. For example: a marginal frame—top, bottom, left and right margins identical—is formal, but how wide is the frame? Is the writer holding back, trying to avoid close contacts (wide marginal frame: very proper, somewhat reserved), or is he just being neat, in spite of his need to relate (narrow marginal frame: concerned about appearances)?

If the left margin is very narrow (starts further back into self), and the right is very wide (holding back from people), then what the writer is not carrying through is his need for self-expression. Look for closed cups, hidden loops, loopy but left-leaning script, and/or other signs of communication problems for confirmation of this possibility. If the script contradicts the margins (for example: a neat script with sloppy margins, or vice versa), see if the signature does, too: the presentation may be a personality mask. Consider all three marginal factors as one script indicator.

B. MATERIALS: The kind of writing paper or writing tool the writer prefers.

What you are looking for here are any personal preferences or idiosyncrasies in writing materials. For example:

1. **The Paper**

As we've discussed, a consistent use of *lined paper* shows the need for established guidelines: a writer who feels more secure when there are clearly defined rules to follow (and any baseline waver on lined paper shows a greater conflict with guidelines than the same waver on unlined paper). The same guideline conflict holds true for paper that has a printed marginal rule—but be careful. If your subject occasionally over-writes a right marginal rule, that can fall into the same "length of message" category we discussed for top and bottom margins. Left marginal rules, however, are as much evidence of guidelines as is the baseline. The writer who chooses to use paper that gives him a printed starting point, but then starts writing further left or further right than the printed guideline, is deliberately (even if unconsciously) fighting the rules.

Notice the *size of the paper*, especially in relation to the size of the script. Small paper confines your expression into a smaller space. Large writing on small notepaper, for example, shows at least one conflict: the writer who needs wider horizons (the large script), but who allows himself very little room for self-expression (the small paper).

Notice if the paper is *eye-catching or unusual*; decorated, imprinted, colored, scented, and so on. Like a flourished script, these are ways to establish an individual identity or to attract attention. But unless the writer has designed his own notepaper, he's using someone else's artistic expression instead of his own originality.

2. **The Writing Tools**

You need a sample written with ballpoint pen to accurately judge pressure. But if the ballpoint is the writer's preferred writing tool, it also gives you some additional personality clues.

A *ballpoint* is a common writing instrument, and it is also one of the easiest pens to use. It gives you a good, clear line, without the extra problems involved in using a fountain pen, and without the extra embellishment you get from a fiber pen. The writer who uses it is practical (the pen is easy to get and easy to use), not afraid of making mistakes (he's writing in ink), and (especially if he uses blue or black ink, which are also more common) generally more interested in getting the job done than in making any particular kind of impression.

A *pencil* can be considered either a less mature writing tool, or a less formal one, depending on other signs in the script. It allows for erasures, giving the writer the opportunity to correct any possible mistakes; and it also smudges and fades more easily than ink (informality).

A *fountain pen* requires extra care. It has to be filled; it has to be cleaned; and the writer has to be careful not to use excess pressure which could damage the point. But more than that, a fountain pen is considered to be, by many people, a writing instrument with a bit more "class" than most other tools. It is a very "adult" pen. The writer who uses it tends to be somewhat more formal (and check the margins and the script indicators), or, at least, needs to make it clear that he's a grownup.

Fiber pens make a stronger impression with less physical effort than a ballpoint. *Colored pens*, like colored paper, attract attention. These are both ways to be more "influential," or at least more noticeable, than you actually are (or feel you are).

And, unless you are dealing with a very young child, you should have second thoughts about a writer who sends you a letter written in *crayon*. It's certainly cute, but it is definitely immature.

As with script styles, there is an endless variety of writing materials available, and which ones the writer chooses are clues to character and personality. People do tend to write on or with whatever comes to hand, or change their overall presentation depending on to whom they are writing, so you may not be able to make a judgement here unless you are familiar with the writer's normal preference in paper or writing tools. But be aware that decorative writing paper shows as much of a need to be noticed as flourishes or circled i-dots; so do colored inks, unusually-shaped penpoints, or uncommon writing tools (such as crayon used by an adult). The person who feels a need to enhance the appearance of his sample probably feels that the message is not much worth reading or that he is not much worth paying attention to—or, that he won't be noticed without embellishment. It's a sign of insecurity, and can also be an indication that the writer feels a certain lack of self-worth.

In general, the overall presentation of a sample tells you what kind of impression the writer wants to make—and whether or not he makes it.

REVIEW

Based on this additional organizational indicator, and the analysis information you already have, this is what you should be able to tell from a sample of script. Let's take it from the top:

1. You know whether or not the writer is in charge of his own life, or if someone or something else is calling the shots (organization).

2. You know whether or not the writer is experiencing self-doubts or has questions about the way he is living his life; and if so, how severe they are (baseline).

3. If he is going though emotional highs and lows, you know whether those doubts exist because he is looking for guidelines (disorganized), or because he is fighting guidelines other people or events are trying to rule for him (organized).

4. If he's emotionally stable, you know whether it's because he's keeping himself on too tight a leash (rigid organization), because he's given up something he feels he can't have (conflicting indicators), or because he has simply found exactly what he wants.

5. You know if he is an original, or at least a flexible thinker (unique formations, organized)—which is to say, if he can change his plans to meet changing circumstances—or if he's simply confused in some way (unique formations, disorganized).

6. You also know how he chooses, or if he bothers, to relate to others (form), at least on the surface; whether he will make an effort to accommodate himself to others (rounded), expects others to accommodate themselves to him (angular), or doesn't particularly care what others may think (scrawled).

7. In addition, you have some idea as to whether or not the writer can plan a course of action and carry through on it; you have a clue as to his intentions, and to whether his intentions will be mirrored in his results (margins).

8. And you can guestimate how much of what he does is to get the job done, or the message across, and how much is to attract attention (unique writing materials), or to appear more forceful than he is (fiber pen). You also know whether or not he's sure he can get the job done right (lined vs unlined paper) the first time (pen vs pencil).

9. You know how he feels about other people; and you know whether or not the writer's decisions, and feelings about self, will be influenced by what he perceives as other people's reactions, and if so, how much (angle).

10. You know what kind of lifestyle situation and/or professional environment would be most productive for the writer, and you know whether or not he knows what it is, and if he is pursuing it (size).

11. You know whether or not the writer is willing—or able—to work for what he wants, and if not, why not (pressure).

12. You know what he wants, whether or not he knows what he wants, and whether or not he's getting it (zone emphasis).

13. Underlying these major traits, you also know how the writer functions, and what is likely to interfere with, or matter more than, his ability to function. And along with priorities, you have some additional clues about his possible talents and abilities (penstroke formations).

14. Finally, and most important, you know whether or not the writer feels he is is a worthwhile person, and with that, you know the source of his ability, or lack of it, to cope with stress (identity words).

Once you have examined in detail all the causative factors in the writer's makeup, stand back and take another overall view of your subject. Especially if you are doing the analysis for counseling purposes, answer these questions *for the writer*:

What matters most to this person? Does he understand what it is that he needs? Is it something he wants, or something he already has and is trying to keep? Is he capable of achieving, acquiring, or retaining this very important thing—and if not, what is preventing him from getting/retaining it (or: what can he do to bring it within his reach)? Is it a positive goal, i.e., in your opinion, will he be better off or worse off if he does get what he wants, and how should he qualify his goal for his own self-protection? And, with the understanding that except in extraordinary circumstances we *can* control our own destinies, what can this person do to make his life more productive, more satisfying, more worth living?

In brief: Who's in the driver's seat? And if it isn't the writer, what can he do to regain control of his life?

Conclusion: *Doing the Analysis*

To understand what you're seeing when you do an analysis, you need to keep in mind, both while collecting your data and forming your conclusions, that a sample of handwriting does not give you an objective picture of reality: it gives you the writer's subjective perception of reality.

The writer's orientation is totally subjective. He is not telling you what is happening to him, but how he feels about it: his reaction to events. And he is not telling you what he has done, or what kind of person he is: he is telling you what kind of person he feels—or fears—he is. In effect, handwriting analysis enables you to stand in someone else's shoes, looking outward at his world and inward at his soul through his eyes.

The analyst's orientation must be totally objective. As an outside observer (and no matter how clearly you see what the writer sees, you are not, after all, experiencing what he is experiencing), you can provide your subject with a different perspective; to uncover and explain for him the nature of the forest, despite all those distracting trees. It is not really necessary for you to know, or even attempt to decide, what kind of advice to give. If you can supply enough of the missing pieces your subject needs to clarify his picture of reality, most people will be able to take it from there.

Impartiality is the most difficult, but the most important, lesson you will have to learn in order to be a good graphologist. You must answer the analysis questions based on the *writer*'s needs, and not on your own opinions as to what constitutes a good person, a capable person, a likable person, or a worthwhile goal. The question which provides *your* guideline is simply this: What comments or counsel can you offer this writer that will make his insights clearer, and his life easier? That is the purpose of the analysis.

In Chapter 10, we'll put it all back together. We'll set up an analysis worksheet that you can use to list and describe your data, and an analysis questionnaire which will give you a general outline to follow for writing up your findings. Then we will do a complete character and personality analysis to demonstrate just what you can learn from a sample of script.

10

Doing the Analysis—
The Form and Style of Script

Handwriting analysis is a skill, before it is anything else. It does you no good to learn the meanings of script and penstroke formations if you can't apply them to an actual sample of writing. And you have not, so far, been shown how to apply them.

The analysis information given in this text was presented one step at a time, and in an order that would make it easier to learn. And the sample analyses that we did in Chapters 1 through 9 were, of necessity, somewhat piecemeal. Each trait indicator was interpreted separately, and the purpose of those analyses was primarily to demonstrate what a specific indicator could mean in different styles of script. As a result, while the analysis conclusions did in the end work out with reasonable accuracy, we also took some unavoidable wrong turns along the way.

When you are doing an actual analysis, you can't interpret each indicator separately; you have to try to integrate each of your interpretations into the overall picture as you go along. You examine the penstroke formations when you measure the major trait indicators. You look for reasons and causes as you define attitudes and behavior patterns. A right tilt, for example, tells you the writer is outgoing—or wants to be. At the same time that you measure the degree of tilt (how much), you have to check the middle zone and the penstroke formations to determine how well—or if—the writer expresses this particular need. Each factor, each trait, has to be drawn together into a coherent whole at each stage of the analysis.

It helps to have all the facts in front of you before you begin your write-up. The worksheet and questionnaire described below will give you one way to make certain you have identified and defined whatever information is available in a given sample of script. Once you have this information, however, you also have to know how to use it. In the second half of this chapter, we will fill in the worksheet, and do a complete analysis write-up, to demonstrate how these script and penstroke measurements can be interpreted and combined—and explained to the writer.

173

This is not an iron-clad procedure for doing an analysis—none such exists—and as you acquire more experience as a graphologist, you will and should work out a system of analyzing handwriting samples that works best for you. The procedure outlined here is a personal counseling format, and whether you will be writing up detailed analyses as a part of professional counseling work, or just using your new expertise to entertain your friends at parties, this guideline will serve to give you a quick (and well-organized!) way to get at the facts until such time as you develop a method of your own.

I. Getting at the Facts

The analysis procedure can involve a lot of work for the analyst—much more work than is actually revealed in the write-up—though you can work quickly and still be thorough if you operate according to a system. You need to be certain that you don't overlook any essential factors; and you can't assume that any particular factor is non-essential (unless, as we've noted, it's a one-time slip of the pen). Despite the wealth of detail graphological analysis can give you, the writer still knows himself better than you do; some small point that you might overlook could be the key to the answer he needs.

The easiest and fastest way get at the facts is to start by listing all the indicators exactly as you find them in the sample: not the interpretations, just the actual usages (with enough practice, you will remember what they mean). And one way to make certain you don't leave out any essential information is to use a worksheet, like the sample shown below. (An explanation of the information you are looking for is given in parenthesis.)

Note: The worksheet information is not part of the analysis write-up. It's for *your* purposes only. Unless your subject is interested in the how and why of graphology, there's no reason for him to see it.

ANALYSIS WORKSHEET

Subject's Name   *Type of Sample*
Age (if known)   *Date written*
Occupation (if known)

Script and penstroke usage

(For self-direction and self-control:)
I.   GENERAL ORGANIZATION
     (A visual scan for control and planning ability, which is always a matter of original intention versus finished product (what was your subject's primary purpose in writing this sample?). You will find clues to that intention in the technique used to write the sample. Check for:)
     A. Inconsistencies/variations
     B. Complications: unnecessary penstrokes, tangling, etc.

    C. Extremes of any kind

    D. Flow impediments

    E. Other irregularities or peculiarities (includes missing necessary accessories, illegible formations, etc., and *also* includes any original or imaginative adjustments that assist script flow).

II. BASELINE

(State its characteristics, and note if under control or extreme. If irregularities exist, add a quick visual judgement of what is causing or affected by that irregularity, i.e., if slant, size, form, etc. appear to alter in shape at the point of baseline variations).

(For social attitudes and self-control:)

III. A. GENERAL FORM

(Note the basic or major usage: round, angular, or scrawled. Then indicate elements of other forms and where or how used (as; pointed m/n in a rounded script, etc.). Note also whether usage is controlled or extreme.)

    B. GENERAL TYPE

(This is an aesthetic judgement, so be careful. Note whether basic style is graceful, awkward, or crude, and what seems to be the reason (what formations cause the type). Also; is this form consistent, original, extreme, etc? In a "graceful" script, flow is smooth, and demonstrates a certain amount of writing skill and/or ease with the (writing) situation; an "awkward" script appears either unpracticed (as, in children's writing) or clumsy, and indicates that the writer is uncomfortable with himself or the situation; a "crude" script is awkward attempting to be graceful (or even artistic) and indicates a need to be valued or appreciated. Any of the three can be organized or disorganized. This is a minor indicator: if you can't place a style, let it go.)

IV. GENERAL PRESENTATION

(State the overall visual impact, then describe:)

    A. Margins (Balance, placement, width)

    B. Materials (Describe the paper and the writing instrument—and if you specified materials, note variation from your specs)

(For conscious attitudes and motivation:)

V. THE MAJOR TRAIT INDICATORS

(State overall or major usage, then note any variations or extremes in:)

    A. Angle (Overall: right, left, vertical)

    B. Size (Overall: large, medium, small)

    C. Pressure (Overall: firm, moderate, light)

    D. Zones (Overall: Balance, any emphasis/de-emphasis)

(For unconscious motivations and reactions:)

VI. PENSTROKE FORMATIONS/USAGE

(Note how usage affects flow and legibility. You are looking for:)

    A. Open/closed formations

    B. Loops/loopless formations (including extra and hidden loops)

    C. Necessary accessories (i-dots, t-bars, punctuation usage if applicable), and unnecessary accessories (pre-strokes and end-strokes, knots and ties, hooks and claws, flourishes and ornamentation, etc.)

D. Connectors/printed insertions
E. Capitals (What is their form and size; is usage throughout consistent; any "special effects"?)
F. Special formations (Original formations, and/or original use of standard formations (as; altered connectors); unique formations (as; circled i-dot); unusual formations, etc.)

(For self-image:)

VII. IDENTITY WORDS

(Indicate *relative* size, usage, and form in:)

A. Pronoun I (And are all pronouns consistent?)
B. Signature (Compared to text style; use of capitals in each name, etc.)
C. You/me formations (Compared to each other *and* to the rest of the script)

You may not have all the script factors you need, especially in a short sample. Whenever that's the case, just note "NA" (Not Available) on your worksheet. If the factor is an essential one, like identity words, you may need an additional sample to complete an analysis; but be aware that not all analyses you do will be, or even need to be, complete (See: Chapter 14: Using the Analysis).

Once you've filled in the worksheet, you have all the available facts in front of you, all in one place, and, in *your* (unconscious) mind, already interrelated. You will find that you do automatically interpret the indicators as you list them; and when you begin your write-up, each interpretation you make will be affected by all the others, which is as it should be.

Automatic interpretation and correlation of analysis data comes with practice, of course. If you want to check yourself to make sure you know what you're seeing, put your worksheet up against the analysis outline shown below. The outline is a "translation" of the worksheet (with the addition of a section for analysis conclusions and summation). With all the usages in a given sample listed and described (and assuming the sample gave you all the data you needed), these are the questions your script and penstroke measurements should have answered for that writer:

ANALYSIS OUTLINE (*completed*)

(For self-direction and self-control:)

I. GENERAL ORGANIZATION: Does this writer have an independent sense of identity and purpose?

A. (Script Style:)

1. Is this writer capable of making his own decisions and/or taking effective action in most circumstances? (If yes, skip to B)
2. If not, is it because he cannot (a) think clearly; (b) act coherently; (c) control his reactions; or (d) something else (and what is it)?
3. What is the possible cause of his lack of self-determination? (a) poor

self-image; (b) conflict with outside opinions or events; (c) ineffective means of coping or acting; or (d) something else (and what is it)?

B. What was his primary purpose in writing this sample? In your judgement, did he accomplish his purpose?

II. BASELINE: Does this writer have usable guidelines, and/or is he sure of his ability to reach his goals and his right to try?

1. Does the writer feel reasonably secure about the direction his life is taking? (If yes, skip to III)

2. If not, is he reacting (to lack of security) with (a) emotional ups and downs and self-doubt, or (b) rigid self-control?

3. What is the possible cause of his feelings of insecurity? (a) lack of inner guidelines; (b) conflict with others or with authority; (c) events outside his control; (d) something else (and what is it)?

(For social attitudes and self-control:)

III. A. GENERAL FORM: What is the writer's basic attitude toward other people?

1. Is this writer (a) concerned about others' opinions and feelings; (b) more likely to make decisions or take action independently of outside pressures; or (c) indifferent to either the quality and/or the effects of his actions? Why? (Penstrokes!)

2. In this particular script, is this tendency a (a) positive or (b) negative factor? Why?

B. GENERAL TYPE: What is the writer's basic attitude about dealing with other people?

1. Does this writer (a) feel comfortable within his basic situation and/or give the impression that (he feels) he knows what he's doing; (b) feel ill at ease or in some way inadequate to meet the (writing) situation; or (c) feel a need to make some kind of impression (and if so, what is it?)

2. In this particular script, is this tendency a (a) positive or (b) negative factor? Why?

IV. GENERAL PRESENTATION: What is this writer's attitude toward the overall appearance and effectiveness of his work?

A. (Margins:)

1. How would you rate this writer on planning ability and carry-through? (a) good; (b) fair; (c) poor.

2. How would you rate this writer on general attitude or pose? (a) formal; (b) casual; (c) careless.

3. How would you rate this writer on manner of relating to others? (a) reserved; (b) friendly; (c) pushing it.

B. (Materials:)

1. Is this writer more concerned with (a) getting the job done; (b) getting it done right; or (c) making an impression?

2. In your judgement, is the impression the writer makes the one he wants to make?

(For conscious attitudes and motivation:)

V. THE MAJOR TRAIT INDICATORS: What kind of person is the writer? Are the writer's greatest problems (a) self-caused; (b) caused by other people; or (c) caused by events outside his control? Why?

    A. (Angle:) How does the writer react to other people? How does he express those feelings (penstroke formations)?

    B. (Size:) What kind of lifestyle or professional environment would suit him best? What kinds of talents, abilities, or potentials does he have (penstroke formations)?

    C. (Pressure:) How determined is he to get what he wants, and does he know his own limitations? How well does he work within those limitations (penstroke formations)?

    D. (Zones:) What does he want most? What does he do best and/or enjoy doing most (penstroke formations)?

(For unconscious motivations and reactions:)

VI. PENSTROKE FORMATIONS/USAGE: What are this writer's underlying feelings, potentials, talents, and needs?

    A. Does the writer know how to go about getting what he wants?

    B. What does he want?

    C. What interferes with his getting what he wants?

    D. Are there any danger signs (traits potentially dangerous to either the writer or others around him)?

(For Self-Image:)

VII. IDENTITY WORDS: Does this writer respect himself as a person?

    A. How does he see himself?

    B. How does he want others to see him?

    C. How does he rate himself in relation to others?

VIII. GENERAL ANALYSIS:

    A. What matters most to this writer?

    B. Does he clearly understand what it is?

    C. Does he know what he has to do (or stop doing) to get what he wants?

IX. SUMMATION:

    A. What is the writer's greatest problem?

    B. What is the writer's greatest advantage?

    C. What aspect of his nature or situation is it most important to make certain he understands? (i.e., what would you emphasize in an analysis write-up?)

Once you have measured and defined all available indicators in a sample of writing, and you know the implications of each indicator within the context of your subject's overall makeup, your only remaining task is to explain it in laymen's terms to the writer.

II. Doing the Analysis

You were told in the Introduction that the most difficult analysis to do is of someone you think you know very well, because you are too likely to allow your pre-conceived opinions to influence your analysis conclusions. However, it's also true that the best way to demonstrate just how accurate and detailed a picture graphology can draw is to show you an analysis of someone you know very well—or think you do!

There's only one person we can assume that both the author of this book and anyone who reads it might know in common. So, let's use that "person" as our volunteer subject. We will do a step-by-step script and penstroke analysis, using the procedure outlined above, and then put that information into a complete character and personality write-up.

Any standard Schoolform style—in any language, in any country—gives you a picture of that nation's "ideal national personality": the type of person that its citizens are encouraged to be, or encouraged to think of themselves as being. Our volunteer subject for this analysis is American Schoolform, and our analysis will reveal the ideal American personality.

Note: Test yourself. You've studied handwriting analysis, and you have a worksheet and analysis outline to use as a guide. Why not do your own analysis of American Schoolform *before* you read the write-up given here? Script pressure is firm and consistent; materials used follow test line specifications. The handwriting sample is on the next page.

ANALYSIS WORKSHEET

Client Name: American Schoolform   *Sample Type*: Test line
Age: Adult   *Date Written*: Middle to
Occupation: N/A   late 20th century

Script and Penstroke Usage

(For self-direction and self-control:)
I. GENERAL ORGANIZATION: Sample evidently pre-planned and following clearly defined specifications. Intention: graceful technical perfection. Form variation only where necessary for unbroken flow (Note: re-shaping of the "r", for example, when connected at the top of the middle zone, or the raised t-bar to prevent butting). A size distinction is evidently made between looped ascenders and loopless ones (the d's and t's are smaller in size); otherwise all factors consistent. Script clear, legible, fairly unadorned.

Note also that this sample is "best behavior" (very aware that it's going to be judged), and therefore very carefully and precisely executed. Overall style would indicate that this writer's decisions are based on what people will think of his work.

II. BASELINE: level (no general upswing/downswing); rigid (no deviation).

FIGURE 1: AMERICAN SCHOOLFORM
First Grade Copybook Size

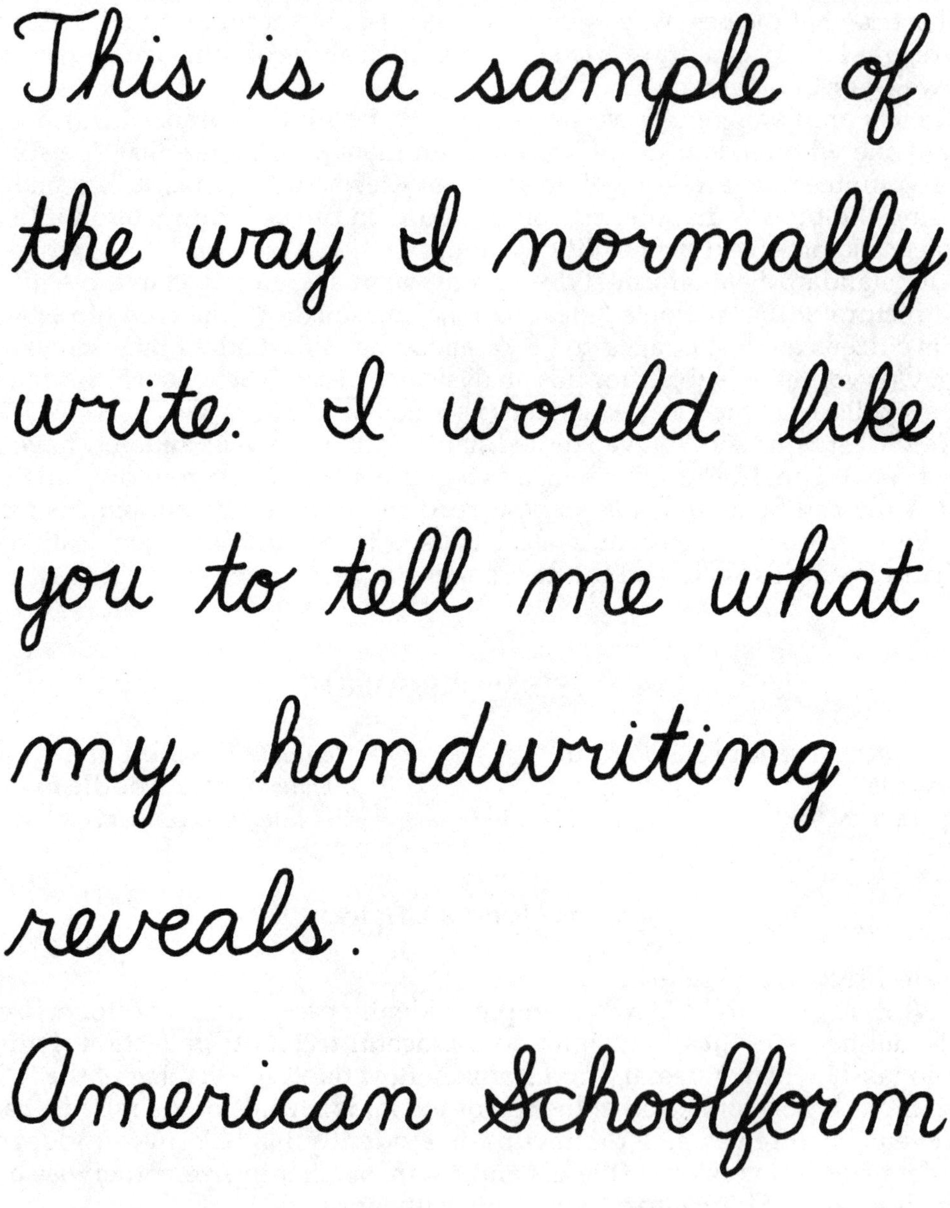

This is a sample of the way I normally write. I would like you to tell me what my handwriting reveals.

American Schoolform

(For social attitudes and self-control:)

III. A. GENERAL FORM: Controlled roundhand; promotes script flow.

Note moderate angularity to distinguish letters ("r"); note also *sharp angularity in all left-swinging return strokes* (see: capital I; capital S; internal return on lowercase k). Minor (very controlled) upper-zone reach exists on initial stem of lowercase r.

B. GENERAL TYPE: Graceful, due primarily to the roundhand style, but also based on the evenness and regularity of formations and usage of connectors. Grace is unusual for such a large size, but obviously well under control.

IV. GENERAL PRESENTATION: No evident peculiarities; generally attractive.

A. Margins are balanced top and bottom; sample has been centered on the page length. Margins also generally balanced right and left, with consistent (straight-line) left margin. Placement regular (framing effect); marginal width consistent with script size (usually 1 to 1 1/2 line space top and bottom); similar measure side to side. Sample overall shows formal presentation and carefully executed pre-planning.

B. Materials (Note: In order to get this sample right, it was necessary to use copybook paper (i.e., first-grade practice paper, which has ruling for zones as well as baseline); that also accounts for the amount of spacing between lines. It's safe to assume, however, that if this were someone's natural style, he wouldn't need all those guidelines to produce it. So for the purposes of this analysis, we will state that materials follow test-line specifications: 8 1/2 x 11, white, unlined paper and ballpoint pen. Note also, however, that this subject is known to adhere to any stated or formal specifications for various types of communications.

(For conscious attitudes and motivation:)

V. THE MAJOR TRAIT INDICATORS

A. Angle: Controlled-right; no variation

B. Size: Large. Letter and line spacing consistent with size; word spacing equals letter width of lowercase (middle zone) formations. No variation except for loopless ascenders, which are also consistent within themselves. Loopless ascenders would appear to be a middle zone extension rather than an upper zone formation.

C. Pressure: Firm. No variation (including no added downstroke or t-bar pressure; any "heavier" or darker lines are the result of covered downstrokes).

D. Zones: Balanced; except for the formation of loopless ascenders, no variation within zones.

(For unconscious motivations and reactions:)

VI. THE PENSTROKE FORMATIONS: Penstroke usage is designed to assist script flow and legibility. All formations clear, simple, and readable.

All formations except cups are closed; cups generally consistent with letter width. Note that on lowercase c (middle zone cup) opening is slightly constricted due to capping; cup on pronoun I also capped, but left slightly open.

Letterform loops moderate, rounded, all originate or terminate in the middle zone. Lowercase o consistently shows diplomatic loop (note this is also

true for uppercase O when used); the only other hidden loop or knot formation in this sample is the (connector) return on the uppercase S. No loops on d
or t; no hidden or extra loops in any zone except where noted; no printed
insertions: covered downstrokes used for returns on loopless forms.

I-dots close to stem and in line with the stem; t-bars centered on stem and
balanced; punctuation precise. Capitals which begin in the upper zone use
moderate, semi-decorative, wind-up strokes (cf: diplomatic knot on o); no pre-
strokes, moderate to no endstrokes in the middle zone; where endstrokes
exist, they appear to be a terminal flourish of the pen. No knots, ties, etc.
except as mentioned.

No word breaks, except where a connection between a capital letter and a
lowercase form would require reshaping of the capital (see: Th formation). No
printed insertions. Letterform shape altered where necessary to assist in the
connection of all (lowercase) letters in a word; capitals connected to lowercase
wherever (original shape of) letterform permits (cf: Am; Sc).

Capitals tall, consistent, slightly more decorative than lowercase forms.

Special formations: altered lettershapes to conform to or assist script flow.

(For self-image:)
VII. IDENTITY WORDS
    A. Pronoun I: As tall as other capitals; moderate, rounded loop; cup
capped by incomplete connector return, but left slightly open. Note sharp
angularity on left (return) stroke. Initial and internal pronouns consistent in
size and form.
    B. Signature: No variation from script style. No variation in signature cap-
itals. Note sharp angularity on return stroke (capital S); interpretation as for
pronoun (critical return affects self-image).
    C. You/Me Formations: No variation; no special size change or emphasis
on either formation.

When you write up your analysis findings (or anything else, for that matter), it helps to follow an outline. The worksheet format can also give you a
means of organizing your written presentation; notice that it groups specific
areas or needs as a unit. Keeping similar factors together, and labeling them
clearly (as; interpersonal relationships, work habits and abilities, etc.) will
make your write-up easier to follow; stating your conclusions in non-technical
terms will make it easier to understand. (Again, this sample write-up is not the
only way to present your analysis conclusions; feel free to alter or rearrange
the presentation for your own purposes, or even for any individual analysis
subject.)

We'll do this write-up in the second person familiar to demonstrate how
an analysis reads when it is being done for the person whose handwriting
you've analyzed. Note that an analysis write-up does not normally include an
explanation of your interpretations (i.e., the baseline shows this; the slant
shows that); however, since this write-up is being done primarily for study
purposes, it will include explanations for all analysis conclusions. The interpretation notes are in parentheses within the text of the analysis.

GENERAL ANALYSIS NOTE:

Obviously this sample was not written by an actual person: it was designed to imitate American Schoolform style—and it was written very carefully, to demonstrate the best side, the most perfect image, of this particular "writer." The only organizational conclusion you can draw is that this writer is definitely on his best behavior, and that he is capable of superb self-control when it counts. And it counts when he is going to be judged, so in a general sense, a sample this carefully executed also tells you that what mattered most *at the time of writing* was the impression the writer needed to make on his reader. Let's find out just what that impression is.

General Character and Personality Analysis

Client Name: American Schoolform
Age: Adult
Occupation: N/A

Sample Type: Test line
Date Written: Middle to late 20th century

Your sense of direction and purpose:

At your best (overall organization), you are level-headed and extremely sure of yourself (baseline analysis). This self-assurance is largely based on your feeling that you know exactly what to do and how to do it (rigid baseline), certainly at least in a technical sense (organization, general pen control) and possibly in the broader social sense as well. In fact, while you are basically a realist (level baseline), you are also absolutely certain that you know all the answers (rigid baseline).

Evidently your experience has borne this attitude out, since your self-assurance both results from and results in a professional and personal self-confidence (capitals/pronoun I). You know that you can do good work (confident capitals); by your definition, good work shows graceful technical perfection: ie; a product that works right but is also attractive to the eye (the style and form of the script). You are also willing to make an extra effort to see to it that a good job is just what you produce (Note: this judgement is not based so much on the sample, which is of course artificial, but on the effort required to form this particular style); it matters to you that your work and efforts be appreciated (decorations on capitals, (slightly flourished) end-strokes, and the reach into the upper zone from the middle zone (lowercase r, and possibly the d's and t's); need to be noticed).

You are capable of thinking clearly and working efficiently (general style, clarity of form), and you are also both willing and able to adapt either materials or procedures to achieve your goals (variation of letterform and connectors to complement script flow). You believe that it is possible and desirable to combine technical perfection with beauty (the graceful style); or, you believe that what is useful must also be attractive in order to be well done (the *choice* of a graceful, clear style). While it is clear that you do enjoy doing a good job for its own sake (upper-lower zone loops, plus the graceful style), and you want to be considered a good craftsman (the emphasis on technical perfection) it is also clear that your overriding reason for attempting to do a perfect job is your genuine desire to please, to be approved of, to be liked—in fact, to be loved (the roundhand).

Your feelings about and reactions to other people:
You basically like other people (right tilt), and you want their approval (plus the graceful roundhand). But you don't lean on them, or even depend on them for very much (controlled right). You also tend to keep your own counsel (closed formations) and even to conceal your real opinions (diplomatic loop on the o). It's unlikely that most people know this about you, however, since on the surface you appear to be very open, hiding nothing (script clarity), and generally outgoing (large script) and friendly (right tilt). Your personal reticence is partly diplomacy, but it is clear that despite your need for approval, you will never entirely open up—and just as clear that you don't really listen to what other people tell you about themselves (constricted middle-zone cup: the c). In effect, you either do not make the effort or do not know how to look below the surface of anyone's "psyche": you judge others, as you judge yourself, on the superficial basis of performance, and you tend to ignore or overlook inner qualities and motivations.

(*Analysis Note*: However much this writer likes company and needs attention and approval, s/he is not particularly philosophical in outlook. The roundhand indicates a desire to please, but also a certain lack of independent judgement; combined with the lack of connectors (literal thinking), it indicates that this person is not someone who looks below the surface of things. Both the controlled-right (mind rules personal relationships) and the upper-lower zone rounded loops (goals matter) indicate the orientation toward deeds and results; with the closures, and especially the cover on the middle zone cup, the result is a tendency in this character to judge people (and self!) by what they do rather than by what they are. It's not so much a lack of foresight as a lack of insight, and it has little or nothing to do with this writer's potential for technical ability (as shown in the well-executed handwriting sample) and originality (as shown in the letterform alterations to permit connectors). But the overall interpersonal attitude is "give someone a well-done job and he will like and thank you for it".)

Your general attitudes and motivation:
You have many interests; you enjoy an atmosphere of "something doing" (size), and you need elbow-room in both your personal and professional life (spacing). You like lots of space, lots of attention, lots of variety in your life (size and spacing).

In terms of professional abilities, you are innovative (the necessary letterform alterations), precise (i-dots and t-bars, plus general script control), and capable of good planning (balanced t-bars confirmed by balanced margins). You need to be able to do a good job (precision of necessary accessories), to enjoy the job you do (the graceful style and the upper-lower loops), and to have that job appreciated by others (the roundhand, the decorations on capitals, the flourished end-strokes). You are not particularly adaptable (large script, not medium); you would be extremely unhappy in any situation where your personal opportunities or actual living space were limited or restricted (size again).

You can be practical (loopless ascenders on d and t); and you can also turn your intelligence, knowledge and experience toward the creation of something actual and useful (practical variation of letterform where necessary). But again, "practical" must include the concept of attractive (graceful style) and personally satisfying (upper-lower loops).

You believe in, and to attempt to live, a reasonably balanced lifestyle (balanced zones); and in general you would subscribe to the idea of a "sound mind in a healthy body." Whatever you get involved in, work or play, you want to enjoy it (upper-lower zone loops are controlled, but feeling is there).

You are willing to work hard to achieve your goals (firm pressure), and you are physically and emotionally capable of the type of sustained effort necessary to carry you through your many work and play activities (consistent pressure). You also, no doubt, look forward to the time when you will be rewarded for your work and your efforts and be able to live—or retire—in comfort (the roundhand again).

Your inner feelings and reactions:

On a personal level (as opposed to overall orientation toward people in general), you have a genuine warmth (right tilt plus roundhand), and you are basically generous (large size plus wide spacing, plus roundhand/concern for others; desire to please). You are capable also of a genuine emotional involvement in what you learn and in what you do (upper and lower zone loops). Because of your general self-control (organization plus controlled-right), you also have control of these feelings: they add enjoyment to what you do, and may influence what you will choose to do, but in the final analysis you will base your decisions on facts rather than feelings (controlled to narrow loops; also, the lack of word breaks/lack of intuitive reasoning). It would appear that neither your ability to function nor your opinion of yourself are susceptible to imaginary hurts or slights (controlled loops; no extra loops. The level baseline is also a clue: no "hope-based" emotions); nor do you drain your energy by worrying about any possible problems until they actually arise (precise i-dots also indicate a limited imagination).

(*Analysis Note*: In any other makeup, all of this would be a very positive collection of traits: but for someone with little to no interpersonal insight, it can be an additional drawback. This writer doesn't get easily insulted, but it's because he also doesn't really understand—or, actually, bother to try to understand—other people's needs or intentions. It doesn't make him gullible; but it does make him very vulnerable, especially to anyone with a clearer understanding of what makes people tick. See below:)

Your self-image:

This is not to say that you *can't* be hurt, however (loops are controlled, but they are there; especially the I-loop); and you should be aware that because you care about the effect of what you do (roundhand, capital decorations, flourished end-strokes, careful style), both your ability to function and your self-image are vulnerable to hurt—particularly if your work does not go right, or does not have the effect you expected it to have. You are also very vulnerable to criticism, primarily because you are sharply self-critical (sharp left angularity in the pronoun I, and in the initial letter S); *your tendency would be to blame yourself if anything goes wrong.*

Because you are not analytical (roundhand) in regard to other people's motives (in the middle zone), if you are criticized you may not understand the reasons for it, especially if you know you are doing the best you can to please. This misunderstanding is partly based on your literal interpretations of what is expected of you and of what is the right course to take (no word breaks). You do not look beneath the surface or beyond the obvious for answers in interpersonal judgements; i.e., despite your technical ingenuity, you either distrust or do not use intuitive reasoning. Part of the misunderstanding also occurs because, despite your need for praise and approval, you are not really trying to please others: not, at least, if it means doing what they want rather than what you want (despite the roundhand, the script does show self-determination). In effect, you expect to be able to do things your way, and win approval simply because you do them well.

Summation:

You can appear obvious on the surface (i.e., to others), but you have a highly complex and contradictory nature: at once self-centered but capable of an open-handed and genuine generosity; self-assured but needing praise and approval; absolutely certain that you know what you're doing and have the right to do it, yet a very harsh judge of yourself; and emotionally dependent on having the quality of your work (and, hence, your value as a person) recognized as superior.

It would help if you could develop a greater insight into other people's needs and motivations; and, in fact, into your own needs and drives. But your greatest problem at this time is your pronounced tendency to be self-critical (sharp left returns run throughout the script). You need to be aware that if ever you begin to seriously doubt your ability, that doubt can damage or even destroy your self-respect and your feeling of personal value.

(*Final Analysis Note*: In effect, the "ideal American personality" is first and foremost "supposed to be" a hard worker who takes pride in the quality of his work. Both the self-critical (pronoun angularity) and the performance-critical (capital letter angularity) traits are probably intended to make him a better judge of his own efforts, but (because of his need for approval) actually function to make him very vulnerable to criticism and even more vulnerable to self-blame. This writer is a wide-ranging, expansive, generous personality with little to no insight into what makes people tick, very little ability (or willingness) to find out what other people really expect, and yet who wants (and needs) more than anything else to be loved.)

Notes on Schoolform as a Writing Style

Schoolform writing *reflects* the ideal national personality; it does not create it. The development of the current American Schoolform style results from what we as a people believe ourselves (or want ourselves) to be. It is possible, by analyzing the Schoolform styles of different nations, to get a picture of their preferred cultural model; and if you know how a people, as well as any individual person, wants to be seen, it makes it that much easier to understand why they behave as they do.

If used as a writing style (by anyone except our volunteer subject!), Schoolform is the prime example of "doing the job properly." It is also a prime example of something irrelevant which interferes with the purpose of the action. The more closely a writer follows, or attempts to follow, Schoolform, the less he thinks for himself; his primary interest is in pleasing authority.

You learned, at a very impressionable age, to express concepts and ideas in a specific way, and it is highly likely that you learned it though repeated drill. In addition, exposure to the original model persists throughout the formative years. Anyone who has ever taken teaching courses will remember learning "blackboard writing"; the style a teacher is encouraged to use, especially in the primary grades, is a graceful Schoolform which is not merely readable from the back of the room, but which also serves as a model of good penmanship for students in the class.

When you exchange that model for a writing style which feels more "comfortable" or "natural," you are expressing *yourself*; your own character and personality, your own hopes, your own dreams. If you retain the original model, you are "just following orders": and, since using someone else's rules of order is always unnatural, the easier it is for you to copy Schoolform (any Schoolform!), the less likely you are to ever be able to make your own decisions—or to become whatever it is you could have been.

Exercise for Chapter Ten

Practice makes perfect. Using the analysis procedure outlined here, do a complete analysis of each sample of handwriting you have collected for study. Discuss your analysis with the writer; how accurate are your conclusions?

Question: How different is the writer from what you knew he "must be like" before you began your analysis?

PART II

*Using the Analysis—
Applications of Graphology*

11

Growing Pains— The Analysis of Children's Handwriting

Since we've just completed a detailed analysis of American Schoolform, let's start the applications section with a close look at the very special people who use that style first: American schoolchildren.

Signs of Growth and Change: Reading Children's Writing

The analysis of children's handwriting is approached from a slightly different perspective than the analysis of adult script. The indicators still have the same meaning!, but many trait characteristics which are interpreted one way in an adult script can have different, and sometimes opposite *implications* when found in the handwriting of a young child.

A prime example of this difference would be, of course, signs of immaturity:

FIGURE 1
Immature Script Styles

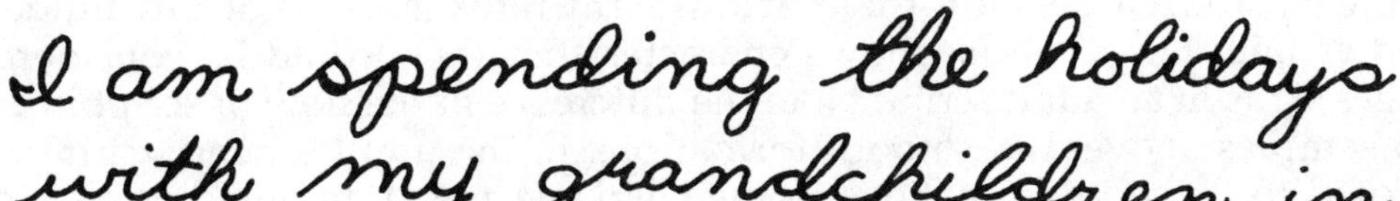

I am spending the holidays with my grandchildren in

Andrea, age 57

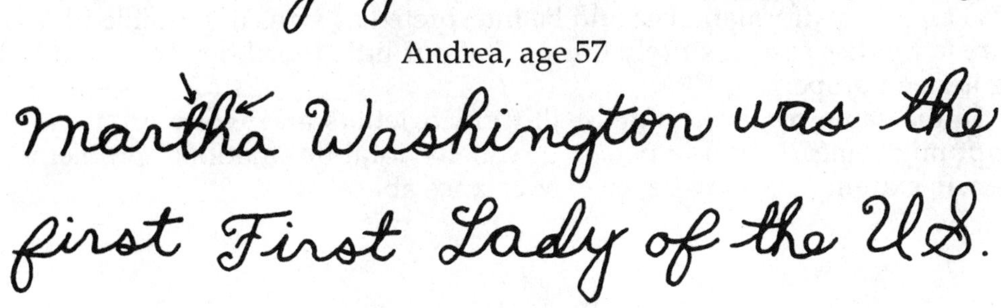

martha Washington was the first First Lady of the US.

Linda, age 9

191

Lack of self-direction, lack of ability to make independent decisions, lack of confidence/self-confidence (or, lack of self-assurance), and dependence on others for emotional (and probably financial) support, among other traits, are very negative signs in an adult's script, since they indicate a person unable to fend for himself. When found in the handwriting of a young child, you are still looking at someone unable to fend for himself—but all it means is that the writer is acting his age (why do you think it's called immature script?); and presumably these are traits the child can be expected, or encouraged, to outgrow.

Variations, especially in size and zone emphasis, are also viewed differently for a growing, developing, experimenting personality than for an adult. It may be just as confusing for both writers, but it is, at least, "socially acceptable" for a young child not to know what he wants to be when he grows up. In fact, very young children are encouraged in their attempts at role-playing; it's part of their learning process. An older child has a harder time of it, especially during puberty and the teenage years (when he is trying to become a "grown-up"). But even if the youngster does not receive the kind of emotional support he needs when these changes begin to happen, he is generally not expected to be able to set adult goals or direct his own life. The same type of indecision is not tolerated in an adult—even by the writer himself.

The actual interpretation of some script factors can also vary, depending on the age and/or educational level of the writer. You should always keep in mind when analyzing a child's script that at least some of the variations, malformations, and structural oddities can be put down simply to a lack of familiarity with the alphabet; though this would also be true for the writing of a semi-literate adult. Handwriting is a very complicated process—in fact, it is as complicated to learn as handwriting analysis—and hesitation, awkwardness, or actual mistakes do not reveal negative characteristics in anyone who is just learning how to do it.

For a very young child especially, script oddities can also be due to difficulty with the actual physical requirements of writing. As a physical skill (and even assuming familiarity with the alphabet), handwriting requires eye-hand coordination and fine-muscle control; these abilities take time to develop, and different children develop them at different rates. Nine-year-old Linda's handwriting, for example, shows characteristics that would be considered danger signs in an adult script. Note the difference in the flow of script in the two samples above: the smooth formations in the adult's handwriting as opposed to the jerky formations in the child's (arrows). In an adult's script, these ragged malformations could be interpreted as signs of possible illness or pain; in Linda's case, it simply means that our little fourth-grader is not holding her pen properly.

In the same respect, crude or ill-formed letters and words in an adult's script might mean a crude personality, behavioral or emotional problems, or even, in extreme cases, evidence of substance abuse:

FIGURE 2
Structural Variations in Adult Script

Really, I'm suprised at They've

Crude Writing

This is a sample of would like

Ill-formed Writing

In the handwriting of a young child, these same misshapen letters, along with letter inversions (such as an "e" printed backwards) and similar eccentricities, again only show the child's inexperience and lack of skill. While this variant interpretation would not be as true for an older child (or a more experienced penman), you should be alert to the possibility, and allow for it in your analysis.

None of this, of course, is to say that negative signs in a child's script are not as serious as they are for an adult: sometimes they can be worse. Children are extremely vulnerable; moreover, they have much greater difficulty than adults in expressing their problems and needs, and certainly much greater difficulty dealing with them. Even if a given child has the insight to understand what is causing his problems, and is not afraid to say something about it, the fact still remains that as a minor child, he is powerless to change the situation that is causing it. No matter what potentials his script shows, legally and emotionally no child is in control of his own life: some adult authority is in the driver's seat.

A left-leaning tilt in a child's script still means difficulty in relating to others, no matter what the degree of skill in writing. And whatever the angle, the tilt as a left slant should be considered more extreme than the same tilt for an adult, and the implications far more serious; children should be able to lean on others for emotional support. A young child who develops a fear of others has less resources, both internal and external, to fall back on than an adult with the same problem; further, the child may carry that fear for the rest of his life.

Certain types of structural difficulties should also be interpreted as having more serious implications for a child than for an adult, even when it is obvious that skill problems are the cause of the difficulty. For example, cross-outs and strike-overs:

FIGURE 3
Dealing with Mistakes

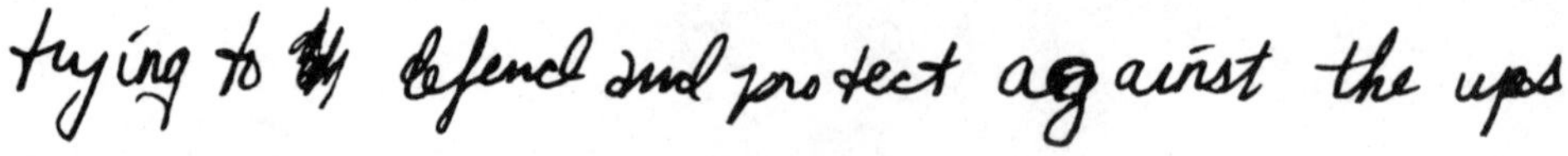

trying to ~~th~~ defend and protect against the ups

Sample from a college sophomore's notebook

I will write ▬▬ carefully.

Sample from a second-grade penmanship exercise.

In an adult's script, these can mean anything from haste (as it does in the first sample, where the writer was trying to keep up with a lecturer), to thoughtlessness or indifference, i.e., indifference to the impression made on the reader (still a valid interpretation, since that sample was intended for the writer's eyes only). Either interpretation, however, gives it an meaning nearly opposite to that of the second sample. In a child's script—and especially when the error is so carefully and thoroughly obliterated—such corrections usually mean that the child cares very much about the impression he's making, and may even be afraid to be caught making a mistake. (Child-view Interpretation Number 1: When you cover something over so that you can't see it any more, it means it isn't there, and maybe even means it didn't happen.)

In both of these samples, we have a writer who made a mistake, crossed it out, and then continued writing, for whatever reason: unwillingness or lack of time to do it over, fear of an inability to do it any better, or a hope that it wouldn't be noticed. But in the second sample, we have to consider the possibility of a serious problem: the child who is afraid to be caught making mistakes may also be afraid to try something new.

And in a general sense, a child's skill difficulties can be a problem above and beyond actual performance ability; or, they can be the cause of other problems even more serious. As an analyst, you make allowances for the child's inexperience; but many parents, and even teachers, do not. Any difficult skill is also frustrating to learn, and you can assume a certain amount of frustration even in a child who does not have unreasonable expectations to live up to. But if the child is being required to perform beyond his ability, the effect on his self-esteem could be devastating, and perhaps irreparable. Writing is not the only new and difficult skill a child is required to learn; nor is it the only skill that most adults forget is new and difficult. Further, even older children lack situational experience as well as skill experience; they simply haven't lived long enough to know that even the worst times can pass.

Any and all identity indicators in a child's script which show any sign of low self-esteem or inability to cope should be considered maximum danger signs. Children are not simply undersized adults. They are a special group of people with special needs and special problems; problems which are very likely to be undervalued by the very people from whom the child needs help in solving them.

Never forget that a child's grief can be just as overwhelming for him as your more adult concerns can be for you; and never forget, also, that the suicide rate for people under the age of twenty-five is one of the highest in the country. In an adult, a positive self-image is one factor that enables him to cope; in a child, a positive self-image may be the only factor that enables him to survive.

The **interpretation** of any script indicator is what it literally means—at any time, in anyone's handwriting. The **implication** of that factor is what it means *only* in terms of that individual whose handwriting is being analyzed. Using the worksheet as an outline, let's adjust the interpretation of our script factors to reflect their implication for children's writing:

Interpretation Versus Implication: Reading the Signs

Graphology sets the age of (chronological) maturity at 25. Until that age, any analysis subject is considered to be still growing and changing; and still inexperienced enough that external events can have a powerful impact on what kind of person that individual will eventually become.

A developmental study of children's handwriting would be a complete book in itself, and would have to include chapters on developmental psychology, case histories, supplemental readings and more, to make certain that the student of graphology had at least an intellectual understanding of what every classroom teacher and every parent of more than one child knows from experience: all children, like all adults, are different, even at the same age.

Further, there are much more radical changes in problems and needs within a shorter span of years for children than for adults. Even ten years, for example, is not likely to produce significant character and personality changes in an adult; but there is no comparison possible between the developmental and psychological needs of an eight-year-old and someone who is 18.

It is not possible, in a book of this nature, to describe in detail the different problems faced by children of different ages. Rather than listing even skill-level stages, therefore, we will focus on only one age: the point at which the child begins to use cursive writing, and therefore, the point at which graphology can begin to identify the origins of problems and needs.

To illustrate how script and penstroke interpretations should be modified for children, we will analyze the script of one young writer; and as we do, also list descriptions and interpretations for script usages that may not exist in this sample, but that can be found in the handwriting of other children. Note that this is not a "well-organized" character and personality write-up: no attempt has been made to correlate the analysis findings. The purpose of this analysis is to examine each script factor individually and discuss its implication for this child, and for children's writing in general.

Note also that this discussion is far from complete: it does not cover every possible variation in children's script, and it does concentrate on only one age category; in fact, on only one child. But it should give you some idea of the adjustments that have to be made when you are analyzing children's writing.

Figure 4 on page 196 is the handwriting of a physically healthy and somewhat precocious eight-year-old girl. Box lines show the actual size of the paper used. How do we read what we see? We'll do the analysis on the worksheet.

FIGURE 4
Pauline, Age 8

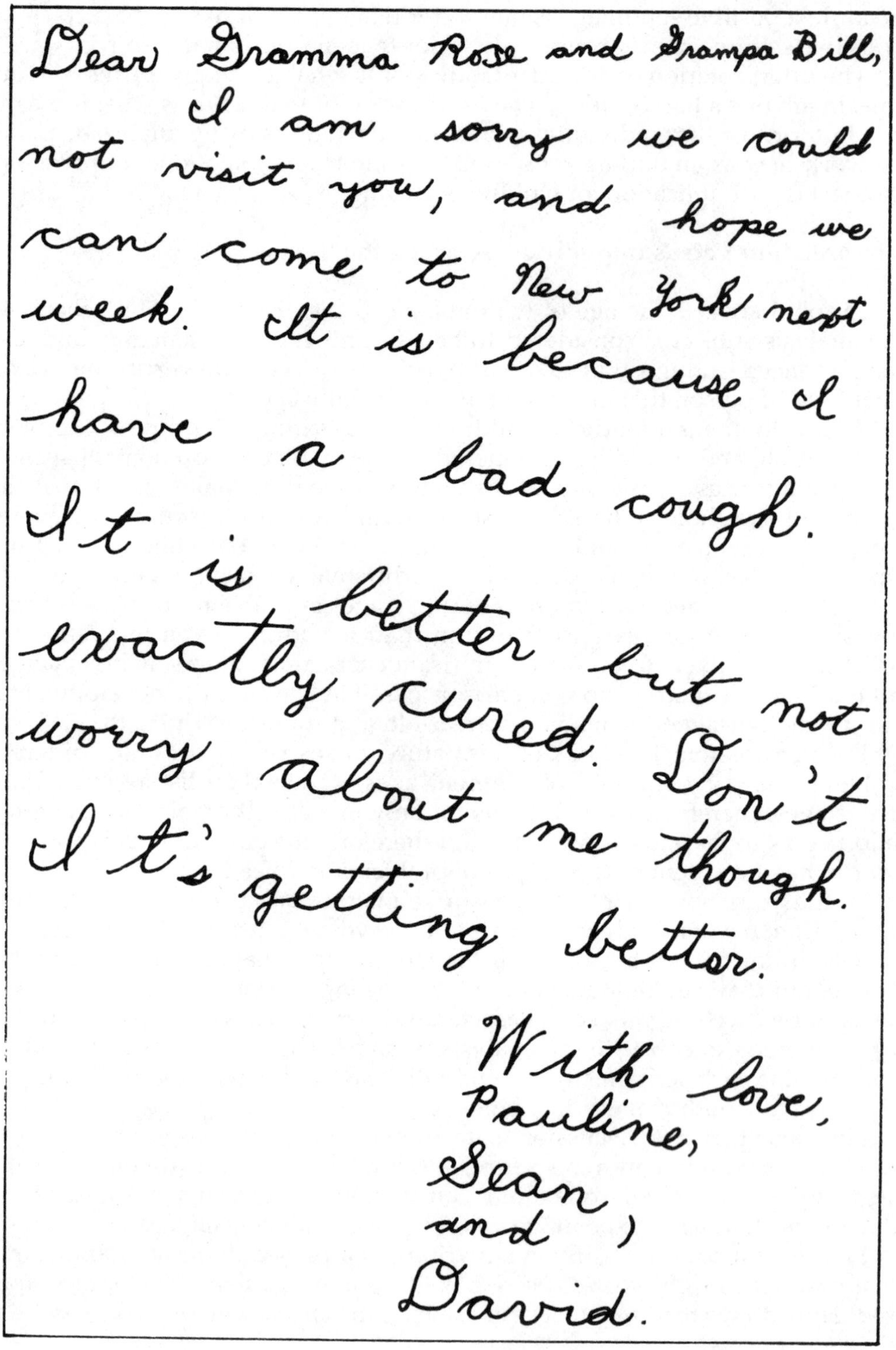

Dear Gramma Rose and Grampa Bill,
I am sorry we could not visit you, and hope we can come to New York next week. It is because I have a bad cough. It is better but not exactly cured. Don't worry about me though. It's getting better.

With love,
Pauline,
Sean,
and
David.

General Organization

Poor planning at this age still means an inability to design a task coherently, but its presence is more "justifiable" in a child's writing than in an adult's (or in a sample by more practiced writer). The verbal content of this letter was probably not thought out in advance; also, this youngster obviously could not predict how much physical space the words she used would take up on the page.

Apparently the intention here was to fill the space allowed with as few actual words as possible, with the exception of the first line, in which those words "had to" fit on one line; see below: Presentation. (Child-view Interpretation Number 2: It *looks like* you've written a lot if the whole paper is covered with words from top to bottom and side to side, no matter what gambit you employed to accomplish that end.) The conflict is most evident in the size variation (note how much bigger the letters get once she could foresee that she would run out of words or patience before she ran out of space); the inexperience evident partly in the size enlargement and partly in those lines where wide word spacing resulted in cramped right margins. As we said, obviously the child could not foresee how the letter would come out until it was written (though she compensated for surprises very well, within her limits) and just as obviously, she didn't do it over.

Other irregularities in this sample are basically technical difficulties. Note, for example, the formation of the "x" in "next" (fourth line down, last word), which is either a connector problem or an error in writing the letter to begin with; and also the way she "fixed" the second "t" in "getting" (last line) when it turned out to be too short for the crossbar. It could be her way of avoiding doing it over, but other factors in this child's script do indicate, despite everything, a genuine concern with getting it right.

In this sample, then, almost all inconsistencies and irregularities can be traced to either immature planning or lack of practical skill; and we would conclude that basically this little girl knows what she wants and has the potential to work out ways of getting it—even if at this particular point she is being made to do something she doesn't want.

General Notes: Irregularity due to lack of muscular control (in this sample, note the "e" in "better", seventh line down, center) is something you should watch for, as a guide to how far the child should, or should not, be pushed to "do it right": no matter how willing the child is, he or she has to develop the coordination first. There are also negative aspects to poor planning which cannot be traced to inexperience or inability: we'll cover those under General Presentation.

Baseline

The extreme downslant to the baseline is fairly typical at this age. It is not pathological depression in most children's script, but poor planning—or clever planning, depending on how you look at it. As you can see, there was not enough room on the paper to fit the words in each line, and hyphenation is not a familiar, or perhaps even a known, option in the second grade. However, the paper width can be "extended" by slanting or curving the baseline; and if the choice of direction is downward, that is also good sense: an upswing would run into the line above.

The downslant here also enables the child to use up more paper (length-wise), and that brings us to our next point. A certain amount of dissatisfaction with events is still indicated by this baseline dip, which, though it is not evidence of general depression, should at least clue the writer's parents as to how she feels in this particular situation. This child does not like writing letters, or at least did not want to write this one; recall also that what to say, and/or what she was writing about, was undoubtedly part of the problem. Her unhappiness with this parentally demanded filial chore is evident in every line of her script.

Children do tend to dramatize feelings and events more than (most) adults: yes, this child is unhappy, but she is unhappy because she is being made to do something she doesn't want to do, and not because she is basically an unhappy child. Neither the situation nor the reaction is uncommon; many children are made to do things they don't want to do, and more power to the parents who are loving enough to insist on proper discipline. The condition of the baseline tells you, better than the child can or is allowed to verbalize, exactly how he feels—*at the moment of writing*.

There is a difference, however, between something the child doesn't want to do, and something he is not able to do: watch any child's script for baseline dip and other irregularities on *lined* paper. The insistence by writing teachers about staying on the line is pretty general, and children—like adults—do find it easier to steady their baseline on ruled paper. If the child's baseline fights the rules, there can be a serious problem. It might be carelessness or indifference (a junior-league form of rebellion), which should be noticed and traced to its causes. But if the child *is* trying and *can't* do it right, then he needs experience with something else that he can do right. As we've noted, handwriting is not a simple skill to learn, yet it is often presented as such; further, each child is certainly well aware that he *must* be able to do it. Failure in this primary skill may lead to a long line of other failures, if the child becomes convinced that he can't do anything right.

General Form

This is a roundhand; most angularity here is due to jerkiness of the pen. But we can see the angularity starting: note the m's and n's. The occasional pointed tops of these letters are too smooth to be lack of control; notice also, that their use is in words which are likely to be more familiar to the child (as: "am," "can," and "me"). This is one of the reasons we called this child precocious—and the precocity is based on *practice* (i.e., the more sure she is of her skill, the more able she is to make her own decisions).

Doing it easily is muscular control, and it is only one sign of a child's development. Trying something new is a more positive sign, and may tell you more about the child's capabilities than the form of the script. Roundhand dominates at this age, even for the quickest learners; but some problems with control, oddly enough, can give you a clue to potential that the form can conceal. Our clue in this sample was the word "exactly" (line eight). The height and position of the "l" was another unexpected surprise to this writer; our reproduction doesn't show it, but the original indicates that she had to retrace the t-stem to make it long enough to accommodate the bar. The word was evidently a problem in other ways as well—but the point is, she *used* it. One sign of emotional health in a child is that new knowledge is not a bogie but a toy; and it comes from praise for trying as well as for succeeding.

General Type

This is awkward writing, which is not surprising. Awkwardness indicates a feeling of unease with a situation. In an adult's script, it can be based on a lack of skill confidence; in children's script, it is simply based on a lack of skill. Awkward writing is to be expected at this age; in fact, awkward behavior in any new situation, or in the effort to make use of any new skill, is to be expected at any age. No matter what the individual's basic abilities and potentials, the learning period is always awkward, and usually nerve-wracking, and because of that, you can build true personal *in*security in your child if you really want to. Just insist on expert penmanship before the child is capable of it.

General Presentation

A visual impact only a parent could love.

The marginal crowding and imbalance results primarily from immature planning. The child thought she would need—or would be easily able to use—all the room on the paper, and so started as close as possible to the top; then she ran out of what to say and had to stretch it out toward the bottom. The cause of the right crowding we discussed earlier; on the left, a good part of it was more likely a matter of the paper edge being the only marginal guideline she had (remember that school paper is normally ruled for left margin). We could assume, then, and in many cases it is true, that left crowding on paper without a marginal guideline is inexperience, resulting from an inability to make an independent decision about where the left margin "should" be. Recall, however, that the plan was to fill the entire page; so the tight left still shows a need to communicate, even if it is a deliberate put-on.

The sample was written on a half-sheet of unlined note paper, in pencil. The pencil is fine. Even the schools don't begin to insist on ink until well into third grade and possibly later, so in this case, the child was simply using a familiar writing tool. It was also fortunate, since it enabled her to make a couple of corrections. The original shows that the word "York" was erased and rewritten at least twice (evidently she had some trouble with the capital "Y").

The choice of paper, however, corroborates our original judgement that she wanted it to *look like* she was writing a full-length (or at least a full-page) letter. If you cover the whole paper with words, you have obviously written as much as you possibly can—and, of course, if you use a smaller piece of paper, there is less writing you have to do before you have written as much as you possibly can.

The combination of marginal crowding, paper size, and (erasable-correctable) writing tool all indicate that the impression this writer wanted to make was of a genuine attempt to do a good, and complete, job of writing.

General Notes: In a free-form sample like this one (where the presentation is up to the writer), the rules of writing it are purely optional. We can see in this sample that the child knows the form of a letter and is willing to follow it: the greeting (first sentence) *had to* fit on one line; the paragraph is indented, and the closing—even if calculated to extend the letter all the way down to the very bottom of the page—is correctly placed and correctly punctuated. It tells us that she uses what she learns; but that's her choice. In a natural sample (although this, since it is being done under duress, is not entirely a natural sample), as long as the child is writing something she is practicing; let her set it up any way she likes.

When, however, presentation does matter, it should be insisted upon. This is not a matter of skill level, or blind obedience, but of willingness to learn. If a teacher, for example, gives specific instructions on how to set up an assignment paper, those instructions should be followed. Certainly after the instructions have been explained several times, there is no legitimate reason why even the most awkward writer cannot place his words in a particular spot on the page. If he doesn't, you are dealing with an attitude problem—he's not listening, or he's too lazy, or he's refusing to follow directions.

Free will aside, it is important for a child to learn *how to* follow directions. Even if the child will never have to work for a living and wants to spend his life making model airplanes, he still has to know how to follow directions. Self-determination and independent judgement are valuable attributes; but the arbitrary refusal to do a simple, standard task according to specifications (and as requested by the person you are doing it for!) is not, and should be actively discouraged. This type of "rebellion" serves no real purpose, except one. It lets you know that the child has some kind of real or imaginary grievance against authority.

The Major Trait Indicators

Skill variations aside, the major trait indicators read pretty much the same in a child's script as in an adult's; your interpretation is largely a matter of how much value you put on what you see. In this category, some usages can be overlooked, while others may be extremely negative.

Angle: This script tends a bit more right than Schoolform, but it's still pretty much under control, and it's about standard for this age. If the script begins to slant beyond pronounced right, the child is not getting enough attention (which may also mean a child who needs extra attention); either way, it's just as well to be alert to the need.

Vertical writing is also not uncommon at this age, and partly traceable to the youngster's greater experience with block printing (see below: Penstroke Usage). But both the vertical and the controlled right show a certain reserve which is also fairly typical, and perfectly normal. And it does reflect a growing independence; the child's need to "do it myself."

A left tilt, as we mentioned, is a pronounced danger sign; and the younger the child, the greater the danger. For many children, the first signs of shyness appear on the lowercase d (a); for other children, it takes a much more serious form (b):

FIGURE 5
The Origins of Shyness—and Fear

you and me and the

a

When I made one it

b

Such a child needs more than attention. He needs encouragement—and he needs it *now*, before the tilt goes completely left, or the script begins to show other signs of feelings of inadequacy. The child who uses a left tilt in his script is afraid; and simply telling him not to be is not enough. You have to find out what (usually interpersonal situation) he fears, and then find a way to make that situation less threatening.

The child who uses a left tilt on his *pronoun* is abused. Remember that a left-slanting pronoun on a right-slanting script indicates that the writer has been badly hurt by someone who matters. The abuse may not necessarily be physical. In fact, it may not even always be intentional. But something in the way the child is being treated has made him afraid to trust, and afraid to love.

Size: The one negative sign in our sample letter is the small script with which it begins; and it is not entirely due to the attempt to squeeze the greeting on one line. It is evidently a more normal style for this writer than the larger size, since the child is more comfortable with it. But the focussed concentration indicated by small size should be discouraged in a child this age. Bearing in mind that the concentration required for the tiny writing in the first line is even more intense for an eight-year-old than for a 28-year-old (based on skill level), this child is shutting out too much. What's more, she knows she's missing something: note the wide word spread where the size is small, and the more consistent word spacing as the script gets larger. She might not like it, but she'll be better off in the long run if her parents insist, at least for now, that she get out and try to make friends and develop varied interests. Eight is much too young to begin to specialize.

Oversize writing, when typical, is another clue that the child needs attention: it's a "see me" style. But a reasonably visible handwriting, at least medium to medium-large, is a healthy size for a young child. In terms of skill level, it is easier for the child to write larger; it is also encouraged in writing practice (check out the size of the lines on paper that beginning writers are given in the schools). A growing, developing personality should at least be adaptable (medium), or even better, willing to grow (medium-large).

Pressure: In this sample, pressure varies with the size. It is moderately firm (for pencil) and very even in the first five lines; as the size gets bigger, irregular heavy pressure strokes indicate at least a growing irritability, if not outright frustration. We can't tell if the frustration is with the task itself, or with the difficulty, for this child, in writing a larger size, but frustration—or anger—it is, nonetheless.

It is more common for young children to bear down hard when they write (writing is an intense physical and mental effort!), and light pressure, especially when the script is carefully formed, is another negative sign. It is evidence of timidity, lack of self-assurance, and/or feelings of inadequacy (and some complimentary comments on how well the child is doing—either at writing, or at some other skill—tend to result in firmer script pressure).

Varied pressure is still frustration, just as sudden heavy strokes are anger, but as we noted, it is difficult in the young writer to determine if the frustration has to to with some event in the child's life, or it if based on a problem with the writing skill itself. If it continues through enough samples, however, something is bothering the child, and you should make an attempt to find out what it is.

Zones: Here's another reason we called this child precocious; the middle zone is only mildly emphasized, and only sometimes—and note the upper zone extensions. It shows a lesser dependence on others (others, at this age, being parents and teachers), and also confirms our earlier conclusion that this child likes to learn, and use what she does learn. In effect, we have a (very) young writer who is pulling away from parental authority and beginning to think for herself.

Also note, however, the de-emphasized lower zone. When we match that to the small size, we come up with a child who is not physically active, either in conjunction with, as a result of, or as a cause of her concentration on specific interests. It is possible to be intellectually curious and work oriented and still be physically lazy—and that physical laziness may be one thing that keeps this child from involving herself in activities with other people.

A lag in lower zone development, certainly at least until puberty, is more than normal (though in this case, because of the extent of the upper zone reach, it is a definite imbalance); upper zone extensions do tend to appear first. By this age, young as it is, writing should begin to pull out of the middle zone. Until the child is older, variations and zone imbalance are not cause for concern unless linked to some other negative sign; middle zone emphasis, however, even in a younger child (and however "normal" it may be), *is* cause for concern. And when you see it developing, you should encourage that child to try something on *his* own. Middle zone emphasis is not insecurity, but it is over-dependence, and indicates that the child (or the adult!) is over-protected.

Penstroke Usage

It's too early at this age to see the variety of individualized formations which appear in adult script; not when most of your subjects have barely graduated from block printing (and still revert to it, on occasion, with what almost seems like relief). What you do see tends to be either related to skill problems or caused by it, and you should adjust your interpretation of any factors from improper punctuation (which might be carelessness but could just as easily be lack of knowledge or understanding) to unusual formations accordingly.

Those formations which are more significant in a child's writing include block printing, extra strokes, the formation and size of capital letters, and, as we mentioned earlier, cross-outs and strike-overs.

Reversion to print, and especially the exclusive use of block printing by a child who has learned script, is a sign of insecurity in terms of skill confidence, often based on a need to make the best possible impression. The child reverts to print because he *knows* he can do it, whereas the cursive is newer, and something he's not as sure of. However, it is not only normal, but healthier, for a child to like to try out something new; if he's afraid to use his new skill there has to be a serious reason.

In the same respect, extra strokes in the cursive may be a special attempt to do it even better. In our sample, the extra strokes are prestrokes or endstrokes—insecurity based on a need for approval—which pretty much dominate the script. Some evidence of this reaction is fairly common in externally-motivated children (those from whom much is expected, even if the expectations are rational), and it can take many different forms. What this little girl is doing about her need for approval is making an extra effort to do the job right (as: the correction on "getting" and the concern with proper format). We might also wonder if the smaller script is such a reaction; as evidence of the extra effort focussed on doing a good job.

Prestrokes and endstrokes are taught as connectors when cursive is taught, and many children may assume that they are part of the letter itself. Just as many children drop these formations, however. An extra stroke, and an extra effort, they remain, and a statement by the child that he's doing his best to win your approval.

This is true also because even an imaginative child, as this one is (note those high-flying i-dots!), tends to be more literal than an adult. Again; a child has less experience with options: the way he was taught to do it is the way it should be done. And our sample shows that literal interpretation; all letters are connected, in spite of the difficulty, with some letters, of making them connect (note the connector problem between the "e" and "t" in "better," line seven).

The fact that almost all capitals are separated from the lowercase is also a literal interpretation at this age: capitals are a "separate alphabet"; a young writer is taught how to make the easier connections (usually those at the baseline), but other capitals are treated as stand-alones. This, again, is the "right way" to do it.

Prestrokes and curled decorations on capitals are Schoolform (see the alphabet chart, Chapter 6). They also tend to hang on longer than prestrokes in the middle zone. Capitals are harder to do, and the child (or any writer) gets less practice with them, so he tends to pay more attention to getting them "right." Depending on the child's aesthetic eye, and whether or not a given writing exercise allows him time to *draw* his letters, he may also find them more fun to do. Decorations on the capitals are not a negative sign in a child's script; they are more likely to be an indication that he is playing. Even so, and as in an adult's script, they show greater attention paid to doing a more attractive job.

Capital letters may also be more vertical than the lowercase (closer to block printing style), and this should not be considered a tilt variation, but (again) more of a skill problem.

The important factor, of course, is how big they are. If capitals are the right size in relation to the script, the child is willing to take his chances in order to show off his new skills; if they barely top the middle zone (hidden in the script), you come again to the child who lacks confidence in his own ability to do—and in fact, may even be afraid to show you what he does do.

Identity Words

Pay extra careful attention to these. The young child especially is very aware of himself, and takes (or *should* take!) an extra interest in anything that refers to himself.

Note in our analysis sample the smaller internal I (fifth line from top) and the smaller capital on the signature. Signatures are practiced; once a child learns to write his own name, he may even do it, at least for a period of time, to the exclusion of anything else. Signatures also begin to develop conscious individualization much sooner than anything else in the child's script. The signature is "my name," and can be fascinating to a child.

We could assume that the signature this size corresponds to the smaller size of writing—but not with the evidence of that internal I, or the fact of the smaller capital, and especially not when her brother's names are written larger. You/me formations help you identify significant others (though it can sometimes be difficult to tell, when the you is larger, if the child himself places a greater value on that other, or if he feels that the other is valued more). When it's a matter of names, however, even with the most significant other, the child's own name should be at least equal, if not larger, in size:

FIGURE 6
Matthew, Age 5

Our young analysis subject certainly has a lot going for her, but it's possible that a good part of her development is based on the fact that she has something to prove. Despite her bravado—and she's dealing with her situation very well within her limits—this child does feel that in some way having to do with what she is, she's not quite good enough. What's more, she feels that her siblings are in some way better.

Analysis Notes: Each child's needs are different, and it is often difficult for even the most perceptive and caring observer to catch the undercurrents which influence an individual child's growth and potential. With handwriting analysis, it becomes less difficult for anyone who cares about a child to watch and encourage his growth and guard his emotional health; certainly, what you find in his writing will tell you, better than the child is able (or, perhaps, permitted) to express, how he feels about himself and what is happening to him—and what he needs in order to cope. It can also tell you whether or not what you are doing about it, in terms of individual attention, concerned supervision, and intelligent discipline, is having the positive effect on the child's self-image that you intended it to have.

The little girl whose handwriting we used as our model is precocious because she has been encouraged to be; her parents, and in fact other adult relatives and most of her teachers, recognize the fact that she is bright; that she enjoys learning and can make practical use of what she learns; in fact, that she has a great deal of potential. But it is obvious that the child herself has arrived at the conclusion, for whatever reason, that she is somehow not a valuable person; or, that there are others more valuable than she is. It may be that she needs more attention than she is getting, or perhaps that she needs a different kind of attention. But she certainly needs assurances that she is in and of herself—and apart from whatever she can or cannot do—a worthwhile person. Without it, she may grow up to spend the rest of her life feeling that no matter what she does, it is not enough to count.

Conclusion: *Tailoring the Analysis*

When you are dealing with a specific category or group of people, your attitude toward that group is at least as important as your ability to adjust your interpretations of penstroke formations; in fact, it may be the basis of your ability to adjust your interpretations. Obviously, you are more likely to be able to make these adjustments accurately if you have your own regular personal contacts with children (or, whatever other special group you are dealing with). But in all cases, *what* you are taking into account in your analysis is the effect of special events and circumstances which are what make those people a special group in the first place.

In the case of children's writing, you are dealing with a developing, changing, character and personality—which means one that doesn't know who or what it is yet—of whom certain things are expected. What is expected may be too little in some ways and too much in others, but it also tends to be something the child cannot clearly define or understand, and yet that he wants to do, because he *needs* to please.

All of this makes a child emotionally vulnerable and highly susceptible to suggestion; incidents that may not even be noticed by an adult can totally alter the course of a child's development, and, for good or for bad, most of what happens to him will stay with him all his life. The indicators may change (i.e., the reaction or the means of coping may alter) as the individual grows older; but it is in the child's script that you find not only a preview of what the adult will be, but explanations of what is responsible for those things he can't be.

Notes on Children's Writing

When you begin to study children's writing, you can also begin to see the origin of some of the penstroke interpretations in adult script. For example: scribbled-out or scribbled-over letters and words in an adult's handwriting is a sign of guilt; of something to hide. It has its basis in the cross-outs and strike-overs used by a child to conceal mistakes, and it has pretty much the same interpretation: a fear of some wrong—in fact, of some inadequacy—being found out.

A young child just learning cursive writing will very often add the pre-stroke to a letter or word. Because the child is unfamiliar with the script alphabet, the connector formed as part of the letter is the "right way" to do it, and adding the prestroke indicates an extra effort to do the job right. Does it really mean anything different in an adult's writing? Prestrokes show hesitation; a chance to think before starting an action; an extra effort added to the job because the writer is unsure of his ability to do it right. In the child's script, the performance insecurity has to do specifically with a lack of knowledge of the proper way to write the letter; in an adult, it can refer to a similar insecurity in just about any area. But it has its basis in the way the child was taught to perform a difficult and complicated task.

Even in handwriting, it is possible to see how the experiences of the child affect the performance of the adult.

Additional Notes on Implication: Other Special People

Many of the injunctions regarding skill insecurities, need for reassurance, and feelings of inadequacy which apply to children's script apply equally, and for many of the same reasons, to the handwriting of immigrants. If the writer was educated in some other country, writing as a physical skill may not be a problem. But language, customs, and an infinite number of other variables do become a consideration. For example:

This is a sample of the way I normally write. I would like to know what my handwriting

This writer is 42 years old. He was born in Italy, and has been in this country for about 20 years. He speaks with a strong and identifiable accent, but he writes (and, according to his report, thinks) in English.

He also works as a typesetter *in English*; a skill which requires considerable linguistic fluency, if nothing else. Originally, he was a linotype operator—for almost all of those 20 years—but at the time this sample was written he had switched, less than two years earlier, to computer typesetting (a skill which requires a good deal more than linguistic fluency, and at which he excelled almost immediately).

He has a wife and three sons. He encourages his children to do well in school. He owns his own home, and also owns other land and investment property. Besides the typesetting, he does high-quality screen printing, and shortly after this sample was written, he finally quit his job of many years and went full-time into the (self-employed) business he had been building up while employed. He reads voraciously, mostly technical or how-to books (he has little patience with fiction); and has enough personal self-confidence to be able to admit when he does not know or understand something, and to ask for an explanation from the person most likely to know—even if that person is one of his own children.

Why does little or none of this show up in his script? The sample is very badly disorganized, and shows insecurity, poor planning, lack of direction and feelings of inadequacy. And the sample is right—because that is how he feels *when writing in English*. And it is, based on the amount of time he's been doing it and however adapted he has become, likely to be the way he will always feel.

The sample shows these negative factors partly because of unfamiliarity; not with the alphabet (the physical skill), but with the language. It also reflects the myriad other adjustment problems involved in being a stranger in a strange land; however much the writer may have wanted to immigrate, and however satisfied he may be with the results of his decision, the problems exist. Everything from idioms to social customs to laws and traditions have to be learned as they happen to come up; always, and probably for the rest of his life, he will be feeling his way like a blind man past circumstances which are obstacles to him, but totally natural to the native-born. It's enough to make anyone nervous, even the generally more assured, more determined, more self-sustaining kind of person who makes a success of his immigration.

These are factors you must take into consideration when analyzing the handwriting of immigrants, even those of long standing. It can make the task of doing an accurate analysis difficult if not impossible; although, if nothing else, you can often provide reassurances to the writer simply by reminding him of the basis for any feelings of inadequacy (certainly, they fall into the category of circumstances beyond his control!).

If the writer remembers his native tongue, as not all do, you might be able to get at least an idea of what kind of person he could have been like without these problems. A sample in his original language can show adjustment problems, too; how accurate a picture it draws will depend on how well your subject remembers his native tongue. But you may also be able to get a sample which will at least give you a standard for comparison.

We asked our volunteer subject to translate the test line—and he did, at 20 years remove from daily use of his native tongue. Observe:

Questo e uno esempio di
come io screvo normale.
io volesse più sapere
la mio scritture dimmie
a me.

Always ask anyone for whom you are doing an analysis how long he has been writing, and whether or not English is his native tongue. Just a comparison of these two baselines alone should tell you why.

12

Body Language— Signs of Illness and Pain

The most negative indication analysis can reveal is not a character or personality trait.

When you're not feeling well, even if all you have is a bad cold, you can't function effectively. And the more serious the illness, the more seriously it will affect your thinking, your behavior—and your handwriting. As a graphologist, you should be alert to signs of illness or pain as a possible reason for script disorganization.

Reading the Signs

Diagnosing physical illness is not a job for a graphologist; it's a job for a doctor. But recognizing the possible existence of physical dysfunction is not only well within your range, but a necessary part of the analysis. Many physical ailments can show up in handwriting first: before the writer himself, or even his doctor, might be aware that something is going wrong. And, as you are aware, the earlier an illness is diagnosed, the better that person's chances of a cure.

As for those of your analysis subjects who already know that something is wrong but have not bothered to check it out, the fact that you can not only spot the problem in their handwriting, but even describe the symptoms, may be just the extra push they need to get them into a physician's examining room.

In most cases, you will not be able to specifically identify a given illness from the pain signs in script (unless you *are* a doctor!). But you can describe the type of pain, and its general location in the body. Discomfort or pain shows up in three types of penstroke formations: (a) pain dots; (b) script hitches; and (c) penstroke wavers:

FIGURE 1
Penstroke Indicators for Illness or Pain

(a)	(b)	(c)
Pain Dots	Script Hitch	Penstroke Wavers

When the body is healthy, its functions operate smoothly, and its impulses flow with even regularity. Writing is a physical activity, requiring the cooperation of both nerves and muscles; if something happens which interrupts the smooth flow of body functioning, it will be reflected in an interruption of the smooth flow of penstroke movement. Just as an example: if you were to somehow stub your toe while writing, you can be certain there would be an obvious "hitch" in the script *at the moment the pain occurred*. The continuing pain pulses of a longer-term illness or injury show up in the same way, and they show up at irregular, but repeated, intervals in the script. How (and where) they show up gives you your first clue as to what might be wrong.

I. Identifying Pain or Illness Indicators
  A. *Pain Dots*
  The pain dot is usually the least severe indicator, especially if it's the only type of pain indicator in the script, and if it occurs infrequently. It looks like a blob of ink (the kind caused by a leaky ballpoint pen), and some "pain dots" may be just that. If it is a pain indicator, however, on close inspection it will show up as a heavier pressure point (caused by the pen momentarily bearing down harder), and/or as a concentrated hitching stroke (caused by the pen "skidding" in that spot). It may indicate either a throbbing pain (as from a sprained ankle), or a sudden sharp jolt (as from a gastric attack or arthritic twinge).
  B. *Script Hitch*
  The hitching stroke may also show heavier pressure, in relation to overall script pressure, at the point where it changes direction. Whether or not it does, it is usually indicative of more serious pain, or of an actual dysfunction. While there are a variety of problems that may be its cause, it is usually referred to as a "heart hitch," especially if it occurs in the upper zone, since it often indicates an interruption in the heart action. In other areas of the body, it may indicate equally serious conditions (or not, since gas pains show up the same way!). It is caused by a pronounced jerk of the pen, in unconscious sympathetic reaction to an interruption of normal body function, or in conscious reaction to a severe jolt of pain.

Be aware that this script formation can also be caused by non-pain interruptions. For example, if someone were to bump against the writer's desk, the pen would jump this way; or, if the writer were concentrating deeply and the doorbell or phone suddenly rang, the startle reaction could cause the same kind of hitch. The script hitch is significant only if it repeats throughout the sample, and diagnosable only if it stays in the same zone.

C. *Penstroke Waver*

Wavering penstrokes have a variety of possible interpretations. They may indicate a condition such as restricted breathing even in a firm-pressured script; when the script is light-pressured and the waver affects most or all of the sample, you may be dealing with an arthritic, someone who has suffered a recent serious illness and is still recuperating, or even a stroke victim. The waver is caused by a general physical weakness and/or by constant pain which makes it difficult for the writer to control hand movements or body shaking.

In wavering scripts, if pain exists it will be indicated by other signs; this formation does not result from a sudden pain surge, but from a general incapacity or weakness which makes it difficult for the writer to control or guide the pen.

II. Interpreting Pain or Illness Indicators

How serious the pain or illness is *for that writer* will be indicated by the frequency with which these formations show up in a sample; the more often they occur, the greater the effect of the physical problem on the writer's ability to function. But it is not always possible to determine how serious the illness actually is. Different people react differently, even to the same problem: some people have a greater tolerance for pain, or better physical control over their body's reactions, than others. If a physical problem exists, however, it will show up in the script eventually: even a sprained ankle which the writer is ignoring will result, in a longer sample, in pain dots about once every 10 to 20 words.

Precisely locating the pain is also a touch and go proposition, as it is not easy to establish whether the problem is located on the right or left side, or the front or back, of the body. But it is possible to generally pinpoint the area of the body where the pain or dysfunction originates. Figure 2 is graphology's "Anatomy Chart":

FIGURE 2
Body Correspondences to Zones of Script

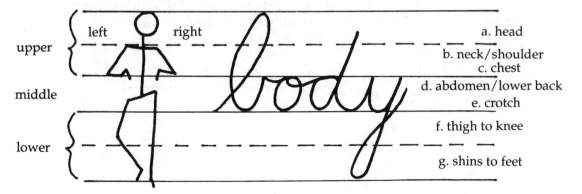

Using this chart as a general guide, you can differentiate with reasonable accuracy between a headache and a stomachache, or a twisted wrist (not the one used for writing!) and a sprained ankle. For anything more specific, temper your conclusions. A pain dot located on the downstroke (right side) of the y, for example, should indicate that something is wrong with the right leg. But many writers reverse left and right in the indicators (as does the human brain, the two halves of which control opposite sides of the body). So all you know for certain is that the writer is experiencing pain in one of his legs, possibly the right one.

Combining Script Indicators

As well as identifying the general type of dysfunction and locating it on the body, you can also use character and personality indicators to assist in your "diagnosis." An emotional problem can be caused by an illness, but it can also be the cause of it.

For example, hitching strokes or dark pain dots on the center to upper section of middle zone formations may indicate either gastric attacks, or a middle to lower back injury. If, however, the script also shows nervousness, emotional ups and down, irritability, frustration, or similar characteristics to an extent not affected by the pain signs (i.e., pain signs sporadic; emotional upset consistent), it is possible that you may be looking at the beginnings of an ulcer:

It could also simply be gas pains, especially at this stage, and also especially with that (possibly respiratory) hitch in the chest area (on the first l in normally). But it doesn't hurt to suggest that the writer have himself checked out.

Sometimes the "illness" indicated by a script waver is at least partially self-imposed by the writer. A shaky, wavering handwriting, light or dark pressured, might be the script of a victim of some serious illness. But that same waver may also indicate that the writer is feeling no pain—at least, nothing physical. If the script also shows strong or dominant physical drives, and few or no pain signs, the cause may be something the writer is taking:

(a)
Alcoholic Dependence

(b)
Drug Addiction

In general, if such a script also shows signs of strain (a difficulty with and therefore an intensely careful effort involved in forming letters, with mistakes made anyway), a tendency to sag or downslant in the baseline, and punctuation or i-dots and t-bars that are misplaced or run into other letters (difficulty seeing or coordinating), alcoholic dependence is a very good possibility. And note also in this sample that laid-down pronoun I: another very common characteristic of an alcoholic script.

Those same strong physical drives in a script showing erratic disorganization and distorted formations (and often including oversized or misplaced looping), can reveal drug dependency even, or perhaps especially, if the waver appears deliberate. In this case, you are not dealing with simple disorganization, but with a script in which words, or even letters in a word, change their style and form randomly, indicating—as it was once very well put—that the writer is mentally not present during the act of writing.

Again, it pays to be cautious before stating your analysis conclusions. In the first case (the alcoholic script), you can state that the writer is having extreme difficulty thinking and functioning coherently, or coordinating his actions; in the second case (drug dependence) that it appears he has lost touch with reality. You may or may not mention what you feel is the reason for the dysfunction, but in both cases you add: *see a doctor.*

And remember, when doing your analysis, that both alcoholic dependence and drug addiction *are illnesses*, and should be treated as such. The fact that they are emotionally caused is beside the point: so is an ulcer.

Tailoring the Analysis

Script disorganization based on an inability to properly form the pen-strokes can have a variety of other causes. You will find it, as we discussed in the last chapter, in the handwriting of young children; it is also characteristic in the handwriting of semi-literates, and of immigrants for whom the language is the difficulty. Skill problems can also be caused by pain: and pain, of course, can cause emotional problems. The same difficulty we noted for an alcoholic could be, especially if there are many lighter-pressured areas and frequent pain signs, the handwriting of an arthritic; and certainly if that writer used to be physically active, he's going to be frustrated now.

Just as formations which appear to be pain indicators may be due to some other factor totally unrelated to either pain or even innate capacity, sometimes what appear to be negative character or personality traits can be due to physical dysfunction. An extremely small, cramped handwriting, for example, may not show stinginess at all but poor eyesight; especially if punctuation, or i-dots and t-bars, tend to be either very clearly placed and carefully done, *or* peculiarly placed. Broken letters are generally considered an indicator for dishonesty or evasiveness (See Glossary), but they may also indicate blood pressure problems, especially if the pen appears to have skipped, rather than been lifted, in the middle of a single-stroke formation (as a downstroke), and the writing is in other ways fairly smooth and fairly clear. And a very light script, as we've noted, could be sheer fatigue, rather than laziness or lack of drive.

With these possible variations in mind, you may want to be less than definite in your diagnosis: but always, when in doubt, counsel medical attention.

Doing the Analysis

In terms of purely personal counseling, and whether or not the writer is or should be under medical treatment, you must make allowances in your judgement of character and personality traits when the writer is ill. The more severe the illness, the more it will affect the writer's control of the pen, and hence the organization of the sample. In some cases, the effect may be severe enough that you cannot do an analysis; just as some illness can be severe enough that the individual cannot function normally.

And the more severe the illness, the more it is likely to cause emotional problems which the writer would *not* have if he were physically well. Beyond "skill allowances," you must also remember to temper your judgement of character traits in other ways. No person who is ill, even if all he has is a bad cold, is going to be himself. And even if the illness is due to something in the writer's emotional makeup (such as the use of controlled substances), he is still not showing you his full potential when he writes a sample of script.

Conclusion: *Signs of Illness and Pain*

You will find that the identification of physical dysfunction in script is not a sure process. Besides the fact that you cannot accurately "diagnose" a specific illness, you may also be mistaken in your identification of pain or illness indicators in the first place. Very often, some other factor can be responsible for what looks like a sign of physical dysfunction.

Nonetheless, if in your estimation it is at all possible that the writer may have some kind of physical problem, tell him to see a doctor. Even if some of the time your reading is totally off base, those physical problems you *do* catch—and those people whose health, or lives, you may very well save—are more than worth some occasional egg on your face.

In the case of pain or illness indicators, even when in doubt, counsel medical attention. If you're wrong, it can't hurt. If you're right—and say nothing—it might kill.

13

Changing the Signs—Graphotherapy

What is Graphotherapy?

You are what you write. How much can be learned about you from a sample of your handwriting is limited by the quality of the sample, by the expertise of the analyst, and by the fact that not every trait that is revealed in handwriting has been positively identified by graphological research (yes, there's even more than you've been shown in this book!).

But the kind of person you are is clearly revealed in the way you form your letters and words; and, more to the point, significant changes in your character and personality are recorded by corresponding changes in the style of your script.

That being the case, it should be possible to change what you are by changing the style of your script.

And that is exactly what graphotherapy does. The therapist and the writer work together to selectively alter specific reactions and impulses by deliberately redesigning their corresponding script or penstroke formations. And this unique form of corrective therapy has proven effective whenever its precepts are properly applied and properly used.

Your reactions and impulses, which are controlled by your own personal makeup, are translated by neuromuscular reflexes into the individualized variation of penstroke formations which make up the style of your handwriting. Any deliberate change in your writing reacts back on those same reflexes and then on your personal makeup (though how profound, and how lasting, the personal effect will be depends, of course, on the purpose for and the type of the change in your script).

Graphotherapy is a controlled change: preplanned and predetermined to react on a specific trait, and on that trait only. It is sometimes used with the aid of other therapeutic techniques, and sometimes used by itself with no aid other than the informed cooperation of the writer. But it is possible, by choosing the right trait to alter (and the right alteration to make!) to change you

215

from the person you are into the person you can be—and, by repetition and determined effort, to make the change stick. You are what you write. And you can write what you want to be.

The actual process of therapy, however, is not a simple one. Once the change to be made has been determined (and that choice by itself can be a long process) it is then up to the writer to enforce the change, and that takes practice. Your present style of handwriting developed over a long period of time, and so did the traits which determined it. It may take much less time to alter it, but it, and you, cannot be altered overnight.

Graphotherapy can make the process of character and personality change easier. Further, it gives you the ability to select and consciously control what that change will be. But therapy it remains, and not a miracle process.

How much time and effort is required varies with the individual and the nature of the change. Some people can change their handwriting more easily than others; and some have less of a change to make. But even under ideal circumstances, you and your client should plan on a *minimum* of two to three months' determined effort to produce any kind of lasting effect; and during that time daily practice, and *continual* practice (including at least five to ten times a day of the therapy exercise and a conscious effort to incorporate the penstroke change into all written messages) is the necessary regimen. You must also caution your client that if he skimps the practice, or skips a day, during the initial period particularly, he runs the risk of losing all progress made up to that point. Writing style is a habit, and like any other habit, it is hard to change.

Given below are the steps in the therapy process, and then a list of procedures that have been tried, and found to work.

Step One: Define the Problem

What to change is a decision based on consultation between therapist and client, after thorough and in-depth analysis of the current style of script. You *cannot* work from the test line, or from a single analysis, alone.

Before you even begin to consider trait changes, you need an extensive sampling of the writer's script style. Your preliminary analysis should be based on a sample that runs at least three full pages, if not more. In addition, you also need the equivalent of at least five to six full pages of writing, in shorter samples *not written for analysis*, done over a minimum period of six months. If for some reason you cannot wait six months before beginning therapy, you still get the longest sample you can at the time, and then ask your client to supply you with earlier specimens written several months previously to the analysis sample.

This requirement serves several important needs. We can assume, in any sample written for analysis, at least an initial restraint, based partly on the writer's self-consciousness in writing for analysis, and also, undoubtedly, on the fact that he is copying something (the test line) and/or following specific instructions. This "false front," whatever its cause, and whether intentional or unconscious, tends to disappear if the sample is long enough.

Comparison of samples done at different times and under different circumstances also enables you to identify pen-control changes in a style of writing (those minor indicators of mood or vitality which continually vary). Pen-control changes are significant in the overall analysis, in that they indicate the various effects of temporary circumstances on the writer; however, it is also important to know which formations indicate only transitory reactions, and which are permanent character or personality traits. It is sometimes not possible to distinguish pen-control factors in a single sample, even it it does run several pages.

Script variables aside, in preparation for therapy you are also trying to distinguish between a symptom and its underlying cause. Is the writer unable to assert himself because he's shy, or is he shy *and* unable to assert himself because he's afraid of being hurt, and therefore protects himself by drawing into a shell? Or, is the writer unable to assert himself because he doesn't think much of himself, and if so, who or what is responsible?

For each different cause there is a different kind of therapy. The writer may have come to you as a therapist specifically because he wants to become more assertive, but if his lack of assertiveness is only a symptom it does him no good for you to treat that. Based on the preliminary in-depth analysis and subsequent progression analyses (See Chapter 14), you can determine, or even just confirm, what it is that is really causing your client's problem.

Personal interviews are also necessary during the analysis process; they give both you and your client the opportunity to clarify your statements, and to ask clarifying questions. Further, once you have determined exactly what the problem is, you must be certain that your client understands exactly what change the therapy is intended to bring about, as well as its possible ramifications, and what he must do to affect it—and he must be certain that he *wants* that change! This is the basis of informed cooperation, without which, even if it could be made to work, graphotherapy is an imposition, not a benefit.

Step Two: Consider Alternative Solutions First

Not everyone needs therapy. Sometimes specific situational advice will provide a more workable solution to a specific problem.

For example: suppose your client has a generalized feeling of incompetence. You might help him by suggesting a change in the way he forms his capital letters (see below: Therapy Procedures). But it would help him more to learn that he can complete specific tasks successfully. Again: explain the purpose of the exercise, and then suggest simple tasks that he can complete successfully: individual assignments which have a known goal and clearly defined instructions for accomplishing it. These could include (depending on your client's interests), following instructions in a cookbook (a basic one!), starting with simple meals and even eventually proceeding to gourmet cooking; or, following a simplified sewing or needlework pattern; or, making a model airplane or completing some other pre-designed craft project; or, learning how to drive a car. The purpose of these exercises is to teach your client that if he plans a project carefully he *can* accomplish a specific goal; and, especially if what he makes in these preplanned projects is something he wants, he can learn to apply this method toward goals that do not have clearly defined instructions.

If your client hates his professional life, lacks direction, feels generally incapable of success, you might be able to help him by straightening out his baseline. Or teaching him zone control. Or working on his self-image—there are any number of effects feelings of failure can have, and any number of causes. But you'll help him more by suggesting that he go for job counseling, and then follow it up by training in a field that will suit his abilities and needs. *A sense of direction can be imposed by graphotherapy, but it won't last if it has no basis in reality.*

There are many other situations in which this type of counseling can be effective. Wherever possible, treat therapy as a last resort, and start with "real life" activities your client can use to overcome a given problem. You'll see the change take place in his handwriting, without graphotherapy.

Step Three: Define the Therapy Procedure

If both client and therapist agree that strengthening a specific aspect of the writer's character or personality will work better than other methods or procedures in helping him achieve his goals, then graphotherapy is indicated. With the problem defined (Step One), the next step is to identify the script factors which affect it, and determine precisely what changes in that formation are required to correct the problem.

Never attempt to change more than one trait (more than one script or penstroke formation) during a single therapy process. Each change you make, however minor, will have a domino effect: it will react on all other aspects of the writer's makeup. Even if your client has more than one problem (and most people do!), choose only the most significant factor and work on that first; often, one change can solve other problems without the need for additional therapy.

Be sure your client is aware that if you choose the wrong problem to work on, or the wrong therapy to deal with it, it might create other problems, or make existing problems worse. Even the right therapy can sometimes have unexpected results: it is not always possible to predict what a given change is going to do for a specific individual, and trying to make more than one change at a time is just asking for trouble. The only way to control the change at all, and to clearly see its effect on the writer, is to contain it; to limit the therapy to a single, specific, and clearly defined goal.

The therapy process is a matter of teaching the writer how to alter his script in such a way as to replace the negative characteristic with a positive one. It is usually a good idea to reinforce the script change with a verbal statement which continually reminds the writer why it is he is doing this in the first place. Whatever (written) statement you use, the exercise sentence(s) should contain as many of the script formations to be changed as possible. This combination of remodeled formation plus reinforcing statement is the therapy exercise which is to be practiced those five to ten times daily for two to three months (or more!).

You should also suggest to your client that he keep a diary, which includes his practice exercises but also records *affective* events which occur during the therapy process (anything that happens to him that relates to the change he is trying to make, or that results from it). The diary gives someone who is not adept at reading penstroke changes (by which you will read the effect of the therapy) a way to chart his own progress, and will also give him a permanent record of the therapy period, which, we have found, many people value.

It also gives him one more important therapy aid: the opportunity to practice his remodeled penstroke formation in a writing environment which is private, and in which he can take more time (and do it right). You should also suggest, of course, that he make the attempt to include the alteration in everything he may write.

It is vital that this running record be watched carefully, whether you are working with someone else, or trying a trait change in your own makeup. *Every factor in an individual writer's makeup is interrelated with every other factor;* and as we noted, changing one script indicator can result in unexpected, and possibly undesirable, changes in some other indicator(s). If that's the case, the exercises should be stopped immediately, and the entire therapy process re-evaluated, or even brought to a permanent halt. Never, even after thorough analysis, simply give someone a therapy procedure and then let him go it alone.

Cautionary Note: For analysis in general, and for graphotherapy in particular, please remember: this book is an *introductory* text only. Its purpose is to teach you the fundamentals of graphology and to acquaint you with its possibilities as a career or as a useful tool in some other career. But it is not a substitute for experience, or for training in counseling techniques.

One of the greatest services any personal counselor can perform for a client is to recognize when that client's needs are beyond the counselor's competence. Because graphotherapy requires the informed cooperation of the client, it is not, perhaps, as dangerous in amateur hands as other forms of psychological therapy might be. But this brief review alone does not make you a qualified therapist. However adept you may eventually become as a graphologist, you should not attempt to use this counseling technique without *first* acquiring practical psychological and/or psychiatric background and training.

Some Don'ts

Even assuming a competent therapist, there are still some conditions under which graphotherapy is not a recommended procedure.

It should not be used as a preferred treatment for anyone under the age of 25. A growing, developing personality is one that "doesn't know what it wants to be yet." Neither can anyone else know or predict what that child can or will be. The character- and personality-changing techniques available to the graphotherapist can cause irreparable damage when used on a subject who cannot make an informed decision as to what kind of change he wants to effect—or what kind of person he wants to be when he grows up.

If handwriting analysis reveals emotional or behavioral problems in a child, those problems are best dealt with on a one-to-one, interpersonal level. Assuming the problems are not severe, the best way to help a child develop his own individual potential is for someone who loves him to show him what is available, and then help him to build the emotional strength he needs to believe that he *can* be what he wants to be (and the self-discipline he needs in order to achieve it). If the child is severely disturbed, to the point where he needs professional help, then he is already beyond the range of what graphotherapy can do for him.

Graphotherapy is not a recommended technique for any incompetent subject. "Incompetent" includes children; it also includes anyone who is mentally defective, or mentally or emotionally disturbed. And in general, it also refers to any analysis subject, even that person is mentally competent, who does not fully understand exactly what the therapy process is intended to accomplish.

This is not a procedure that you recommend casually, nor do you offer to give someone a therapy exercise without their informed consent. "Informed consent" means, specifically, that the writer knows exactly what trait or characteristic is going to be changed and agrees with the reason it should be; further, he also knows exactly what trait or characteristic the change will produce, and agrees with the reason it should be.

If, in the course of general analysis, you discover that your subject has a problem graphotherapy could solve, you still do not suggest a therapy exercise without extended analysis, consultation, and *the writer's* permission to do so. Some people can change without therapy; some people will not benefit even from therapy; most people do not require therapy in the first place. You are not the judge of whether or not a trait should be changed. Only the writer can decide that, and only the writer can decide what he wants to change it *to*—or if he wants to change at all.

If graphotherapy cannot be used casually, then why bother to explain this technique in a book which is likely to be read and used by people who are not qualified therapists? Because it can be used for self-improvement. Without extensive counseling and therapy background, you should not use this procedure for someone else. But you can use graphotherapy for yourself, to help you strengthen positive qualities or overcome negative traits. The writer knows himself best—and that makes you the best judge of what kind of help you need, or of whether you need any help at all.

If you do decide to try a therapy technique for yourself, however, use it carefully, and follow the procedure exactly as outlined. This technique is a powerful mind-changing tool; and it can produce changes—though not the ones you hoped for—even if applied incorrectly, or if the wrong therapy is used. Always be certain that you know exactly what you are changing, why you are changing it, and what that change is doing to you. Handwriting analysis can be used as a party game, with no harm to anyone. Graphotherapy cannot.

With these cautions in mind, let's take a look at some specific therapy procedures.

Graphotherapy Exercises

The following section lists some of the ways graphotherapy can help eliminate negative traits, and replace them with positive self-reinforcement. Note that these examples are all *primary factor* therapy procedures (in which a change in a single significant indicator can bring about other positive reactions in the person's handwriting and in his general makeup). Any problem a given writer has which involves more factors than just a primary should not be handled with graphotherapy.

General note: Whether or not identity problems are indicated, and with or without a change in the signature, the writer should *always* sign his name after each practice exercise. This personalizes the procedure: in effect, it acts as a continual reminder to the writer that he is the one making these statements, and that they refer specifically to him.

Also note: if your client is embarrassed by an exercise sentence you suggest, remind him that no one need see his notebook except himself, and you.

Therapy Procedures

I. *Problem*: Poor Self-Image

Indicators: Very small and/or left-slanting/extreme right, and/or "foetal" pronoun I (as you can see, reasons or reactions vary). Usually, but not always, there also will be small capitals on the signature as well; over-flourished capitals on the signature also indicate this problem when combined with the pronoun formations described above.

Treatment: Every time you write the pronoun I, use a single, *firm* downstroke; keep the letter as vertical as possible and at least twice the size of middle zone letters, and slightly taller than ascenders.

(If only the signature shows poor self-image: When you sign your name, the capital letters should be at least twice the size of all middle zone letters, and fairly plain; i.e., almost like a printed form. Note: Do not combine signature change with pronoun change. *You work on only one factor at a time*.)

Write the following sentence or one like it at least ten times a day and sign your name each time (sentences for this exercise should contain as many pronoun I's, initial and internal, as possible):

I am a worthwhile person, and I believe that I can accomplish what I set out to do. This is how I write.

Remember that the altered pronoun formation should be included in everything you write (or, the signature change whenever you sign your name).

The effect of this exercise, sometimes even *without* a reinforcing statement (though, not without a practice exercise!), can be literally spectacular. Where poor self-image is the cause, it affects everything else the person tries to do—or fails to do. With this problem solved, other problems become solvable, and sometimes seem to solve themselves.

The I-formation we chose, as you remember (Chapter 9) is the one least affected by emotional battering, so in addition to the confidence (height) and determination (firmness), you help your client become less vulnerable.

Caution: Do not suggest the single downstroke if the script indicates strong emotional involvement (as, wide looping) or emotional vulnerability in other ways (as, hypersensitive d-loops, etc.); ignoring feelings will not make them go away. In such a case, let the writer retain his own I-formation (though you can suggest narrower loops on the I), and concentrate on height and firmness; if that eliminates the hypersensitivity (as it sometimes does), then you can either suggest the single-stroke I or, if the writer is feeling better about himself, leave well enough alone.

II. *Problem*: Lack of Confidence

Indicators: Small or variable-size capitals; also exaggerated or overflourished capitals. Often, other signs of insecurity or hypersensitivity show up as symptoms as well.

Treatment: Form your capitals simply and clearly (like the printed form), using a firm pressure, and make them at least twice and no more than three times the size of letters in the middle zone.

The practice sentences, and there should be more than one (for extra capitals!), may be any combination of statements which use different capitals for practice. To start you off:

> *Because I know I can. Anything is possible. Every day in every way I'm getting better. (or even:) Why not? This is how I write.*

III. *Problem*: Self-doubt/lack of direction.

Indicators: A *badly* disorganized baseline (and remember, a slight waver, especially on unlined paper, is normal and healthy, and can be partly a skill problem even for an experienced writer).

Treatment: Use lined paper for at least the initial period (the first month to month and a half), then write half the exercises on lined and half on unlined paper, gradually progressing to only unlined paper. Do not change the script size—if the script is too large even for standard-rule, skip lines. Make every effort to keep the bottom of the middle zone *on the line* at all times, and also use lined paper outside the therapy situation, when possible. As long as and whenever your baseline continued erratic on unlined paper, revert to lined paper to straighten it out.

Almost any practice sentences will include formations you need for this exercise, but try to get a combination of formations which hit the line (like the m or n), and which curve at the line (like the a or o). For example:

> *I have the right to plan my own life according to my own needs and abilities. I'm sure I can plan my life well. What I am doesn't hurt any one; it's just what I am. I have the right to choose my own path, and I can succeed. This is how I write.*

IV. *Problem*: Feelings of Inadequacy

Indicator: T-bar low on the stem; usually "weak" (light-pressured). Note that other self-image or confidence problems may or *may not* also show up; in any case, correcting the t-bar tends to "repair" capitals as well.

Treatment: Form your t-bar with a single, clear stroke halfway up the stem (raise it above the top of the middle zone); be sure it is balanced (equal on either side of the stem) and firm.

The practice sentences should use as many (lowercase) t-bars as possible;

in the beginning, middle, and end of words, and preferably following or followed by middle-zone formations (as a, u, m, rather than th formations):

> *There is no reason that I cannot accomplish anything I set out to do. I am good at what I do. I have the ability to do it well. This is how I write.*

V. *Problem*: Shyness to Fear

Indicators: Left-tilting script, controlled to extreme; also, left ending strokes. The stronger the tilt, the greater the problem, of course, and the more likelihood of accompanying problems.

Treatment: Change the writing slant to controlled-right. If necessary, suggest the use of a calligraphy pad or similar lettering-art aid; these are preprinted, and can make the difficult task of forcibly altering your slant a bit easier.

The practice sentences should use a fair scattering of ascenders and descenders:

> *I can tell people how I feel and they will listen, because I listen to them. I am not afraid, because I know that my life has value, too, and others will recognize it. This is how I write.*

Note: This therapy procedure can also be used for a variable tilt. In that case, its purpose is to help the writer overcome his feelings of interpersonal confusion. The same or similar practice statements can be used as well.

VI. *Problem*: Lack of drive/lack of assertiveness

Indicators: Very light pressure, or handwriting that fades off the page. (And, again, usually other negative signs as well.)

Treatment: Make yourself press down firmly when you write, and try to make upstrokes fairly firm, as well as downstrokes. Cross your t's evenly and firmly as well. When you have finished writing, you should be able to feel an indentation on the paper by running your hand across the back of the sheet; it is not necessary, but it is possible, to also make at least a slight impression on the sheet below the one you're writing on.

Use as practice sentences phrases which contain up and downstrokes and t-bars:

> *I am determined to get something definite accomplished. It is possible for me to work hard and to do well. This is how I write.*

VII. *Problem*: Frustration

Indicators: Uneven pressure. Note: this is not the same problem as lack of drive or aggressiveness, and should not be treated in the same way. Observe:

Treatment: Moderate your script pressure. Notice which type of pressure occurs most often in your sample, and/or which level of pressure shows less other script problems, and stick to that.

Practice sentences should also contain upstrokes, downstrokes, and t-bars, but the message is different:

I have to learn to work at my own pace. It is not necessary for me to work myself into the ground to get something accomplished. All I need is to maintain a steady pace. This is how I write.

Also note: If the script also indicates a cause for the frustration (such as procrastination: t-bars short of stem plus extra loops), then work on that *first*; counsel the writer to eliminate the extra strokes and cross his t-bars firmly. (Remember: work on *only* one problem at a time!)

VIII. *Problem*: Hypersensitivity, and similar emotional over-reactions.

Indicators: Pronounced to extreme looping, especially on normally loopless forms; also hidden loops and double looping. Note: For guilt, which can also fall into this category; cross outs, strike overs, scribbled out letters (guilt based on feelings of inadequacy), also peculiarly twisted forms, especially in the lower zone, accompanied by other signs of evasion or insecurity.

Treatment: Note: You do not want to eliminate all loops, just control them. It might be a good idea to re-introduce your subject to Schoolform (except for that self-critical pronoun I!). Eliminate loops on d's and t's and tighten (narrow) loops on other letters. Practice the covered return stroke in both upper and middle zone (on d's and t's, and on letters such as the lowercase a). Eliminate loops inside letters, and form middle zone letters especially as simply and clearly as possible.

For guilt: If you make a mistake, just draw a single line through the word and write it over; don't try to "fix" it or disguise it. Smooth out lower-zone loops and eliminate knots or extra strokes, as well as narrowing the loop and controlling the angle. And again: these are two separate problems, and should be dealt with one at a time.

Practice sentences should include formations in all zones which use loops or could attract hidden loops:

I am a worthwhile person. People like me because I like them. It is good to feel good about myself and I am good enough to have that right. (For guilt: It is okay to make mistakes. Making a mistake does not make me a bad person; it only means I'm human.) This is how I write.

IX. *Problem*: Mental confusion

Indicators: Tangled script. Note: if combined with depression, fear, self-critical and/or suicidal tendencies, see to it that the writer gets professional help. Unless you are a trained suicide counselor, you are risking his life. This therapy is *only* for confusion, not for emotional pain.

Treatment: Here again, the calligraphy-type pads are a tremendous help (but check to make sure the angle is controlled-right); certainly at least use lined paper. We suggest the writing pads, by the way, because they also give a middle zone rule, and sometimes other helpful guidelines. If the tangling is severe, don't even attempt to use cursive at first; return to print, and use careful letter and word shaping and spacing. You may also want to ease the task of diary writing somewhat, to not more than a few extra sentences or phrases a day (or however long your client's concentration and patience holds out).

Gradually, during the therapy period, begin using script again, starting with trial connectors between printed letters, and finally going to the cursive form. Don't drop the lined paper until the script flows easily.

In effect, you are teaching your client to write again; you are also—and most important—giving him something he can do successfully. We've had some good results from having clients trace Schoolbook, in either a medium or large size, before beginning to write cursive again; also (and here is where other therapy methods come in), by having them do simple tasks with a definite procedure and a known result (see above, Step Two) is also helpful for this problem. Make certain, however, not to suggest (or, if possible, not to permit) any task too elaborate or too new: the feeling that they don't know what they are doing or how to do it is part of the problem in the first place.

Practice sentences should include as many letter combinations as possible, both round and angular, in all zones:

> *I can think clearly and write clearly. I take the time to organize my thoughts before I write or speak, and when I do, I find that I can do it right. I can learn to do anything if I want to, if I work carefully or have a good enough teacher. This is how I write.*

DON'T worry about the speed of writing; that will pick up. In this case, *clarity* is the object.

Conclusion: *Using Graphotherapy*

In all cases, it's advisable to check self-image and confidence indicators *first*, and if that is a problem, to deal with it first. For a surprising number and variety of people, the primary causative factor which therapy should address will be related in some way to their self-image. More often than not, where there is some other causative factor, it has resulted in a self-image problem, which then in turn reduces that individual's ability to cope. Very often, establishing a sturdy self-image, while it may not solve all problems, at least gives the writer the inner strength he needs to deal with them.

Some problems, of course, may require more unusual solutions than those we covered; and sometimes, solving one problem brings another to light, one which may either have been put aside (by the writer), or which may have been the actual base cause but was overlooked in the analysis. When or if this occurs, don't get bent out of shape, and don't let your client go off on tangents, either. Deal with one thing at a time; and don't keep switching therapies every time something new comes up. You don't want to do too much remolding in any case; but if, in your judgement and that of your client, there is another change that would be beneficial, you can tackle it next, *after* the first therapy process has been completed and has had time to sink in. Always keep in mind that winning one battle decisively will make the next battle that much easier; it proves to the writer that he can control his own destiny.

Again: do *not* attempt to deal with more than one problem at a time. Change only one indicator, and monitor it carefully. Once the writer has integrated the change into his own makeup, if he wants further assistance, and if further assistance will in fact be beneficial, you can begin the analysis process again.

But: be aware that some people are gluttons for therapy. If you've established a good working relationship with someone and your advice or emotional support has proven beneficial in the past, it is not necessarily unreasonable for that person to come back on occasion for more of the same. But continual character and personality changes don't benefit anyone; and if your client keeps wanting to fix things, then his real problem is outside the range of graphotherapy. Tell him to get professional help.

14

Using the Analysis—
Applications of Graphology

We began this book by telling you to use what you learned; we'll end it by showing you how. In this chapter, we'll look at some of the more common applications of graphology. Part One describes some of the types and uses of personal counseling analyses; Part Two lists some of the ways you can apply your new skill either as part of your current profession, or as a way to earn extra income as a full- or part-time graphologist.

PART ONE: The Analysis as a Counseling Tool

The use of handwriting analysis as described here is basically a client-centered approach; that is, that the *writer* is the person best qualified to identify and solve his or her own problems, and that the function of the analyst is to provide a supportive atmosphere which will make that self-discovery possible.

I. General Personality Analysis (GPA)
Graphology's primary emphasis is individual personal counseling, and the basic procedure for personal counseling is the GPA.

The General Personality Analysis is done at the request of a given writer (your client) from a sample supplied by that writer; and it is intended to be used by the writer for his or her own guidance. It is usually the first, and often the only, analysis or type of analysis most people will need: because usually what most people need is hearing someone else say "I know exactly how you feel." If further advice or assistance is necessary, the GPA can be used as a springboard for more specialized forms of analysis, including graphotherapy (if indicated).

As an analysis, the GPA is a comprehensive character and personality study of the writer; as complete as possible, based on the sample available. The write-up—the written report of analysis findings which is presented to the client—identifies major traits and characteristics (those elements of the writer's makeup which have the greatest influence over his or her *behavior*). In addition, it should at least mention what appear to be minor indicators but which occur often enough in the sample to suggest that they could influence the writer's thought or behavior patterns. Generally, the analysis will also attempt to pinpoint at least one major problem the writer is currently having and its probable cause.

While any analyst's client generally does expect to get some kind of advice, it's a good idea to avoid making specific suggestions unless they fall within your field of expertise. For example: if the analysis reveals that the writer's main problems are occupational, you can suggest job counseling. But unless you are a vocational guidance counselor, then no matter what talents and abilities the sample may reveal you do not suggest training in a specific profession. If your analysis is accurate and thorough enough most people will be able to make their own decisions, based on its findings. For those who insist on advice (and especially for those who may actually *take* someone else's advice) you must be even more careful *not* to tell them what to do. You cannot make someone else's decisions; even if you feel, after you have completed the analysis, that you know this person better than anyone else. It's still his life, and he must be encouraged to make his own decisions regarding the information you've given him.

In the long run, your emotional support is much more important (and will be appreciated much more than any advice, however apt). If the onetime analysis does nothing more than let the writer know that someone else knows how he really feels (and let the writer know that he is not the only person in the whole world who feels that way), it will have served its purpose. You will find that very often an accurate GPA enables a writer to "open up"; to talk about his or her problems. And almost always, this is all the help, or even therapy, most people need.

The GPA is called a "personality analysis," despite its in-depth approach, because it is primarily socially-oriented, as is handwriting itself, of course. The emphasis, for the analyst, is on the writer's concepts of socialized behavior; and for the writer, on how those concepts affect and are affected by his or her relationships with other people, and by events involving other people. While you certainly can mention any abilities or potentials you note, you are not really attempting, in the preliminary analysis at least, to give either vocational or therapeutic advice. Your concern is with the writer's ability to function in the context of his environment; in fact, with the writer's ability to communicate.

The analysis we did of American Schoolform (Chapter 10) is an example of what is meant by a preliminary GPA: a General Personality Analysis. There are, however, additional versions and applications of handwriting analysis as a counseling tool:

II. "Mini" Analysis

The mini-analysis is a brief sketch of the writer's current situation. It may be a concise description of his lifestyle as affecting or affected by dominant traits or (if you can pinpoint it quickly) by some underlying orientation or attitude; or it may be no more than a simple statement of an obvious problem (as indicated by a usage which runs through the entire sample, and/or which stands out in some way). Unlike the in-depth character study of a detailed GPA, the mini-analysis is not intended to examine cause and effect or the interrelationship of traits, but to get a quick, if somewhat superficial, perspective on the writer's current problems or general circumstances.

A mini-analysis can be presented either verbally or in writing. In its verbal form, the mini-analysis is not even a counseling tool as such, but more of a "party trick." It can be used to entertain and amaze your friends, or (as many professional graphologists often find practical) as a means of demonstrating to either the skeptical or uninformed exactly what graphology can and does do. As you are now aware, given a knowledge of penstroke formations it is possible to apparently just glance at a sample of script, and then tell the writer more about himself in a few minutes than his closest friends and family have been able to find out in years. This casual statement of an absolute stranger's inner thoughts can be very impressive.

For a verbal mini-analysis, what you are looking for *is* the obvious; bearing in mind, of course, that what is obvious to you is not necessarily obvious to anyone else. And the fastest way to get at what is currently on your subject's mind is to check the script for either variations or unusual/unique formations:

FIGURE 1
Looking for the "Obvious"

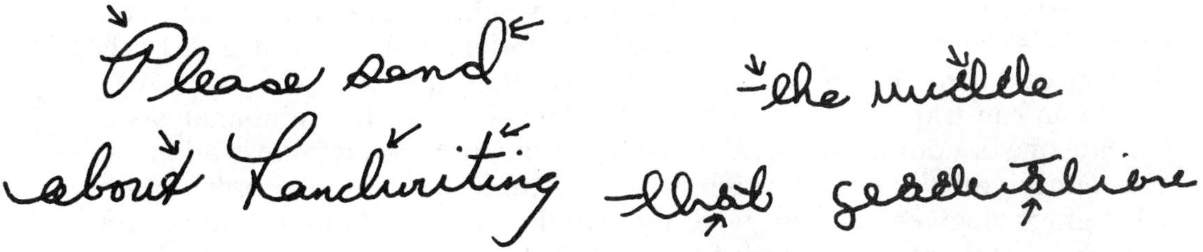

(a)	(b)
Major Trait Variations	Unique Penstroke Formations

If, for example, you see a variable tilt (sample a) which swings from pronounced right to vertical (and especially when it is the sensitive loops that pull back to the vertical!), you tell your subject that right now he is having difficulty making up his mind about how to relate to others; he would like to be outgoing and friendly, but feels he should be more reserved. And if the sample shows a combination of extraneous knots and ties with incomplete (left of stem) t-bars (sample b), you can explain to the writer that the reason he can't seem to get anything done is because he keeps getting bogged down in unnecessary details.

It's best to try to stay with the major trait indicators if there are other people listening; what you find in penstroke formations does tend to be much more personal and may be unnecessarily embarrassing. But in neither version of your snap analysis will you be telling your subject something he doesn't already know; though you will be telling him something he doesn't ordinarily tell. And, if nothing else, the audience reaction can be very supportive to *your* self-image.

As a write-up, the mini-analysis takes itself a bit more seriously. It can be a starting-point: a means of determining what kind of analysis the writer may need (as; personal counseling, vocational analysis, etc.); or, it can form the core of your detailed GPA. In this use of the mini-analysis, you are looking for a *controlling factor* (an underlying orientation, often unconscious, which determines the writer's attitudes and therefore accounts for his actions and reactions); and you do want to find a trait or characteristic which the writer may not be aware of, but which can determine his attitudes or behavior, for good or for bad, without his volition.

Most often, you will find it by checking the script for conflicting indicators and determining their cause; in other cases, you will find it in a formation which is unique *to that script style*, though it may not be an unusual formation per se. Here again, you may find the worksheet useful for listing your data, but the analysis itself is still only a sketch; it focuses on that one piece of information which it is most important for the writer to understand about himself.

As an example: a mini-analysis of American Schoolform was stated both in the summation of the GPA, and in the final analysis note. This writer does have a strong need to be loved, and a verbal analysis would make the point that he expects, and in fact needs, that kind of approval as a response to his performance. But the controlling factor which should be stated in a written analysis is that intense, self-critical tendency which runs through the entire script style. And what this writer needs to understand is that it could act to damage or destroy his self-image in negative situations.

If you can train yourself to get at the facts quickly, the mini-analysis can become one of your most useful tools. It can function as a demonstration analysis, either verbally or in written form; a means of showing people not only what graphology can do, but what *you* can do with graphology. You can offer it to your clients as an alternative to the GPA, for which (if you use graphology professionally), you would have to charge a great deal more. It can also be used to answer specific questions, as long as those questions fall within the realm of what handwriting reveals (i.e., instead of deciding what to tell the writer about himself, you let him ask you about some current problem he wants clarified). If you do use the analysis for this purpose, however, be sure your clients clearly understand what you can and can't tell them. Many people expect something mystical (and not necessarily only from you), and they need to be told that you can't predict the future, you can only predict the writer. The best statement we've found to explain that the graphologist is not a seer is this one: "No; I can't tell you whether or not you'll win the lottery. But I can tell you whether or not you'll be happy if you do—or don't."

It does get easier. And while the GPA always remains a lot of work, you will find, with practice, that the "at-a-glance" mini-analysis can tell you up front, and without hours of preparation, what kind of person you're dealing with. The more analyses you do, the more each sample you see will begin to "speak" to you. You'll find yourself reaching "instinctive" conclusions (which you should, of course, check against the worksheet), and those conclusions will become more and more accurate. They are not instinctive at all, of course; but simply a result of the fact that you will begin to see handwriting in terms of its formations, and that you do begin to know, without looking it up, what those formations mean.

III. Comparative Analysis

The procedure for any comparative analysis is fairly straightforward: a point-by-point comparison, for similarities and differences, between two or more samples of handwriting. It can be used in any circumstances where a comparison of script and penstroke usage is needed. For example, the analysis may compare two samples by the same writer, or it may compare samples by two or more different writers. Comparison analysis can also help settle legal questions (as; whether or not a given signature or sample of writing is a forgery, or whether or not two or more samples were written by the same person).

The worksheet is an especially useful tool for doing this type of analysis. You take each sample separately, and describe in precise detail the actual usage of each script and penstroke formation. Then you compare the usages in each sample, one at a time, matching trait indicator to trait indicator, penstroke formation to penstroke formation.

If you are doing the analysis for counseling purposes, a write-up would be part of the procedure; how detailed it has to be would depend on the reason for the analysis. But for the most part, you are not concerned with correlating data as for a detailed GPA, or even as for a mini-analysis. Your primary concern in this type of analysis is exactly how and where the samples match up, and exactly what form any differences may take.

When used for counseling purposes, the two most common forms of comparative analysis are Progression Analysis, and Compatibility Analysis.

A. Progression Analysis

Progression analysis enables a writer to chart his progress over a period of time; it is also the next stage, after the preliminary GPA, in establishing a graphotherapy procedure. This is a comparative analysis based on a series of samples from the same writer which were done at different times and under different conditions.

What kind of sample you need for each successive analysis depends on the reason for repeating the analysis in the first place. Very often, you would be doing progression analysis for a writer who simply wants to know how he's doing *now* as opposed to *then* (the last time he was analyzed). In this case, and assuming no serious problem, the test line may be more than adequate for your purposes; and, in fact, may be easier to work with. If the end is to be graphotherapy, you should be working from more than just the test line, and at least the majority of your samples should be "natural."

How detailed each analysis must be (i.e., whether you need a full GPA each time or can handle it with a version of the mini-analysis) is a judgement you will have to make depending on your individual client's needs; however, you should complete the worksheet for each new sample. For this particular type of comparison, what you are primarily looking for is differences—for changes—and however detailed your write-up, in successive analyses it is usually only the changes you need to describe.

And yes, everyone's handwriting changes, and it changes all the time. The question for progression analysis is *how* did it change, and *in regard to what*. You can mention situational changes as; lighter than normal pressure, which may only mean that the writer was tired when he wrote his second sample, or more of a scrawl than usual, which means he was in more of a hurry. But what you are looking for is *significant differences*: the solution to an existing problem, the start of a new problem, or some kind of character, personality, or attitude change which may not necessarily be a problem at all, but which is going to influence how that person will live his life from now on.

Be aware that *you may not always find something*. In fact, in most cases, you won't find any significant differences, and those changes you do find will be very minor, especially if the samples are close in time. But if something has changed, however minor, you will find it by matching equivalent indicators.

For example: In Figure 1, our writer with the social conflicts might, by his next sample, have managed to steady up his angle of tilt; if he does, he has resolved that particular conflict (and *that* is your mini-analysis). A full analysis would have told you that not only were there a variety of reasons for the conflict (as; the sensitive "d"), but there were also a variety of reactions beyond the tilt waver itself (as; the deep double-looping in the middle zone). Does the later sample show that he resolved the conflict by becoming more reserved or by becoming more outgoing (i.e., what tilt did he end up with)? And, did he accomplish it by becoming less hypersensitive or more secretive (i.e., were there any changes in the loops)?

Just as important: Were there any other changes in the style of his script, either co-incidental with or as a result of this particular change, which might affect either his social relationships or his self-image?

There are a variety of reasons people do what they do, but there are also a variety of ways people can change, and every change affects something else. Because everyone does have some current problem, it is too easy for the analyst to work only on that problem and overlook other developments, especially in this type of analysis. This is why you should use the worksheet even if you are only doing a mini-analysis, and even if your client's stated concern is only one specific problem. For example: did the second sample also show word breaks where the first showed none? Did the baseline go off whack? Did the zone emphasis, as well as the tilt, show a change, and if so, what? You are looking for *any* significant changes, whether or not they appear important at the moment, and whether or not they have any apparent bearing on the problem under consideration.

Certainly if there is a specific problem, and/or if your client is particularly concerned with a specific area of his life, you can concentrate on that in each succeeding analysis. But as the analyst (and as the objective observer) *you* must be the one to avoid using tunnel vision. As long is someone is coming to you for a better understanding of himself, you tell him *everything* he needs to know—not only what he wants to hear.

B. Compatibility Analysis

A compatibility analysis matches the handwriting of two more more different people, to determine points at which they are likely to agree, and where conflicts between them are likely to arise. It is used just as often by people thinking of joining a company or starting a business partnership as by those who are considering marriage or some other live-in arrangements; many such analyses have been done as a means of helping people choose roommates—or, at least, as a means of letting them know what they're getting into *before* they sign a lease together! The reasons people need to know if or how well they will get along are as many and varied as people themselves.

The test line can be adequate for this purpose, although, as with any analysis, the longer the sample you have, the better the job you can do. Your write-up of the comparison can be done from the worksheet as a mini-analysis, but, unlike progression analysis, when you match indicators you are looking for similarities as well as differences. All your conclusions can be stated in a single write-up, with copies for each person involved in the comparison.

From a business point of view, it is also generally a good idea to include a complete GPA of each party to the proposed partnership as part of your service. The best way for a non-graphologist to test the validity of graphology is to read his own analysis, and the detailed report gives each of your clients confidence in your conclusions regarding their compatible traits. The GPA, of course, is given *only* to the person for whom it was done (if they want to share the results with each other, that's their decision, not yours!).

It goes without saying that the fewer people you are working with, the easier your job will be. For a comparison involving only three people, for example, you have to know how A will get along with B, how A will get along with C, how B will get along with C, and how all them will get along with each other. And, as you may also sometimes be asked, should it happen that B and C get along best, how they will both get along with A. If you are doing a multiple comparison, just take it one step at a time. Compare your samples in pairs, instead of trying to combine all your results as you go along, and you are likely to get less confused.

For your clients, just having this information about each other, whatever they may decide to do with it, gives them a distinct advantage over starting a long-term or contractual relationship blind (or on intuitive "feel"). It is certainly an advantage, for example, for A and C to know that B is shy, rather than to believe he is just "stuck up": that they already know without having to be told is also an advantage for B, who can't express his feelings easily. If C is a procrastinator, and A and B know about it in advance, they will not be as annoyed or as inconvenienced by his delays; if they still want him as a partner for his other qualities, they'll find some way to work around this one—or to work on *him*. And if A has a tendency to shade the truth, it is just as well for his potential business partners to know that he does it, and what kind of truth he shades (i.e., if he does it because he is dishonest, or because he's insecure). Remember that people can use information about each other to help each other, not only to get the low-down.

As a matchmaking service, this type of analysis can be used to help people find compatible mates; or, if two people have already found each other, it can tell them in advance how they are likely to get along. If one person in a proposed relationship is extravagant, for example, and the other is a penny-pincher, some problems are bound to arise. It's always best to have at least one marriage partner who is willing and able to manage the family finances intelligently. But it also helps if the saver knows just how much his or her partner is likely to defeat any efforts to keep their financial heads above water; and it helps the spender to know just how much pocket money he or she is going to be allowed. If person A is neat, precise, and very concerned about appearances, and person B tends to be somewhat sloppy, this odd-couple arrangement would probably be unpleasant for both of them; and if A is a bully and B can be easily bullied, you should certainly advise caution before those two people take their marriage vows. The situation might be ideal for the bully, but the intended victim is likely to find the rest of his or her life somewhat less than pleasant.

As with the GPA, your only responsibility is to do a thorough analysis. *You* make no judgements and give no advice (not, at least, as regards the final partnership decision). If people want to get together, then get together they will, no matter what you say, and even if they have paid you to find out they shouldn't: more important, there are times when the most unlikely partnerships turn out to be highly successful. All you are attempting to do in a compatibility analysis is to provide your clients with as much information as you can, based on the data you have; to tell them where their needs are similar, what character or personality traits may differ, and how each person can expect the other(s) to react under certain kinds of circumstances. You let them take it from there.

IV. Aptitude and Inclination Analysis

An aptitude and inclination analysis lists as many abilities and potentials as the available sample reveals; it also specifies what type of employment situation would suit the writer best. It is assumed, in doing the analysis, that work atmosphere is just as important as work type: two people with identical abilities but different personal needs should be looking for two different kinds of jobs.

There are usually three circumstances under which this type of analysis is called for. It may be done for a specific individual as part of personal counseling; an aptitude and inclination listing may also be requested by either a vocational counselor or by a personnel manager as an aid in job placement for a given writer.

As *personal counseling* (as opposed to employment counseling), providing someone with a detailed description of his abilities and potentials can often help him turn a very necessary corner. For those people who feel that there is nothing they have to offer, a long list of marketable qualities can certainly help them think better of themselves. For others, your analysis may identify qualities they didn't realize they had, or pinpoint a trait or characteristic that is the reason they can't seem to make much use of what they *do* know they have.

It's not always a negative attribute that could stand in someone's way! For example—and this misunderstanding is much more common than most people realize—a simple explanation of the difference between ambition (a desire for personal advancement) and determination (the need to accomplish some task or goal) can often bolster a writer's self-esteem. Determination is a very positive attribute in any individual for its own sake, and a very desirable one in an employee. It may enable that person to accomplish more actual work than ambition would; and, in fact, to produce a better quality of work. But without ambition, he is unlikely to get commensurate recognition. If the writer is working in a job where office politics is the key to advancement, he at least needs to be aware that personal inadequacy is not the reason he isn't getting promotions. Even if he's self-employed, he needs to understand that what is keeping him from fame and fortune is not lack of ability in his chosen field, but a lack of interest in pursuing that kind of success. This is at least one bene-fit of handwriting analysis in an aptitude survey: personal needs are as impor-tant as specific abilities in determining how well someone will do a given kind of employment situation.

Other than supportive personal counseling, a list of miscellaneous attributes is meaningless in and of itself, even with definitions. To help your client choose—and find—the right job for him, you require an additional pro-fessional background that handwriting analysis does not provide.

For *vocational guidance* (job placement), you would need an extensive knowledge of the requirements of all current employment opportunities, in order to decide which profession(s) might best suit the nature and extent of the writer's abilities. Lacking that, you would have to work with a trained vocational counselor who does have that knowledge.

Occupational analysis is a less generalized task, and the graphologist can give more direct assistance. Most employers or personnel managers can speci-fy for you what traits and abilities they are looking for in an applicant; all you need do, then, is determine whether or not a particular applicant has those traits. It's almost a kind of compatibility analysis between the job (or the com-pany) and the job seeker. You should list any additional attributes you find, of course; the writer may not be suitable for some immediate opening, but if he has a combination of traits that will suit another position, the personnel man-ager will undoubtedly want to know about it. Astute companies have been known to *make* a job for someone who is highly qualified in order to have that person available when the position they want him to fill is open.

A full GPA is generally not necessary for this type of analysis, unless the writer wants it for his own purposes: a listing of aptitudes and preferences is more than sufficient, especially if someone other than the writer is the one who will be making use of the information you provide. It is also not neces-sary for you to identify specific abilities (as; "artistic"), except as special inter-ests or potentials, even for employment counseling. An aptitude test will tell any vocational counselor what a job applicant can do, and a resumé will tell a prospective employer what he has done. Your job is to tell either or both of them what he *will* do, and what he is apt to do best, and that can make all the difference: especially if the work he should be doing is of a type he has never done before.

For either vocational or occupational counseling, the test line might be suf-ficient, but a full-page letter is often a better idea. The text of the letter is not important: it can be anything from a neutral subject to the individual's reasons for wanting a particular job. As in any analysis, you don't need a lot of personal information; you simply need as many handwriting formations as you can get.

But it is important in this type of analysis that you specify exactly how you want the sample written: and a full sheet (sufficient room for self-expression) of unlined paper (ability to function without guidelines), plus ballpoint pen (energy and determination level), should be included in your specifications, whatever else you may or may not require. When you have completed the trait listing, you take a very close look at the overall quality of the sample itself, particularly in terms of general organization, appearance (presentation), and the *ability to follow directions*. You are, after all, using this person's handwriting skill as a guideline for determining effective and successful behavior. The behavior any writer is attempting to perform successfully is communication, and if he is communicating in an attempt to get a good job, he should be on his best behavior. How well, and with what kind of attitude, he performs this simple task is certainly at least one significant indicator of how well, and with what kind of attitude, he will perform any other.

PART TWO: Income Opportunities in Graphology

Now that you have this new skill, how can you use it? Graphology can give you an extra, and very useful tool in many different professions; you can also use it to go into business for yourself. These are some of the ways professional graphologists earn a living.

1. Consultant Services
    A. *Aptitude analysis* can be offered to major businesses as an accurate (and generally less expensive) means of evaluating the abilities and attitudes of prospective employees. It can be used for both executive recruitment and general employee screening.

The aptitude analysis can also be offered to employment agencies, schools, or counseling services which provide vocational guidance, as an added means of testing people who are looking for what kind of work they should do. As we've mentioned, unless you have vocational training you should not offer occupational counseling without the cooperation of these professionals.

Beyond the fact that a complete analysis reveals not only potentials but preferences—and therefore indicates what kind of work environment the individual needs to function best—it has an additional advantage as a tool for vocational placement. The analysis does NOT reveal sex, race, or age; and that makes it, without question, an equal-opportunity employment tool.

    B. *Social services* in general can make use of the GPA or other forms of attitude and personality analyses. Schools may need assistance in evaluating and helping problem students. Graphology is also a useful guide in working with the emotionally disturbed, both children and adults. In these areas remember: your field is handwriting analysis, not diagnosis. All you are offering is a way to help uncover hidden reasons for puzzling or disturbed behavior.

    C. *Legal services* are also an option. It is possible for you to learn to authenticate (as opposed to analyzing) any handwriting on questionable documents, such as checks, wills, extortion letters, etc. Comparison analysis can tell you, and your client, whether or not the person who is supposed to have written something did in fact write it, or whether the signature or document is likely to be a forgery. A qualified graphologist can also be called in by police departments to perform character analyses on samples of handwriting found at crime scenes or written by possible criminals. An analysis of the personality and potential behavior patterns of a kidnapper, for example, could be of great value to local authorities or the FBI.

Doing this type of analysis could make you an expert witness in a court of law, so it is essential that you be extremely accurate. Again, stick to analyzing just the handwriting. Even if you eventually become very experienced in this field of work, let the authorities deal with analyzing the paper, ink and other material evidence.

D. *Marriage counseling*, dating services, and, as we mentioned, compatibility analyses for prospective business partners or even roommates, are also excellent opportunities for the graphologist. If you are interested in this type of field, you should either have psychological training or be working with someone who does. Listing the traits you find and interpreting what they could mean to the people involved are two different skills!

E. A *newspaper column* can also give you an opportunity to use your new skill. For this, you would have to become adept at using the mini-analysis to answer specific questions. You would also have to make certain that your readers know what kinds of questions you *can't* answer, as well as what kind of samples you need. But there are and have been successful advice columns which use handwriting analysis as the basis for solving reader's problems. If writing as well as graphology is one of your abilities, there's no reason why your byline can't be on one of them.

2. Teaching

You can offer to teach this skill in the regular school system supervisors of evening classes for adult or continuing education may be interested in adding graphology to their program, and so may colleges or universities.

It is also possible to start your own classes or instruct individual students for a fee. A good format for independent classes is from 12 to 20 hours of instruction in equal sessions over six to eight weeks; you can use this text and/or any teaching materials you have developed yourself as a means of organizing your lessons. You can offer to teach in your own home or office, or make arrangements with local social service organizations, such as church or community groups, for lecture hall space. You'll find that teaching graphology makes you a better graphologist; explaining it to someone else reinforces your own skills and understanding of this complex art-science.

3. Going Public

Everybody likes to hear about himself, and everybody's got problems. Handwriting analysis can be done through the mail, thus offering not only a comprehensive character and personality portrait but also absolute privacy; and for many people, the fact that they don't have to meet a counselor face to face could definitely be an added attraction.

It's also possible to "perform"; to lecture or give demonstrations at various social functions. You'll find the mini-analysis a useful tool for this type of situation; and many local organizations do look for guest speakers and interesting topics as a way of attracting people to their planned events (or even just entertaining those who come).

What you choose to do will depend on your background, personality, and special interests, of course; and whether you use graphology as a tool or as a toy will depend on how well you learn it and how interested you are in making use of what you learned. But there are self-employment possibilities for qualified graphologists in many different fields, and job openings in businesses, government services, or private institutions—many more than we have mentioned here. If you learn this discipline thoroughly and use it accurately, your expertise can open doors to an almost limitless variety of employment opportunities.

APPENDIX A

Glossary—
And an ABC of Traits
and Characteristics

"When I use a word" (Humpty-Dumpty said), "it means just what I choose it to mean—neither more, nor less."

Every discipline has its own vocabulary, and very often that vocabulary is made up of familiar-sounding words or phrases which have been assigned apparently arbitrary meanings. To add to the confusion, any discipline which falls into the realm of psychology also uses, in addition to its technical terms, a wide range of emotionally-charged words and phrases which describe human actions or reactions—and it assigns it own specific meanings to those terms as well.

A professional idiom is not really designed either to create an "in-language"or to confuse the layman. The use of an exact vocabulary gives you a precision tool for the recording and transmission of data. Especially in a field like psychology, where there are so many other variables, a specific definition of descriptive terms is essential: it can often be your only means of ensuring that your explanations of research and findings will be understood as you intended by someone else. Its purpose, then, is *communication*.

This glossary lists and briefly re-defines the technical terms used in the text, along with some additional vocabulary. Wherever applicable, glossary entries include the number of any chapter(s) in which a given term is more fully explained.

Also listed, in most cases with script samples and in all cases with specific definitions, is a fairly comprehensive selection of those traits, characteristics, and emotional reactions which can be clearly identified by a graphologist.

Most of the definitions of words and phrases are not too different from standard dictionary denotation, but where they differ, there is a reason. Graphology can only identify any attribute *as it appears in handwriting*. If that attribute has little or nothing to do with communication, or with the mechanical ability to write, then only a part of it, or a clue to its possible existence, may show up in the script. Where that is the case, our definition must be limited to the part or clue which can be inferred from script, and cannot include any other aspect of that characteristic (see, for example, graphology's definition of "creativity" under *Ingenuity*).

Like symbols, words which describe human reactions have a different quality of meaning for different people (even a dictionary gives you more than one definition for most words!), and you should be careful, when using any of these terms in an analysis, to explain your intended meaning clearly and precisely. The intention of this glossary is partly to help you do just that, and partly to illustrate how these attributes appear in script—and in doing so, perhaps to demonstrate a means by which you can infer the presence of traits and characteristics that were not defined in the text or this listing (as; COMBINED TRAITS).

When graphology uses these words, then, this is exactly what they mean:

Aa

ABILITY: A trained talent; a usable skill. Ability is the power to perform in some capacity. See also: POTENTIAL; TALENT.

ACCESSORY, to script: Any penstroke formation (qv) which is added on to the basic letterform. It may be formed as a continuation of the original pen movement (i.e., without lifting the pen from the paper), or added later as a separate penstroke.

Necessary Accessories are those additional formations which are (1) taught as part of the script letterform, and (2) used to clarify meaning or to identify a letter or word. They include the dots used to complete the i or j (i-dots), the bar formation used to complete the t or x (t-bars), and, in some cases, punctuation.

Unnecessary Accessories are exceptional formations which serve to complicate, decorate, or obscure letter or word forms. They include such formations as knots and ties, prestrokes and endstrokes, and ornamentation in general.

The type of formation and how it is used serves to identify the writer's actual intention (as opposed to the implied intention of the sample, which is communication). All accessories, in one way or another, interfere with the smooth flow of script; in analysis, the judgement of positive or negative is made on the basis of whether their presence or absence impedes communication. (Chapter 7)

Acquisitive (drive): Having the need or desire to get something as your own; to have, gain, or earn some material possession. It is indicated in script by initial hooks (also called "acquisitive hooks") on letterforms or t-bars:

The strength of the drive can be determined by the size of the hook in relation to the size of the rest of the letter; how much it influences attitudes or behavior is indicated by its frequency of occurrence. Acquisitiveness may be either a positive or a negative attribute; see also: Ambition; Greed.

Adaptable (trait): Having the ability to adjust to external pressures or changing circumstances. Adaptability is indicated by any medium-size script (see: SIZE). It is generally considered a positive trait; but see also: Conformity.

ADULT'S WRITING: In graphology, an adult is anyone 25 years of age or older; by this point, physical growth is complete and major character and personality traits generally established. Attributes indicated in an adult's handwriting are considered to be an expression of such established (or, "normal") behavior patterns, though judgmental exceptions are made for the newly literate or foreign born. See also: CHILDREN'S HANDWRITING, Immaturity, LITERACY.

Affable (trait): Having the ability or the need to get along easily with others. Affability is not synonymous with either cooperation or conformity, though it may use either or both as a means to an end; the affable individual will be courteous and even-tempered, but with the intent to avoid argument or unpleasantness, or to stay out of trouble. A single script indicator for this trait is the upswinging end-stroke (also called the "affable lift"); note its relationship to the defensive upstroke or backstroke (qv):

As a combined trait (qv), the affable script will include two or more of the following indicators: (1) the affable lift; (2) open roundness of formations (receptiveness, cooperation); (3) prestrokes (desire to please based on insecurity); and (4) light-pressured t-bars (lack of firmness). It is usually a negative personality trait; see also: Defensive.

Affectation (trait): Artificial behavior, usually exhibited as an attempt to claim or exhibit qualities not natural to or actually possessed by the individual using it. See: Artistic.

Affection (attitude): A general feeling of sympathetic good will toward or warm regard for others. Unlike affability (qv), affection does not involve any defensiveness or insecurity; it is a positive attribute which is based on a genuine liking for others. Affection is indicated by a tendency to roundness in the middle zone in any style of script; it usually shows its best side in a vertical to controlled-right tilt. See also: Warmth.

Aggressive (trait): Self-assertive; having the ability or desire to demand recognition of your own potentials, accomplishments, or prerogatives. Generally considered a positive attribute but *only* in a well-organized script (see: Ambition). Aggressiveness is indicated by forceful, blunt-tipped or slashing, terminal strokes up from the lower zone (a transference of physical/material drives into social contexts):

q↓ y↓ : you may think so but

As a combined trait, an aggressive script style includes (1) firm pressure (energy); (2) strong t-bars and heavy downstrokes (determination); (3) tall capitals (confidence); (4) a sturdy pronoun I (self-belief); and (5) controlled angularity (independence of thought).

Where the script shows disorganization (lack of control) or anger signs (qv), aggressiveness may become **hostility** (open antagonism, esp. toward the status or achievements of others): the slashing terminals indicate a potential for this trait as well.

Altruism (trait): The purely positive version of what affability pretends to be; a sincere regard for the well-being of others. Its potential is indicated by the presence of fluid letter forms, such as the figure-eight f, g, or j:

8 f j : my handwriting

As a combined trait, the altruistic script will also show evidence of self-confidence (qv); idealism (tall strokes into the upper zone), and usually some sensitivity (qv); in its most positive aspect the script style as a whole will be original (self-expressive), very fluid (showing a relaxed use of necessary social custom or rules), and very easy to read (consideration for others). Altruism rarely shows up in rounded (cooperative) scripts, or in styles showing insecurity or conformity.

Ambition (combined trait): A need or desire for personal advancement, which may be defined (by the writer) as preferment, honor, power, or similar kinds of attainment. Ambition is indicated in script by a combination of several traits and drives: (1) energy and (2) determination (which together, in terms of work capacity, translate as will-power); (3) pride or (4) a desire to please (prop-strokes); and, of course, (5) acquisitive drives. See also: *Determination*. To learn whether or not the writer will be able to get what he wants, check also for positive signs of ability: (1) independent thought and mental alertness (controlled angularity); (2) self control; and, most important, (3) clear objectives (see: BASELINE).

AMERICAN SCHOOLFORM: see: SCHOOLFORM

ANALYSIS: We agree with Webster: "The separation of anything into its constituent parts or elements; also, an examination of anything to distinguish its component parts, (either) separately, or in their relation to the whole."

ANALYSIS WRITE-UP: A written report in which analysis findings are explained to the person for whom the analysis was done.

Anger (emotion): A strong, and sometimes controlling (or, overriding) feeling of active antagonism, caused by a sense of injury or insult. It is indicated in script by sudden pressure surges, usually on downstrokes, and/or by slashing strokes on t-bars, i-dots, or terminals:

See also: Frustration

ANGLE, or tilt: A measure of both the *direction* and the *degree* of slant of individual letters in a sample of handwriting. Script angle is a general indicator of the writer's overall orientation toward other people, but by itself does not reveal how or whether the writer is able to act on those feelings or communicate his intentions or needs. (Chapter 3). For communication indicators, see also: Chapter 7, Penstroke Formations.

ANGULAR WRITING: Any script style in which individual letters are shaped so that they come to either a blunt or sharp point; angularity refers specifically to letter forms which are traditionally rounded, such as ovals, connectors, or the tops/bottoms of cup-shaped letters.

Controlled angularity shows smooth flow, usually attained through the use of curved connectors and similar inverted-cup strokes, lack of distortion in letter forms, and generally moderate to firm pressure. It is an indicator in script of such attributes as independence of thought, mental alertness, and maturity.

Rigid angularity is the extreme for this style. It exists when letters are sharp-pointed top and bottom, tightly crowded or distorted (i.e., illegible), and usually very heavy-pressured. Extreme angularity may indicate rigidity of thought, as well as critical attitudes, prejudice, and similar antagonistic reactions. (Chapter 8)

Anti-Social (attitude): The act or intention of injuring someone else; also, a deliberate rejection of behavior patterns designed to facilitate or generally accepted as a means of ensuring cooperative social intercourse. Anything from insulting to criminal attitudes or behavior can fall into this category; however, breaking laws or codes or violating taboos may not. See also: GUIDELINES.

Argumentative (attitude): In disagreement or at odds with others, and expressing it by attempts to prove them wrong or in some way incompetent. A single script indicator for this negative attitude is the down-slanting t-bar which aims at or hits into the middle zone:

This formation may be found in any style of script (i.e., round or angular). Whether the writer tends to be blunt or critical can be determined by the bluntness or sharpness of the endstroke on the t-bar.

Artistic (potential): The practice or appreciation of aesthetic activities; also, having or showing taste or skill. Any graceful script style (qv) indicates the possible existence of artistic ability, including the fluid, altruistic indicators:

As a positive indicator, fluid, graceful forms show an appreciation of the beautiful, as well as an ability to translate it into action (i.e., by expert control of the pen); where they aid the smooth flow of script, they also show originality. If both factors are combined with indicators for imagination, this style reveals artistic potential. If grace, originality and imagination are also combined with indicators for ambition (and especially for work capacity), the script style may reveal an actual artist.

Graceful letterforms become a negative indicator when they interfere with the smooth flow of script or obscure the legibility of letters and words; when they take over the handwriting, they become an indicator of affectation (qv), especially if combined with rounded writing (desire to please). If the script style also indicates need for attention, pretense, or inadequate ego (see: Self-Image), the affectation is based on insecurity. As an analyst, however, you should be aware that your subject may still have artistic potential, but be unaware of it, or unable or unwilling to make use of it.

ASCENDER/DESCENDER: Typographical terms for upper and lower zone formations. An *ascender* is that part of a letter which normally extends above the middle zone, such as the upper half of the b, d, h, etc; a *descender* is that part of a letter which is normally formed below the baseline, such as the lower part of the g, j, or p. The terms apply only to lowercase letters.

Ascetic (characteristic): Denial of the body for development of the mind, especially spiritual development. The potential for this characteristic is shown by de-emphasis of the middle and lower zones (no social life; no physical drives), accompanied by tall, narrow or loopless ascenders (high spiritual aspirations):

f g h : This is how I form my handwriting.

In its combined form, this zone imbalance would be pronounced to extreme, and the script angular (independent), small (withdrawn), and vertical (cold); the handwriting may also show a rigid baseline and/or other evidence of tight self-control. It is generally considered a negative social characteristic.

Athletic (potential): Trained, fit, or disposed to contend in exercises requiring physical agility, stamina, and often strength. Lower zone emphasis indicates physical drives; if descenders are long, narrow or pointed loops which hit or extend into the line of script below, it indicates athletic potential (wider loops may only show a need for physical outlets):

g y f : does my writing show? it have to do with

If combined with firm, consistent pressure (vitality) and other signs of energy, especially in a medium-large (adaptable but needs "space") right-tending (other-oriented) script style, the writer has not only the potential but probably the ability for sustained physical activities; combined with evidence of ambition, he also has the competitive drive. As with anything else, of course, control (organization) and self-direction (baseline) provide the key. The handwriting of a successful athlete also shows a reasonable balance between upper and middle zones, with upper zone loops also narrow (practical) and upper zone formations generally simple (clarity of thought) and often original. Note that the upper zone is not de-emphasized: the professional —and successful—athlete must use his head as well as his body. See also: ZONES.

ATTITUDE: General orientation or stance in relation to external influences or events; usually based on emotional reactions.

ATTRIBUTE: A quality or characteristic inherent in the individual. See also: TRAIT; CONTROLLING FACTOR.

$$Bb$$

BACKSTROKE: Any pen movement which moves or returns to the left. Normal backstrokes move toward the left but return right; most loops are formed in this manner, as are most knots and ties. A backstroke which ends at the left generally indicates defensiveness or insecurity. (Chapter 7)

BALANCE, in script: A fairly equal size relationship between upper, middle, and lower zones; it indicates a corresponding balance in general orientation or lifestyle. See: ZONES.

BASELINE: An imaginary line which follows the bottom level of middle zone letters or formations. The ideal, or normal, baseline is that part of letters and words which should rest on the line if the writer were using ruled paper. As a positive or negative indicator, the actual baseline is judged by its deviation from that standard. Baseline is a primary organizational indicator; its steadiness or lack of it is a measure of whether or not the writer has useable or reasonable guidelines (qv), and/or feels secure about his right to define and pursue his own personal goals. (Chapter 2)

BEHAVIOR: Actual performance; open (or visible) responses to modes of conduct on the part of the individual, usually in reaction to his environment. *Behavior cannot be determined from a sample of script*; formations in handwriting indicate potentials or inclinations, not accomplished acts. See: HANDWRITING.

Bitterness (attitude): A general unhappy displeasure with the state of things, or with a personal relationship; usually expressed as a caustic or sarcastic emotional reaction. The script indicator is down-turned initial hooks; usually found on the t-bar, but also possible as a pre-stroke on other letters:

Bitterness is generally a negative indicator even if controlled; see also: Cruelty; Vindictiveness.

Bluntness (trait): Tactless honesty or frankness, generally deriving from a basic insensitivity to other people's feelings. It is generally not a deliberately anti-social characteristic, though it may be perceived (by others) as such; if controlled, it can be a positive attribute. It is indicated in script by blunt endings on t-bars, or on downstrokes and other terminals:

If these formations become club-like (i.e., especially thick or heavy-pressured), the bluntness can become **brutality** (unfeeling or sometimes savage cruelty). Brutality is generally considered an anti-social (qv) attitude or characteristic.

Calculating (trait): Designing or adapting behavior to achieve a specific purpose which is not revealed *as* the intended purpose; premeditated or contrived behavior. Depending on other signs in script, it may be based on either insecurity or dishonesty, but either way is generally considered a negative trait. A single script indicator is any deliberately contrived forms, especially those which impede the flow of script or obscure the meaning of the message:

When contrived forms are hidden in the script, as in the "s" above (arrow), dishonesty is also indicated; if based on insecurity, these forms will appear as wind-up strokes, especially on capital letters which begin a sentence; or as attention-getting and distracting formations, such as the circled i-dot.

CAPITALS: Those letters in an alphabet or style of writing which are normally larger than, and sometimes different in form from, corresponding lowercase forms; also those letters which are normally used as the initial letter of a sentence, proper noun, name or title, or as a means of emphasizing (the importance of) some other word. As a script indicator, the size of capitals in relation to lowercase and middle zone letters is a measure of the writer's confidence in his ability to perform. See also: Confidence. (Chapter 8)

Careless (trait): Negligent; not concerned with doing a job right, or with the consequences of doing it wrong. Carelessness is indicated in script by the absence of necessary accessories. See: ACCESSORY.

CHARACTER: The sum and interrelationship of distinctive qualities belonging to an individual; also, the inner (or "real") self, as opposed to any social mask or pretense. See also: PERSONALITY.

CHARACTERISTIC: A trait, quality, or attribute basic to or normal for a given individual; also, a typical mode of behavior.

CHILDREN'S WRITING: In graphology, childhood is defined as a formative period, and includes any age from the time the child first learns to write (usually at about age six) up until character and personality are relatively stabilized (see: ADULT WRITING). Children's writing shows the problems and trial-and-error process involved in forming the (eventual) adult makeup; analysis generally takes a developmental approach. See also: IMMATURITY. (Chapter 11)

Clannish (attitude): Selective in personal associations; the tendency to associate with or see value in only one's own social group or clique. A single script indicator for this tendency is found in lower zone loops which swing far left, sometimes underlining a word; stubbornness is also indicated when the loops show knots or ties:

Often based on insecurity, this attitude is generally considered a negative factor in script. See also: PREJUDICE.

CLOSED FORMATION: Any penstroke which ends at the point where it began; or, formations producing a circling or boxing effect (no way in/no way out). Closed formations in general are indicators of reticence, secrecy, or cautious expression. (Chapter 7)

COMBINED TRAIT: An overall behavior pattern usually requiring two or more attributes to produce; it affects the individual's general outlook and lifestyle. See, for example: Ambition.

COMMUNICATION: The interchange of thoughts, opinions, or feelings with some other person; also, the ability or willingness to do so. It is the primary purpose of handwriting, and in most cases analysis judgement of positive or negative is based on whether or not the script style makes communication facile or even possible.

COMPARATIVE ANALYSIS: Analysis which systematically examines elements and qualities of two or more samples of writing for the purpose of discovering their resemblances and/or differences, and thereby establishing any possible or probable relationship between them. See also: CORRESPONDING INDICATORS. (Chapter 14)

COMPARATIVE SELF-IMAGE: How the writer rates himself in relation to others. It is determined by the relative emphasis of "you-me" formations in the text of a single sample of script. *Me formations* are any words (usually pronouns) which refer back to the writer of the sample; *you formations* are any words or proper names which refer to the person being written to or a third person being written about. (Chapter 9)

COMPATIBLE: Capable of co-existing in harmony or of working effectively together toward some common end. Compatibility may refer to attributes within a single sample of script (for incompatible factors, see: CONFLICT); or to traits and characteristics compared between two or more individuals. Judgement of interpersonal compatibility is determined by comparative analysis (qv). For the trait, see: Cooperative.

COMPLICATIONS, in handwriting: Any unnecessary pen movements used in forming letters or words; strokes added or included which interfere with the process of writing or the legibility of the end result. See also: ACCESSORY. Script complications are a factor in poor organization, and an indicator of mental or emotional confusion. (Chapter 1)

Concentration (ability/trait): Close mental application (the ability) or exclusive attention (the trait) to the subject or activity at hand. Generally any small script shows concentration in the sense of both close and exclusive attention to detail; concentration is also indicated by precision in the placement of necessary accessories (see: ACCESSORY), regardless of script size. Other indicators for the ability are i-dots close to the stem and firm, short, t-bars; good (consistent) spacing; and clarity or simplicity of form. See also: SIZE.

Confidence (characteristic): Faith in your own ability to perform a task or accomplish a goal; a positive evaluation of personal skills and potentials. A single indicator in script is sturdy capitals (consistent with or slightly larger than script size and clearly or simply formed). Note that capital size may vary with subject matter without indicating a basic lack of confidence; such variation, however, does indicate a relative increase or decrease in confidence in terms of that subject matter. As a combined trait, confidence is indicated by (1) sturdy capitals; (2) a clear, readable script (nothing to hide: security); (3) the absence of unnecessary strokes, especially pre-strokes (self-assurance: security); and (4) a firm baseline (clear objectives: emotional security). *Lack of confidence* can take two completely opposite forms in script: undersized capitals (barely topping the middle zone), indicating that the writer underrates himself; and over-large or over-elaborated capitals, a form of bragging, or egotism (see: Self-Image). See also: Self-Confidence.

CONFLICT: Mental or emotional struggle caused by incompatible or antagonistic needs or goals. In script, conflict is indicated where trait indicators or penstroke formations contradict each other or themselves (as; large letters /tight spacing: size contradiction). In emotional terms, conflict affects the writer's ability to function effectively or coherently (confusion), and if extreme can be dangerous to both mental and physical health.

Conformity (attitude): Absolute adherence to the guidelines of a social group; this attitude is based on an inability or unwillingness to think for yourself. Any Schoolform writing presents the appearance of this attitude (see: SCHOOLFORM); in general, a medium-size script showing rounded formations and other evidence of careful moderation (as; controlled slant, controlled pressure, balanced zones *or* middle zone emphasis, etc.) is an indicator of conformity. See also: Adaptability; Cooperation; SIZE.

Confusion, mental or emotional: Bewilderment; the inability to choose and/or follow an effective course of action. See: COMPLICATIONS; CONFLICT; BASELINE.

CONNECTORS: Penstrokes which are used between letters to join them into words, usually in a script alphabet. See: Logical; WORD BREAKS. (Chapter 8)

Conscientious (attitude): Governed by a sense of right and wrong and acting in accordance with what is (understood as) right; having a sense of responsibility for the results of your own actions. In general, this attitude is indicated in any script that is clear and readable, and which shows careful attention to detail (see: ACCESSORY); if reliability is also a trait, the script will include indicators for honesty (qv).

CONSCIOUS/UNCONSCIOUS: *Conscious* impulses or motivations are those which the individual is aware of or deliberately uses as causative factors in his reactions, behavior, or general circumstances and relationships; *unconscious* factors are as strongly causative, if not more so, but their impact is not evident to or recognized by the individual. See also: MOTIVATION.

CONTROLLING FACTOR: An underlying orientation, often unconscious, which determines the writer's attitudes and therefore accounts for his behavior and reactions. A trait, characteristic, or attitude so basic to the writer's nature that it can take control of his reactions or behavior without his acknowledgement or volition.

Cooperative (attitude): Willing to act jointly with others (positive), or tending to act in accordance with their wishes (negative). Any tendency to roundness in script is an indicator of this attitude; rounded writing in general shows a greater indication of obedience and the desire to please. Carried to extremes, cooperation may become conformity (qv); and if the script is concentrated in the middle zone, the inability to think independently. See: END-STROKES/PRE-STROKES; SCHOOLFORM. Cooperation is also indicated by any clear, readable script with all necessary accessories in place (see: ACCESSORY).

CORRESPONDING INDICATORS: A term used in any comparative analysis (qv); the same script factors as used in two or more samples of script. In comparative analysis, these factors are matched between samples (as; size to size, or loops to loops, etc.) to determine similarities and differences in usage (qv).

COVERING STROKE: Any penstroke laid down on top of or across the impression of a previous stroke. In cursive writing (see: SCRIPT), covering strokes are normally used to alter or reverse the direction of pen movement without adding to or changing the shape of the letter or lifting the pen from the paper. Examples are the return stroke on a d or t stem in traditional American Schoolform cursive.

Creativity: See: Ingenuity.

Critical (attitude): Having animosity toward and expressing sharp dissatisfaction with faults perceived in others or in events. Generally considered an anti-social attitude; it is indicated in script by inverted-v (arrow-head) i-dots, and sharp terminals (as on t-bars and lower zone ending strokes):

i t y : like winter better than

If these strokes are forceful (heavy-pressured), anger is also indicated; how much this attitude will influence the writer's behavior is indicated by frequency of occurrence.

Critical Judgement (potential): The ability to make a reasoned assessment of the value or quality of an object, idea, or course of action. It is indicated in script by pointed tops on m's and n's:

m n : then when I asked her

Most often found in angular writing; however, critical judgement can appear in roundhand. It is also usually the first sign of maturity found in a child's writing. See also: Maturity; Mental Alertness.

Cruelty (trait): The deliberate intention of hurting or giving pain to some other living being. A single script indicator is downturned terminal hooks or claws, especially if sharp-pointed. In graphology, this is also called the "felon's claw":

t g : I won't go with

As a combined trait (viciousness), the handwriting will also show most or all of the following factors: (1) pressured, long, descending t-bars, dagger pointed (anger plus argument: antagonism); (2) rigid angularity (uncompromising, unfeeling); (3) heavy to extreme pressure (brute force); and (4) slashing (anger) or inverted-v (critical) i-dots. The script may or may not also show signs of brutality (heavy-pressured club-shaped terminals, especially in the lower zone). As a combined trait, cruelty is dangerous (to others) in either an organized or a disorganized script; but bear in mind that in a disorganized script the writer himself has no control over where his viciousness will lead him.

(NOTE: For a contrast and clear example of the difference between an *antisocial* and a *negative* attribute, compare cruelty (anti-social) with suicidal (negative).)

CUP FORMATIONS: Any letter formed to look like a cup; a letter formation open on one side (such as the middle zone portion of the b or y, and the letter u). Letterforms like the m and n are called *inverted cups*. See also: OPEN FORMATIONS. (Chapter 7)

CURSIVE WRITING: See: SCRIPT.

Dd

Decisive (trait): Having the ability to make up your mind about a course of action; also having the ability to take action on that judgement, especially in the face of opposition or possible (fear of) failure. A single script indicator for this trait is a firm baseline (clear objectives); the potential for decisiveness is seen in firm, level, t-bars, especially if evenly balanced (determination; planning/carry-through):

t : as I told you

A lack of decisiveness is seen in short, light-pressured t-bars (see: Fear; Timidity). As a combined trait, the decisive writer will use: (1) a firm baseline; (2) firm pressure; (3) large capitals (confidence) and large pronoun I (self-confidence); (4) heavy down-strokes (aggressive); and (5) the firm t-bars. If the decisiveness extends to an ability or willingness to make decisions *for others*, then t-bars will also be lengthened to cap letters in the middle zone (see: Dominant).

Defensive (trait): On your guard; prepared at all times to protect yourself from attack or from hurt. This is a totally non-aggressive trait; the defensive writer is not trying (or able) to strike back, or even to prevent attack, but only trying to ward off a blow. Defensiveness is a combination of fear and insecurity, and as such is a very negative trait *for the writer*. There are a number of indicators in script which show a defensive reaction; listed from bad to worse, they are (letters refer to formations indicated in the sample): (a) the tented t-bar (caution); (b) upswinging end-strokes (peacemaking gestures like the "affable lift" or somewhat higher); (c) the defensive backstroke (shielding or covering); and (d) a left-leaning script (the more pronounced, the greater the fear):

(a)   (b)   (c)   (d)

Many otherwise positive script styles can show some sign(s) of defensiveness; many people feel the need to be on their guard in one way or another. Wherever they do show up, it means the writer *has been hurt*; where they dominate the script, the writer may be so afraid of being hurt again that he is also afraid to try reaching out.

Depression (emotion): In its milder form, or as a passing feeling, depression is unhappiness or sorrow, accompanied by the feeling that something has gone wrong that cannot immediately be set right; any baseline sag is an indicator of this feeling (see: Chapter 2). As a combined trait, depression adds the helpless feeling that nothing is ever going to go right, and the script will show some or all of the following indicators (letters refer to formations indicated in the sample): (a) a descending, sagging, and/or plunging baseline (depression plus pessimism); (b) descending signature baseline ("It's my fault"); (c) weak-pressured t-bars, especially if low on the stem (lack of firmness/feelings of inferiority); (d) sagging final letters and/or (e) descending finals (i.e., ending strokes) on letters that do not have a lower zone (physical and emotional exhaustion); and (f) crossing strokes below the baseline, especially if in the signature (drives cancelled):

A scrawled or illegible signature in this kind of handwriting is just another sign of feelings of inferiority ("Nobody wants to know who I am") or of self-denial. Depression is not just unhappiness, and you may want to look up the symptoms in an abnormal psychology textbook. For however long it lasts, it can be totally incapacitating—and as a combined trait, it means the writer has given up hope. See also: Pain, emotional.

Determination (attitude): The need, desire, or ability to get something accomplished, or to bring some act or work to a successful conclusion. The script indicator for determination is firm pressure, which may exist as strong t-bars, heavier downstrokes, or in the script as a whole (energy):

The possibility that this potential exists even in a lighter pressured script is seen in dashes used for i-dots, indicating drive and, if nothing else, enthusiasm (qv).

DEVIATION, sexual or social: Abnormal or psychopathic acts or behavior; moral perversion or criminal activities. *Cannot be determined from a sample of script.* See: Guilt; Sexual Hangups.

Diplomacy (trait): The willingness or ability to tell those little white lies where they'll do the most good *for others*; tact. A single script indicator for this trait is small, tight loops (or knots) at the top of a closed letter or oval, especially if found in the middle zone:

As tact, diplomacy is considered a positive trait as well as a positively-socialized attitude; if accompanied by corresponding negative indicators, however, keep in mind that it does involve concealment (and a certain amount of circumlocution). See, for example: Dishonesty; Insincerity. For its opposite, see Bluntness.

DISCIPLINE: In general, a system of knowledge or behavior which has a specific application; or, trained use of such a system, generally developed by instruction and exercise.

Dishonesty (trait): Characterized by fraud; in one way or another deliberately misrepresenting yourself or the facts of a situation. A single penstroke in script which indicates this tendency is an extra, especially a deep, loop at the left of a letter (self-concealment), or in the bottom of a loop or oval; since this evidence of something to hide is usually formed by a pre-stroke, it also indi-

FIGURE 1
Something to Hide: Indicators for Dishonesty

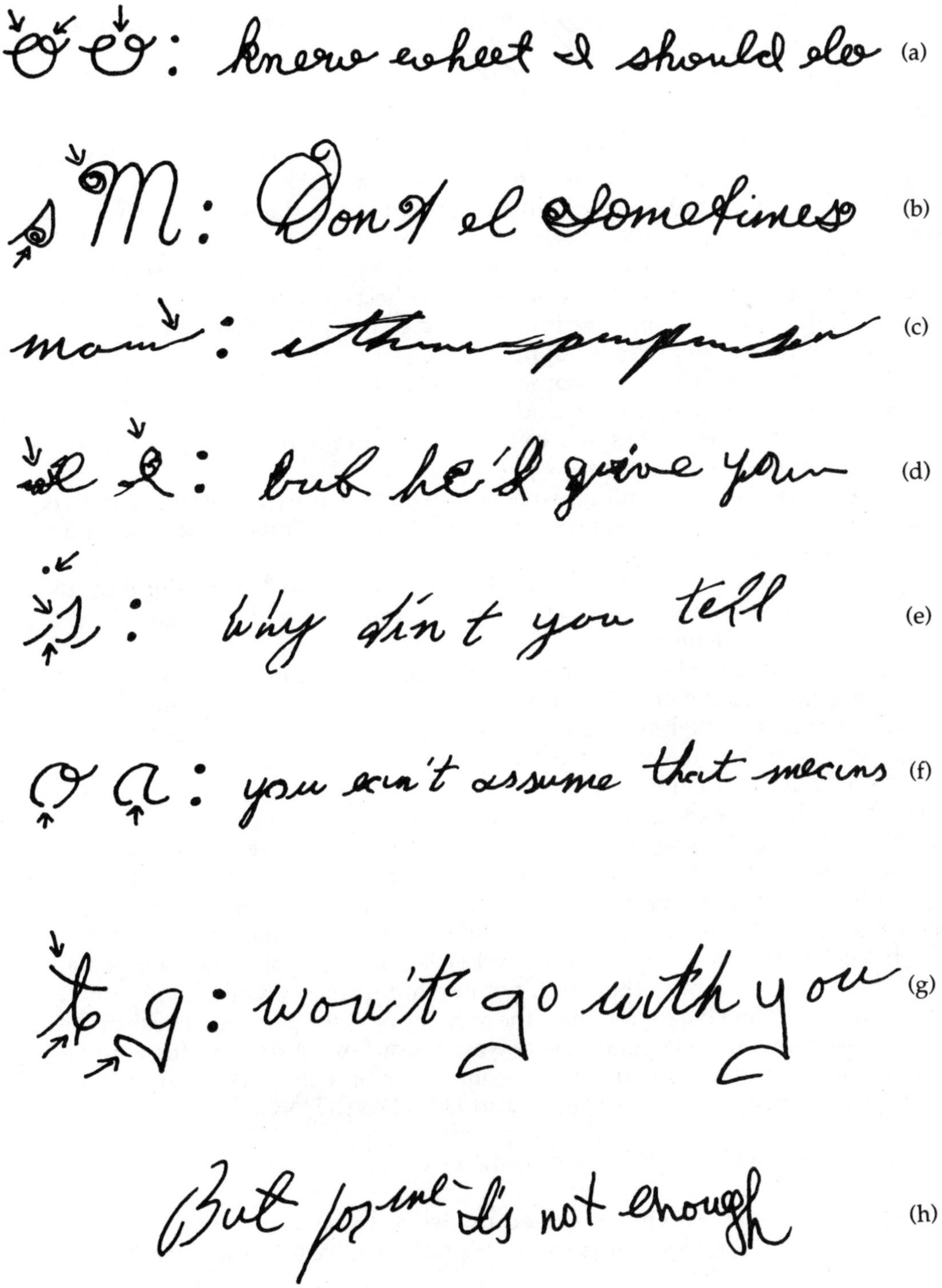

knew what I should do (a)

Don't el *Sometimes* (b)

them purpose (c)

but he'd give you (d)

why ain't you tell (e)

you can't assume that means (f)

won't go with you (g)

But for me it's not enough (h)

cates at least some insecurity:

a d g: hope you can read

Other kinds, and causes, of dishonesty are demonstrated by the following indicators (letters refer to samples in Figure 1, page 255):

(a) ovals with deep double loops (concealment); if the ovals are also open, they indicate insincerity (or lying);

(b) artificial or contrived forms, especially those which obscure meaning (see: Calculating); also, wind-up strokes on the beginnings of words or sentences, and/or slow, hesitant writing (a need to pre-plan what you're going to say—or remember what you said: Insecurity);

(c) scrawled endings on words, or the omission of letters or clarifying strokes (fear of being too clearly understood);

(d) excessive corrections and overstrokes (guilt: and this also qualifies as hesitant writing. Try it and see.);

(e) misplaced punctuation, especially if mixed in with letters, and even more so if with broken letters (partly careless, but it is misrepresentation and concealment of meaning);

(f) ovals open at the base, or traced in two parts (the "embezzler's script": a grasping love of money or material gain combined with hidden motives); and, along the same lines:

(g) left-turning or left-ending strokes which should normally return right, including the "felon's claw" (see: Cruelty); both a grasping nature and concealment and, in the felon's claw, used as a weapon. And finally, the one indicator which can be a major cause of any kind of dishonesty:

(h) a sinuous baseline, indicating a total lack of guidelines. Note that "sinuous" is not the same as "erratic": it can be erratic if pronounced enough, but the sinuous baseline shows a definite, often smooth, wavelike flow. This formation is usually found to some extent in any script showing signs of dishonesty.

Dishonesty may be either defensive or anti-social, depending on the writer's reasons for misrepresenting the truth. When accompanied by indicators for insecurity or sensitivity, then the writer is lying to protect himself, usually because he is convinced others will not like him if they "really know him"; if there are no defensive signs, then the writer may see lying or cheating as a means of achieving some goal. Either way, a word of caution on this very negative judgement: before you call someone a liar or a thief, be careful of your facts. See: BEHAVIOR; DEVIATION; and HANDWRITING.

DISORGANIZATION: See: ORGANIZATION

Dominant (drive): Having the need or desire to be in charge of or to run things; in a confident, well-organized script, the ability to do so. Dominance is indicated in script by a long, overlapping t-bar (capping the middle zone):

tbar : can you tell me

Generally considered a positive trait; certainly any manager or supervisor needs this ability. However, in a less than well-organized handwriting, the writer may simply be **domineering** (demanding his own way no matter what the circumstances), or just plain bossy.

DOMINANT TRAIT: A central characteristic in the individual's makeup which takes precedence over other traits or characteristics; it may act as a controlling factor (qv) over his behavior or reactions. See also: TRAIT.

DOODLING: A neuro-muscular reaction to emotional impulses or external stimuli which takes the form of independently determined penstroke formations. (Welcome to the world of scientific definition.) Emotionally, doodling is a spontaneous act of self-expression; intellectually, it is an unconscious problem-solving activity. As a behavior pattern, doodling is unstructured play; in comparison to handwriting, doodling is non-socialized behavior (*not* unsocial or anti-social: *non*-social). In graphology, a doodle is considered to picture a flash of intuitive insight which explains or defines some problem or situation in relation to a current need or drive; properly interpreted, it can give the writer the same kind of insights into his reactions and needs as the messages of dreams. Doodles are largely interpreted as penstroke formations.

DRIVE: A need or desire to some end, which compels or impels the individual toward that end. It both gives him his force, and forces him to use it. See also: MOTIVATION. For the trait, see Determination.

DYSFUNCTION: Literally: "ill-function" or "bad function." In medicine, an impaired functioning of an organ or part of the body, generally resulting from illness or injury.

Ee

Egotism/Ego-Strength: See: Pride, Self-Image.

ELABORATION, in handwriting: See: ORNAMENTATION

EMPHASIS: Additional attention given to or greater value placed on one object, idea, or activity, sometimes to the exclusion of another. In writing, an emphasized word or phrase is one which is capitalized, underlined, bolded, or in some other way marked out from the text as a demonstration of its greater significance.

EMPHATIC PUNCTUATION: By definition, the use of exclamation points and/or underlining to call attention to something the writer considers, or wants to have considered, more significant or worthy of notice than the ordinary; overuse of capitals would also be considered "punctuation" in this sense:

to do!! Can you imagine such a wierce wiee of acting?!!

An extreme use of emphatic punctuation is most often used by the writer who feels that he can't get his message noticed in any other way. It may also be used by a writer who feels that the language itself is not strong enough, or that his command of the language is inadequate without some kind of visual aid. But it is also, obviously, an attention-getter—a kind of written shout—and for whatever reason it is used, attention is what the writer needs.

EMOTION(S): In psychology, the affective experiences of an individual (or, more simply, how a given person feels about his experiences); in graphology, it is also the subjective perception of self and events (or, how the writer feels about himself and what is happening to him). Emotion is a central concept in handwriting analysis, since any sample of script is not so much a record of what the writer has actually done or experienced as it is a picture of how those experiences have affected him. Any analysis of handwriting must take into account the possibility that events may not have occurred, or that situations may not exist, as the writer perceived them; and also that the writer may not actually be the kind of person he believes he is—or accuses himself of being. See also: HANDWRITING.

Emotional (trait): Depending on feelings rather than facts to determine a course of behavior; and, in behavior, overly demonstrative. The tendency for emotional involvement in a given area or activity is shown by the width of loops in different zones of script (see: ZONES); the wider or fatter the loop, the greater the emotional involvement:

h e g: like to know what

The probable tendency to express that emotion (**demonstrative**) is shown in the script angle; the more extreme the slant (right or left), the greater the effect of emotion on the writer; and the further right, the greater the possibility of emotional outbursts. It should be noted that any emotional reaction, whether or not it's extreme and whether or not it's expressed, results in physical agitation (as; faster heartbeat and breathing, muscle tension, and even changes in glandular secretions); and this neuro-muscular reaction affects the individual's ability to reason. The more pronounced the emotional indicators in a script, the less able the writer will be to think coherently or cope rationally in in the areas(s) they affect.

Two extremes of emotional reaction are apathy and euphoria. **Apathy** is the inability to feel or to express feelings. It is indicated by light pressure rather than by loopless formations; extreme apathy is indicated when a script shows a combination of very wide loops and very faded pressure. **Euphoria** means being in a constantly stirred-up state, and is indicated by extreme looping combined with extreme slant (left or right), and usually variations of pressure.

Emotional Stability: The ability to function rationally even in situations which strongly affect the writer's feelings, or in face of events which affect something the writer feels strongly about. Emotional stability is indicated in any style of script which shows a firm baseline (qv).

END-STROKES/PRE-STROKES: Penstrokes added on to the beginning or end of a letter or word (see: ACCESSORY; CONNECTORS). Depending on the form they take, they may indicate such traits as: (a) insecurity (prop stroke); (b) contrived thought (wind-up stroke); (c) hesitation or uncertainty (tail prop); (d) affability (up-swinging end-stroke); and (e) defensiveness (back-stroke), among others:

$$\overset{\vee}{\prime}a \qquad \overset{\downarrow}{e}a \qquad a\underset{\downarrow}{\smile} \qquad a\!\!\!/\leftarrow \qquad \overset{\downarrow}{a}$$

(a)   (b)   (c)   (d)   (e)

These are generally negative indicators, especially if pronounced. See also separate entries for these traits.

Energy (characteristic): Physical vigor or strength; and we add the definition used in physics: the capacity to perform work. Physical energy is shown by firm pressure; the ability to sustain a given energy level is shown by steady pressure. As a factor in script, energy is the basis for such positive traits as determination, will power, and forcefulness. Where it is lacking in a style of script, there is the possibility that any other positive trait cannot be translated into action. (Chapter 5)

Enthusiasm (trait): *Joie de vivre*; the ability to become excited about a possible event or a task at hand; and the willingness to enjoy an experience or to find enjoyment in any experience. It is indicated in script by dashes for i-dots, especially if placed right of stem:

$$\overset{\vee}{\textit{i}} \quad : \qquad \textit{doing now? I miss}$$

Enthusiasm is a very positive trait. It is a controlled emotional reaction (i.e., the writer thinks the feeling, or decides its occurrence, rather than being dominated by it), and it can override such otherwise negative traits as (apparent) lack of energy or ambition. See also: Determination.

Evasive (trait): Using some subterfuge to hide the truth about yourself; self-concealment. Evasiveness may take the form of ambiguity, untruthfulness, or downright lying. As a combined trait, evasiveness includes several of the indicators for dishonesty (qv), such as deep double-looping or left-tending loops, contrived wind-up strokes, and words ending in scribbles or an illegible scrawl. It is distinguished from dishonesty, however, by signs of: (a) defensiveness (backstroke); (b) introversion, causing or caused by lack of carry-through (hesitant, left-side t-bars); and (c) lack of confidence (small capitals) or (d) lack of self-confidence (small pronoun I, especially if left-tending):

Unlike dishonesty, there is no self-indulgence in this trait, nor anything to be gained; it derives from feelings of personal inadequacy.

Another indicator for evasiveness is found *only* in samples written for analysis. Once you have told your subject that you can't analyze printing, and have also indicated that script can reveal very personal information about his makeup, if he then prints his sample, he is being evasive.

Exaggeration (characteristic): The tendency to dramatize, to make more of something than it is, either to show it off, or to attract attention (to it, or to yourself). A single script indicator for this tendency is the use of an over-size middle zone letter (as; an a, c, or s) to begin a word in the middle of a sentence; if the letter is printed, or set apart in some way, it amounts to an internal capitalization:

In a generally well-organized script, particularly if letter size is otherwise consistent, this formation indicates an appreciation of the dramatic. If the script as a whole also shows practical thinking and/or material drives, the addition of this formation is one indicator of possible sales ability. If, instead, the script is graceful, or shows signs of artistic potential (qv), it indicates a flair for the dramatic (though it does not necessarily indicate an actor: rather, the writer is someone who knows how to use dramatic emphasis, or who simply enjoys using it or seeing it used). If the exaggeration is overdone (as in this sample), it is a negative factor, generally practiced as a means of showing off (insecurity). In a disorganized script, and especially one that shows signs of emotionalism, it indicates a tendency to blow things up out of proportion.

As a combined trait, exaggeration is definitely a form of insecurity, and it is based on a need for attention. A single indicator here is the high-reaching endstroke up from the baseline (wants to be noticed); but note how easily it can swing back into defensiveness:

Other indicators for the combined trait are: (1) unneeded capitals, as in the middle of a sentence or a word (the need concealed but not suppressed; ineffectiveness); (2) abnormally large or flourished capitals (bragging); (3) frequent underscoring or excessive use of exclamation points (unnecessary emphasis); and, when found with these indicators, (4) over-wide spacing in words or letters (Extravagant (qv): the writer who is trying to take up more space than he needs or is able to use).

Extravagant (characteristic): Wasteful—which is exactly how it shows up in script. Over-widely spaced words and letters, wide spacing between lines, and wasted margin space: a wasteful use of writing materials. See also: Generous.

EXTREMES, in handwriting: Any overemphasis in script or penstroke formations or general style at either end of the spectrum, as: too much or too little, too big or too small, etc. (or both extremes together). Script extremes are a factor in disorganization; they indicate extreme reactions in related behavior, and a corresponding lack of self-control. See also: Emotional. (Chapter 1)

Fatigue (physical condition): A lack of physical energy, which may be the result of either overwork or illness. In terms of character/personality analysis, fatigue is an *unnatural condition*: i.e., due to (often temporary) circumstances which affect physical health, and not caused by the writer's normal emotions or innate incapacity to function. Light pressure is the indicator for lack of energy or forcefulness. In a well-organized, mature script, especially if angular and/or showing indicators for ambition, confidence, or similar self-assertive factors, it can be assumed that the light pressure indicates fatigue; it is also evident if a comparison of samples written at different times shows light pressure used in only one or two of the samples. It is generally not possible to be certain of this condition in other styles of script.

Fear/Timidity (emotional state): A state of apprehension or awareness of possible danger; in handwriting, referring specifically to concern for the self-image as potentially threatened by the actions of other people. A single indicator in script for this state of mind is a pronounced to extreme left tilt. As a combined trait (timidity: the inability to take decisive action), the script will also show: (a) very light-pressured, short, weak t-bars (indecisive), especially if low on the stem (feelings of inferiority); (b) small capitals, barely topping the middle zone (lack of confidence); (c) small and/or left-tending pronoun I (lack of self-confidence and/or fear of being hurt); (d) i-dots (or j-dots) left of stem (caution, suspicion); and (e) over-round double-looping (cooperation based on a fear of not co-operating); see: Insincerity:

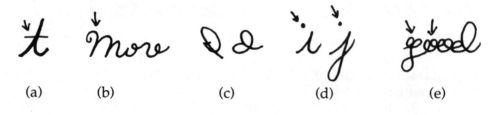

(a)   (b)   (c)   (d)   (e)

Timidity based on a sense of inadequacy is also indicated by any light-pressured, very rounded script; it is not uncommon, but should be carefully discouraged, in children's writing. See also: Insecurity.

FORM, in handwriting: The shape of letters (round, angular, scrawled) and penstrokes (slash, blunt, "original", etc.) in a sample of script. The overall letter and word form, including connectors, in a sample of script is an indicator of social attitudes; the shape of individual penstrokes reveals unconscious motivation (see: MOTIVATION). See also: ANGULAR; ROUNDED; SCRAWLED. (Chapter 8)

FREQUENCY, of usage: How often or how consistently a given formation shows up in a sample of handwriting. Frequent usage is an indicator of habit. See also: HABIT; PRONOUNCED USAGE.

Frustration (emotional state): The feeling of being unable to accomplish a goal or purpose; it may result either from a sense of personal inadequacy or a sense of external roadblocks. It is indicated in script by variation of pen pressure, and is thus both cause and effect of an inability to sustain determination or drive:

Indicators for frustration should not be confused with the use of heavy down-strokes or firm t-bars; see: Decisive; Determination.

Generosity (trait): Willingness or ability to share what you have, or to grant to others what is rightfully theirs; the trait is based primarily on strength of spirit. Genuine generosity is found in conjunction with other positive self-image indicators (it's hard to be generous when you're insecure!), plus indicators for friendliness (see: Gregarious; Warmth), and/or similar other-oriented factors. Basically a combined trait, a generous handwriting will show some or all of the following indicators in a well-organized script: (1) medium to large open ovals (qv), especially in the middle zone (receptivity, honesty); (2) wide, but *even*, spacing between words with (3) generous margins (in both cases, enough space allowed to make reading easy on the eyes and general presentation appealing); and sometimes, but not always, (4) the altruistic, or figure-eight g or f formation. In a disorganized script, indicators specific to generosity (2 and 3) may show wastefulness; see: Extravagant. For an example of a generous style, see American Schoolform handwriting sample, Chapter 10.

GRAPHOLOGY: The study of character and personality through the analysis of penstroke formations found in handwriting. Forms of handwriting analysis are described in the Introduction and in Chapter 14; see also: HANDWRITING.

Greed (drive): Avid acquisitiveness beyond reason; sometimes including or displayed as possessiveness (qv). Pronounced use of acquisitive hooks show the potential for this drive (sample a), especially in a disorganized script. As a combined trait, greed is also indicated by (b) tight over-crowding of letters and words, especially if combined with narrow to no margins (stingy: sample b); and (c) over-inflated lower zone loops (material acquisitiveness), especially if found in an extremely angular script:

(a)

(b)

(c) →

In reference to initial hooks, the basic difference between greed and acquisitiveness is *emphasis*; see: EXTREMES; FREQUENCY; PRONOUNCED USAGE.

Gregarious (attitude): This is graphology's word for "extroverted": outgoing, social-minded, and people-oriented. In general, any large size script, especially if right-tending, shows the tendency for this attitude. As a need or drive, gregariousness is indicated by wide loops in any script size; with wide, shortened loops showing a need for social involvement, and/or wide tall loops showing the need or drive toward social success:

As a combined trait (**friendliness**), gregariousness would include large size and tall, wide loops in a pronounced-right script. The better organized, the more comfortable the writer is in social contexts.

GUIDELINES: A structural format within which an action may be taken without questions as to its validity or propriety, and with a fair amount of confidence in its probable success. Guidelines for socialized behavior may be either acquired or established: that is; the individual may either accept the rules of order as laid down by his social group, or he may work out his own. In either case, the writer's feeling that he knows what to do, as well as the right way to do it, is shown in the relative firmness of the baseline (qv).

Guilt (emotional state): The feeling of having done something wrong (in the sense of immoral or illegal, as opposed to incorrect: for correct/incorrect, see: BASELINE; GUIDELINES). In its more extreme form, guilt is the feeling of being sinful; i.e., (a "bad" person in general). The script indicator for this debilitating emotion is the presence of excessive corrections and overstrokes throughout a sample; partly concealment of (what the writer sees as) mistakes, and primarily an obsession with getting it right that results in doing it wrong:

When guilt feelings are excessive, the script will also show other hesitant forms (as: prop and tail strokes), and twisted formations (see: Sexual Hangups), as well as indicators for insecurity, self-doubt, and similar self-paralyzing negative traits. As with any other attribute of this kind, its presence in script does not necessarily indicate that the writer has done anything to warrant feeling this way. See also: HANDWRITING.

Gullible (trait): Credulous; believing anything you're told, and hence, easily duped. It is indicated in script by wide-open formations both in closed and open letters, and/or by the cupped t-bar:

Gullibility is especially indicated if rounded forms show an immature or slow thinker. The writer who recognizes, as many do, that somehow his receptiveness to others is a cause of his being hurt or taken advantage of will also show indicators for emotional pain (see: Pain, emotional), sensitivity, withdrawal (left tilt), and similar reactive traits. See also: OPEN FORMATIONS.

HABIT: A customary way of doing things, acquired by repetition and showing itself both in ease of performance and in lowered resistance to avoidance. In handwriting, habit is shown by repeated use of any formations (and note: not all habits are bad!). Any "natural" (see: NORMAL) sample of handwriting shows habitual behavior patterns, in that the style has been acquired over a period of time. Individual habit reflexes, or specific habitual responses, are also shown in script by the repetition of individual penstroke formations; the nature of the writer's habits can be defined by analysis of these formations. See: FREQUENCY.

HANDWRITING: A learned motor-reflex skill which requires eye-hand coordination and fine-muscle control. Intellectually, it is a means of communicating thoughts and ideas; emotionally, it is a means of relating to others. As a behavior pattern, handwriting is a form of socialized behavior; and in graphology, it is a cohesive portrait of the interrelationships of individual character and personality traits. For purposes of the analysis, any sample of handwriting is considered to be picture of *tendencies* and *potentials*: what the writer believes himself to be, and what he feels himself capable of doing, rather than what has actually happened to him, or what he has actually done. Based on the analysis, however, probable behavior patterns can be predicted, and probable causes for these patterns defined.

Health Signs: See: Pain.

HIDDEN CAPITALS: See: INTERNAL CAPITALS.

Honesty (trait): Both truthful and frank in communication; free from deception or fraud. See also: Dishonesty. Like dishonesty, this trait has many facets and purposes; in general however, clarity of form shows nothing to hide, and any unadorned, legible, confident script style, especially if showing little to no internal looping (no double loops or diplomatic knot), and including clear, open ovals (open expression) shows the necessary qualities for this trait. Honesty is best determined by the absence of *all* indicators for dishonesty. See also: Conscientious; Bluntness.

HOOKS: Cup-shaped formations added onto the beginning or end of a pen-stroke. In letters or words they are generally placed where connectors would be if the letter were joined to another at that point; they can also appear on t-bars. Down-turned hooks (inverted cup) are also called **claws**. See: Acquisitive; Critical; Vindictive. (Chapter 7)

Humor (trait): The ability to see, and to enjoy, the ludicrous or comical, even in yourself. Humor is indicated in script by wavy horizontals in the i-dots and t-bars, especially if graceful:

If over-done, or if found in a script showing lack of determination, or the presence of other unusual attention-getting formations, it can indicate a generally frivolous nature.

Note that the sinuous t-bar is not the same as a sinuous baseline; it's the difference between a deliberate formation and an uncontrollable one. The t-bar equivalent of an erratic baseline would show change of direction in individual t-bars in relation to each other throughout the sample.

Hypersensitive: See: Sensitive.

"IDEAL" FORMATION: In graphology, that use of any given script factor in a form which indicates that the writer has a greater internal sense of security, and/or a better chance of controlling his environment, than he would if he used some other form of the same script factor. For example: firm or steady is the "ideal baseline," because it reveals that the writer has a clear sense of objectives and is therefore not as vulnerable to negative circumstances as he would be if he used any other baseline formation. A specific formation is described as ideal not because it is necessarily the best usage, but because it has proven to be positive for most people; its use indicates that the writer finds it easier to cope in that particular area of his life. The ideal form of most trait indicators and penstroke formations was described in the text as that usage showing good organization.

"Ideal National Personality": See: Schoolform.

IDENTITY WORDS: Names and pronouns used by a writer in reference to himself. See also: Internal Self-Image. Identity words include the pronoun I, the signature (or any other use the writer makes of his own name), and "me" formations (all other words, pronouns, or titles in a sample which the writer uses as descriptions or references to self). The formation and usage of these terms reveal the writer's feelings about and attitude toward himself. A description of identity words also includes usage of "you" formations as an indicator of how the writer rates himself in reference to others; see: Comparative Self-Image. (Chapter 9)

IDIOSYNCRASIES, Mechanical: The physical materials used in writing a sample of script (as: type and size of paper, type of writing tool, etc.); also the use made of such materials. While notes and memoranda may be scribbled on or with anything that comes to hand without indicating much more than the unavailability of better materials, a consistent use of unique, and especially of eye-catching, materials are an indicator of a need to be noticed. What the writer wants to be noticed for depends on the choice of the attention-getter: elegant materials are generally a play for social acceptance or admiration, while deliberately crude or unattractive materials may show disdain and lack of consideration for others, etc. See also: Insecurity. (Review II)

Illness, physical or emotional: See: Pain.

Imagination (potential): The ability to experience sensations or visualize objectives not physically present or which have no actual existence, or to synthesize original ideas from events or information experienced separately. Imagination can be either a positive or negative trait, depending on both the type of mental image and the purpose(s) for imagining it. A single indicator for either possibility is high-flying i-dots: placed to the right of stem (a) imagination is positive and often creative (see: Ingenuity); if placed to the left (b) the writer has a tendency to suspect (or even fear) the worst. Imagination used in an unsubstantial way (as; fantasizing to no practical purpose) is the trademark of the day-dreamer or visionary. This tendency is indicated in script by t-bars above (and not touching) the stem (c):

i: This is a sample of my (a)

i: but its not as if he didn't (b)

i: Three years. Can it be (c)

As a combined trait (**creative thinking**), imagination is indicated in script by: (1) high-flying i-dots, especially if right of stem; (2) tall strokes into the upper zone (mental reach), with (3) full upper zone loops, especially if the upper part of the loop is very wide (the more enlarged and flourished, the greater the emotional involvement with imagination and fantasy); (4) long, upswinging t-bars (added mental reach); and (5) intuitive breaks in words, and/or printing mixed with script (intuition; see also: WORD BREAKS). For applied imagination, see: Ingenuity.

Immaturity (characteristic): Defined in graphology as a lack of confident self-direction or self-determination, resulting in or characterized by mental and emotional dependence on others. Immaturity is indicated in script by childish writing: ie; concentration of writing in the middle zone, especially if primarily rounded forms are used. It is generally not difficult to distinguish the hand-writing of an immature adult from that of a young child, since the adult's script formations will be smoother and more coordinated (i.e., more practiced):

I am spending the holidays

Immature writing is normal in a child's script, since the need for physical and emotional security is dominant in the growing years, and obedience to authority is considered (or, is taught as!) a behavioral plus. In an adult's script it still means immaturity but becomes a much more negative indicator. See also: Cooperation; Schoolform.

Impatience: See: Patient.

IMPLICATION, of a script factor: Relative interpretation; a definition of meaning in terms of the script being analyzed. Also, an adjustment of script or penstroke interpretation based on individual differences or circumstances; as, for example, skill allowances made in the analysis of children's handwriting. See also: INTERPRETATION. (Chapter 11)

Impulsive (trait): Tending to take action without preplanning or forethought (or sometimes, premonition!). In handwriting *as an action*, planning starts at the left and is completed at the right, and a single indicator in script for impulsiveness is the t-bar that begins right of stem:

$$\mathcal{t}\ \mathcal{t}: \quad \mathcal{I}\ can't\ seem\ to\ do$$

This usage is typical of the writer who tends to act before he thinks. An extreme right tilt also shows a tendency toward (emotional) impulsiveness: i.e., more in the sense of impulsive reactions than in the area of planning ability. See also: Procrastination.

Inconsiderate (attitude): Not regarding or concerned with the rights or feelings of others; sometimes deliberately ignoring them. Any scrawled writing style indicates a lack of concern for other people's reactions, especially when it is a "natural" style (normal for that writer) and/or is used in a communication intended for someone else's eyes. (The writer who scrawls a note to himself is not thinking of other people's convenience either, but other people are not involved in this action, and it does not mean he might not consider others under different circumstances.) A scrawled style that is also sloppy or crude indicates contempt for others.

INCONSISTENCIES, in handwriting: Variations or contradictions in trait indicators or penstroke formations (as; a combination of right and left angle), or "out of place" formations (as opposed to "one of a kind" formations: repeated appearance of some penstroke usage which is at odds with the general style; for example, a consistently left-tending pronoun I in a right-angle script). Script inconsistencies are a factor in poor organization, and in general indicate stress (qv).

Independence (characteristic): Self-governing; the ability to make a decision or take an action without the advice or emotional support of someone in a position of authority (or, someone seen as being in a position of authority by the writer). Independence takes two forms, which are not necessarily related: (1) **self-sufficiency**, or independence of social pressures, which is shown in a vertical script, or in a tall, loopless, vertical to controlled-right pronoun I (independent self-image); and (2) **self-determination**, or independence of thought and action, shown in any writing which is not dominated by the middle zone, or by angular formations in the middle zone. Either of these last two indicators, when they first begin to appear in a young writer's script, can be the first sign of developing maturity. See also: Immaturity.

INDICATOR: In general, any device or apparatus which registers or measures something. In graphology, these "measuring devices" consist of script and penstroke formations, and they measure *symptoms*, or potentials for behavior.

Inferiority (emotional state): A sense of being inadequate, in ability and/or in comparison to others. It is indicated in script by a t-bar placed low on the stem:

Feelings of personal inadequacy are also indicated by the use of small capitals (low confidence) and a small pronoun I (low self-confidence). See also: Comparative Self-Image.

Inflexible (attitude): Unwilling or unable to adapt to changing circumstances; also, unwilling or unable to accept the possibility of (your own) error. Inflexibility is a negative aspect of decisiveness, and is indicated in script primarily by a rigid baseline; rigid angularity is also an indicator for this attitude, but more in the sense of uncompromising than unadaptable.

Ingenuity (potential): Graphology's word for *creativity*: the ability to produce something which did not exist before, or to make unique or creative use of something common or ordinary. As a positive trait, ingenuity is indicated by the use of original formations (qv), specifically those which enable the writer to take short cuts without sacrificing legibility ("improving the use"); it becomes an indicator of creativity when found in a medium (adaptable) size script. As a combined trait (see Figure 2, next page), ingenuity is shown as practical, or applied, creativity, and is indicated in script by:
(a) a medium-size script showing *both* original formations and a careful attention to detail (i-dots, t-bars, punctuation precisely in place); and in all script sizes, indicators for:
(b) imagination (high-flying i-dots);
(c) versatility (t-bars varied as needed to suit script flow);
(d) intuition (word breaks, especially at logical points in long words and/or following capitals; or mixed printing and cursive styles, where it clarifies meaning without slowing down writing speed);
(e) intellectual orientation (tall upper zone verticals); and
(f) mental alertness (pointed inverted cups, such as the m and n).
Overall good organization is a graphic demonstration that the writer's ingenuity can be practically applied.

Inhibition (attitude): Graphology's "introversion": the inability to communicate or act freely; impeded self-expression. Its effect may range from shyness to paralyzing fear. The tendency to inhibited expression is indicated in any left-tilted writing, in either the overall script angle, or in individual identity words. As a combined trait, inhibition indicators include: (1) a pronounced to extreme left tilt (inability to communicate), especially in a small script (withdrawal, an attempt to go unnoticed), or in a very light pressured script (lack of

FIGURE 2
Creative Writing: Forms of Ingenuity as Shown in Script

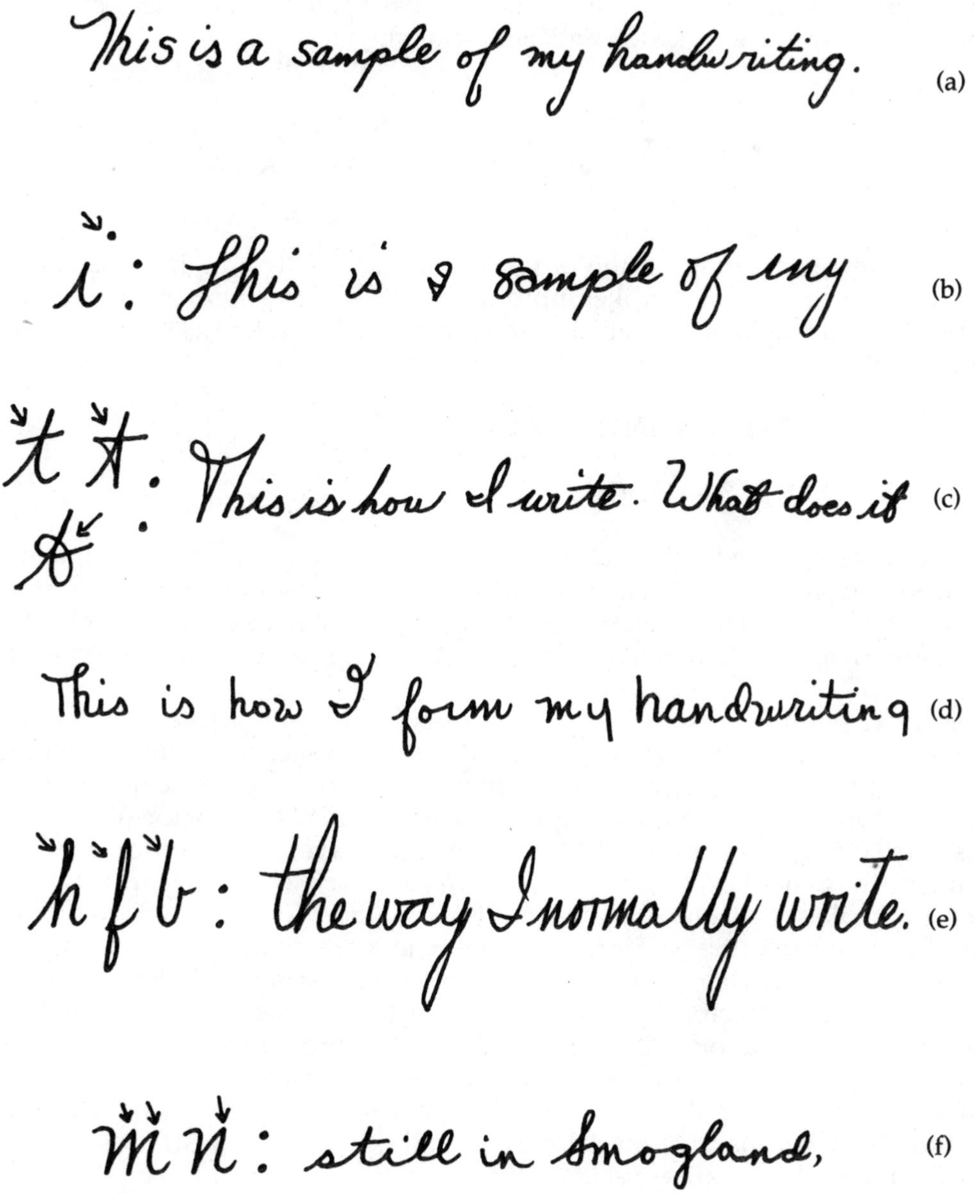

This is a sample of my handwriting. (a)

i: This is a sample of my (b)

t t: This is how I write. What does it (c)

This is how I form my handwriting (d)

h f b: the way I normally write. (e)

m n: still in Smogland, (f)

assertiveness); (2) a small, left-tending pronoun I (fear of being hurt); (3) inferior illegibility (as opposed to a deliberate scrawl: guilt, concealment), especially if found in a compressed, jammed-together script (trying not to take up too much space. This compression exists specifically where there is room on the paper for more writing; it is not stinginess); (4) a convex t-bar ("capping": showing control of expression and aspirations):

and/or similar capping on the pronoun I; and (5) left-swinging finals, especially the defensive backstroke. Inhibition as lack of self-assertiveness is indicated in a very light script which also shows sensitivity or insecurity (i.e., not "pushy").

INITIAL CAPITAL: See: INTERNAL CAPITAL.

INITIAL HOOKS: See: HOOKS.

INITIAL/TERMINAL: Penstrokes that begin (initial) or end (terminal) a letter or word, regardless of whether or not they are accessories. In general, initial strokes refer back to the self, or to planning (as; initial hooks: acquisitive); terminal formations refer to others, or to carry-through (as; terminal hooks: critical).

Insecurity (emotional state): A feeling of being unsafe or threatened, and of needing assurance; in its more pronounced form, insecurity is the graphological **anxiety** (in psychology: apprehension or a continuing and painful uneasiness of mind over an impending or anticipated ill). As a factor in behavior, insecurity may be expressed in a variety of ways, from conformity (see: Immaturity; Schoolform) to anti-social attitudes such as jealousy (qv); whatever form it takes, however, it is dependence on others for ego-support, or, more simply, means that the writer is someone who lacks an adequate internal self-image. In handwriting, it is indicated by a variety of script styles and formations, including specifically: (1) pronounced to extreme left *or* extreme right tilt (over-reaction to other peoples' behavior); (2) pre-strokes and end-strokes, especially prop-strokes (need for assurance); (3) light-pressured, loopy script (lack of assertiveness due to sensitivity); (4) a wavering baseline (indecision, self-doubt; due to lack of guidelines); and, more than the rest, (5) the "fetal" pronoun I (withdrawal), especially if small:

Insecurity can also take some unrecognizable forms, and you should be on the alert for them. One such reaction in particular is egotism, shown in over-sized, over-flourished capitals or an over-blown pronoun I. In any analysis judgement, look for insecurity first (and sensitivity next) as the probable causative factor in any negative trait or attitude. You may be surprised at where you find it.

Insincerity (trait): Either hypocrisy or false pretenses, usually based on a need to conceal what the writer feels are unlikable qualities in himself; a form of insecurity. See also: Dishonesty. A single script indicator for this trait is double looping on open formations (or, frankness overridden by concealment, of both self and attitudes toward others). Note that this formation also decreases the legibility of the letter, often making it unidentifiable (or, altering its intention):

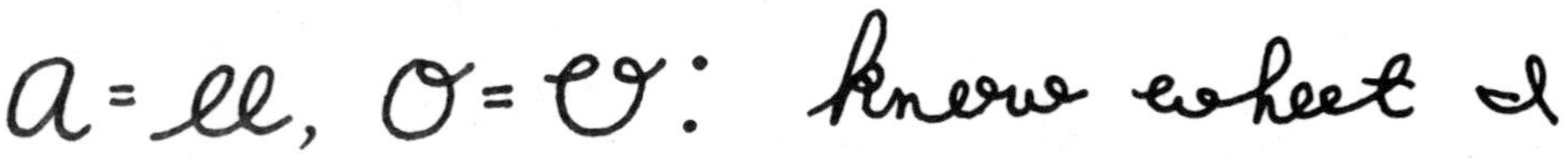

$$a = ll, \quad O = \mathcal{O} : \quad \textit{know wheet d}$$

As a combined trait (see Figure 3 below), insincerity as an overall hand-writing style will show:

(a) a fanciful, stylized (or, designed) script (false pretenses: and a school-form style, when adopted for a particular occasion, also falls into this category); or

(b) over-ornamentation or flourishes, especially if crude or resulting in decreased legibility (a false front).

Within a script style, indicators are:

(c) fancy curled or twisted wind-up or end-strokes (hesitant communication showily disguised: guilt);

(d) misplaced capitals, as in the middle of a word, and/or

(e) excessive underlining or use of exclamation points (an attention-getting device; overrating the importance of a statement, to distract attention from the writer, or from what the writer considers a general inadequacy of performance); and

(f) ovals open at the bottom (concealed motives):

FIGURE 3
Insincerity Formations in Script

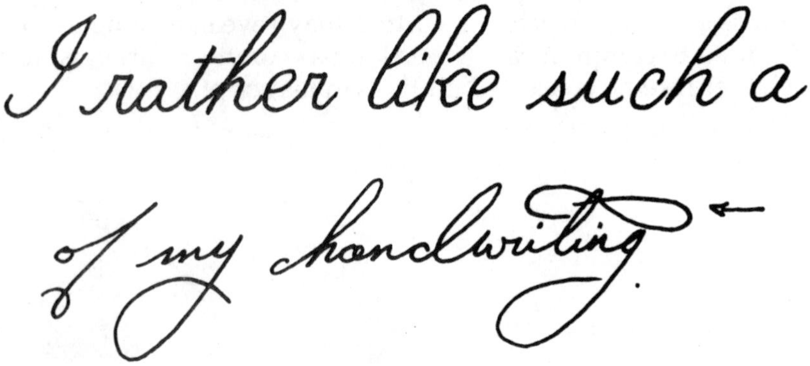

I rather like such a (a)

of my chandwriting (b)

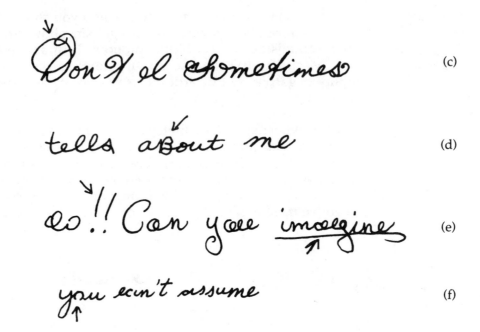

(c)

(d)

(e)

(f)

Insincerity is distinguished from dishonesty in its motivation: the insincere writer genuinely, and sometimes desperately, wants to be liked, and his script will also show indicators for sensitivity (loopiness), emotional dependence on others (extreme tilts), or attempts at gregariousness (large or bold writing). He is lying *about himself* only because he is convinced that the others whose approval he wants and needs would not like him if they really knew him.

Instability: See: Unpredictable.

Intelligence: See: Mental Alertness.

INTENTION: The purpose for any action or behavior. Analysis makes a distinction between *implied intention*, which is stated as the reason for an action, and *actual intention*, which is the doer's true purpose. In handwriting, for example, the implied intention is communication: the purpose of writing is to transmit thoughts and ideas. The actual intention may vary from writer to writer, and is determined from the meaning of any formation which impedes script flow or conceals meaning. See also: ACCESSORY. Note that intention is not synonymous with meaning; whatever the writer may be saying, and/or whatever traits or characteristics his writing may reveal, as long as he is genuinely attempting to communicate (or, as long as communication is his primary objective), there are no concealed motives in his script.

INTERNAL CAPITAL: In general, any capital letter which is used in the middle of a sample or in the middle of a sentence (as; the pronoun I, or capitalization of proper nouns). As a measure of the writer's ability to sustain confidence or self-confidence, the size and formation of internal capitals are compared with the usage for the **initial capital** (usually, the capital used to begin a sample; also a capital used to begin a sentence). See: Confidence; Self-Confidence.

Hidden capitals are any capital letters which appear in the middle of a word. This form of internal capitalization is a reach into the upper zone from the middle zone; it indicates a need for recognition:

What kind of recognition the writer requires depends on the form the capital takes; see also: ORIGINAL FORMATIONS.

Internal Self-Image: How the writer sees himself; his own judgement of his value and adequacy as a human being, or lack of it. It is determined in analysis by the formation of the pronoun I, and by its relationship in size and form to other letters and words in a given script sample. See also: Confidence; Self-Confidence; Self-Image. (Chapter 9).

INTERPRETATION, of script factors: In graphology, stating or explaining the actual meaning of a script factor; also, the generalized meaning of that factor at any time, in anyone's handwriting. The interpretation of a script factor gives its "pure meaning": i.e., as unaffected by the significance of any other factors found in the same script sample. See also: IMPLICATION. (Chapter 11)

Intuition (potential): Insight; the ability to know or understand without conscious reasoning. It is assumed that intuitive perception results from a sudden recognition of the interrelationship of events, facts, or causes and effects, which data have been stored in the memory and then correlated and released by the unconscious in reaction to some final stimulus. In handwriting, the probability that the individual has, uses, or is affected by intuitive flashes is shown by word breaks (qv), especially scattered word breaks, which may be found even in very short words (the sporadic interruption of the flow of reasoned thought). It is not being stated that every word break in a script sample indicates the occurrence of a flash of intuition on the part of the writer; rather, that their presence implies that the writer is someone who recognizes, or who has the capability of using, intuitive thought. Since this type of perception does interrupt the flow of writing (and, hence, interferes with a conscious intention or planned action), it is considered a positive indicator only in a well-organized script.

IRREGULAR FORMATIONS: See: INCONSISTENCIES, in handwriting.

Irritability (emotional state): A diffused form of anger (qv); general impatience or fretfulness which makes the individual unreasonably susceptible to annoyance. The potential for this reaction, or its current existence as an emotional state of mind, is indicated by v-shaped or inverted-v i-dots, or by sharp down-turned initial or up-turned terminal hooks on t-bars:

ĭ ĭ t̆: vacation any season is fine

As a combined trait, irritability is indicated by frequent or pronounced use of slashing strokes or sharp terminal hooks, as well as: (1) heavy-pressured angularity; (2) down-slanted sharp or club-like t-bars and lower zone terminals; and (3) tangled words and lines (sustained anger discombobulates you!), sometimes with pressure variation. See also: Anger; Critical; Frustration.

Jj, Kk

Jealousy (emotion): Extreme possessiveness in relation to some other person; the need to "own" that other, often expressed as suspicion or mistrust of that other's faithfulness, truthfulness, or motives. Note that our definition does not include the concept of envy; for its possible existence, see Greed. Jealousy is not love, nor based on it; it is a reactive form of insecurity. The potential is indicated in script by an extreme right tilt (emotional dependence on others). As a combined trait, jealousy is indicated by: (1) any extreme tilt, left or right (insecurity in personal relationships); (2) an extremely small pronoun I (no internal resources/lack of self-belief), especially if showing extreme tilt (left: insecurity; right: emotional dependence); and (3) small capitals (lack of confidence in general), all in a script showing pronounced to extreme use of acquisitive hooks (avarice).

Kindliness (attitude): A sympathetic, or sometimes empathetic, affection for others. Like a combined trait, kindliness is a general, or overall, attitude, and is indicated in script by: (1) a controlled right tilt (warmth for and trust of others but without emotional dependence); (2) indicators for generosity (qv); and (3) the absence of anti-personal or anti-social indicators such as critical or sarcastic hooks or slashes, anger signs, etc. It is more likely to be found in a medium or medium-light pressured script, and may or may not also show signs of sensitivity (qv).

KNOTS AND TIES: Just what it sounds like: any penstroke formation shaped to look like a fastening knot or tie. Knots and ties may indicate tenacity, stubbornness, or, in a disorganized script, ineffectiveness in the sense of getting bogged down in unnecessary complications. (Chapter 7)

Ll

Laziness (trait): The unwillingness to make an effort, or to exert either mind or body toward the accomplishment of some task or goal. Extremely light, or "fade-away" pen pressure in a very rounded script (where the handwriting shows no signs of either pain or sensitivity) indicates a primarily physical laziness; if the script emphasizes the middle zone, then mental laziness is indicated as well. As a combined trait, the light, over-rounded style may also show: (1) varied slants (a tendency to follow the course of least resistance); (2) uneven pressure and spacing (carelessness); (3) hesitant t-bars and i-dots left of stem (lack of carry-through); and very often (4) "garland" form roundness (see: ROUND WRITING).

LITERACY: The mechanical ability to read and write. It improves, like any other skill, with practice, and is shown in handwriting by ease and fluency of letter forms. The degree of a writer's literacy is in no way a reflection of his intelligence, but it is important in forming analysis conclusions. Many otherwise negative indicators, such as hesitant forms, awkward to disorganized styles, unaggressive or even "lazy" writing, are found in a semi-literate script, and indicate nothing more than unfamiliarity with the skill. Exceptions of this nature (i.e., a judgement of lack of skill as opposed to a judgement of negative character or personality traits), should be made for the writing of young children, the newly-literate, and anyone who normally speaks or thinks—and originally learned to write—in some language other than the one in which the sample was written.

Literal (trait): Absolute adherence to the (learned as) best and correct way of getting a job done. Literal reasoning is extremely rational, effective, and structured, but it is also unimaginative and not particularly creative. It is indicated in script by a complete lack of word breaks, even in the longest words; if the script also lacks indicators for imagination and ingenuity, you have a writer who prefers to just follow orders. See also: Conformity; WORD BREAKS.

Logical (trait): Able to make reasoned judgements based on the facts available. Logical reasoning can be imaginative, but it does not generally rely on, make use of, or even particularly trust intuitive leaps. It is indicated in script by word breaks at logical points: ie; at the syllable break, or hyphenation point of the word, especially in longer words. See also: WORD BREAKS.

LOOP: Any penstroke formation in the general shape of an oval, half bow, or (closed) fold; the effect is of an open space, elongated in shape, which is surrounded and enclosed by boundary lines. In handwriting, loops are formed by return strokes for ascenders and descenders; their presence and width indicates (the writer's) degree of emotional involvement. See also: CLOSED FORMATIONS; KNOTS AND TIES. (Chapter 7).

LOWER-CASE LETTERS: All letters in an alphabet style which are not capitals (qv); whether or not these letters also extend into the upper and lower zones of script, they all begin and end in the middle zone.

Mm

MAJOR TRAIT INDICATORS: Script formations; larger blocks of writing, which affect the style of a sample as a whole. In terms of the analysis, they picture general character or personality traits which the writer is usually aware of, though he may not be able to control or use them. These traits are called *major traits*, partly because they are the most obvious, and partly because they are the most "natural" to the writer (i.e., they would be the writer's normal behavior if nothing else interfered). See also: MOTIVATION; PENSTROKE FORMATIONS. For the script formations which picture them, see: BASELINE; ANGLE; SIZE; PRESSURE; and ZONES.

MARGIN(S): White space framing a sample of handwriting; the unused portions of a sheet of paper above, below, and on either side of a block of writing. Marginal quality is a minor (or, secondary) organizational indicator, and is used to measure both general planning ability and social attitudes. Marginal width combined with a measurement of space between lines of writing is also an indicator of generosity or thrift. (Review II)

Materialistic (attitude): Placing value on physical possessions; a collecting and/or hoarding tendency, which may or may not also involve acquisitiveness, possessiveness, or greed. Inflated lower zone loops are indicators of both physical and material drives. If the drives are materialistic, then angularity will appear in the loops, and/or be pronounced in the middle zone:

Where the writer intends to earn what he wants to own, or directs most of his planning ability toward these ends, the script will also show upper zone extensions (but with a greater lower zone emphasis). Greed is indicated if acquisitive hooks (qv) are pronounced. The further left the lower loops swing as a unit, the greater the possibility of possessiveness. In a script like this sample, where ostentation is also indicated, material possessions may be seen as a means of buying security or friends.

Maturity (characteristic): Mental and emotional independence; the ability and willingness to assume personal responsibility for your own behavior and the results of it. In handwriting maturity, *whatever the chronological age of the writer*, is considered a function of mental and emotional growth, and is shown by extensions into the upper and lower zones (a growing away from emotional dependence on significant others) and/or at least some angularity in the middle zone (independence of thought). For example:

Mark, age 12

This sample is a child's script (chronological age 12), but a mature (or, maturing) handwriting. It shows both balanced extensions and the beginning of independent opinions (note the middle zone angularity, as well as pointed ascenders and descenders). Emotional dependence is retained here only in the pronounced to extreme right tilt. See also: Immaturity; Independence.

Mental Alertness (trait): Graphology's clue to the existence of intelligence; the ability to recognize the difference between a recommended procedure and a more effective one. It is indicated primarily by pointed tops on m's and n's (a quicker and more effective way to write these letters). These are usually the first letters to go angular in a maturing script, and may also be angular in an adult roundhand; they are considered an indicator of mental alertness because they fall into the middle zone (i.e., a challenge to imposed group values). Mental alertness is also indicated by additional evidence of controlled angularity throughout the handwriting.

High, narrow, upper zone extensions, showing mental activity with control (or, if loopless, with suppression) of emotional involvement are also a clue to this trait, as an indicator of intellectual curiosity:

As a combined trait (**applied mental capacity**), the script would show mental alertness and curiosity, plus indicators for good planning, determination, self-control and self-confidence, and similar attributes. *Note* that actual level of intelligence cannot be determined from script: only the nature of its use.

MOOD: A temporary and usually quickly passing emotional reaction. It may or may not be caused by some event outside the individual's control. The form it takes, however, will be dictated by his own internal makeup.

MOTIVATION: A force *within* the individual, as opposed to any external event or stimulus, which determines his reaction to situations or events; any idea, drive, emotion, or organized state (need) which prompts or incites him to action. **Conscious motivation** is intellectually controlled: the individual mentally determines a course of action or is acutely aware of the reason for or causes of a given reaction. **Unconscious motivation** is an underlying cause for behavior; basic elements in the individual's makeup which influence his choice of action or type of reaction, but generally without volition. While the individual may be aware of the existence of these inner forces, he is generally unaware of the extent of their influence on his behavior in a given set of circumstances, or unable to control them.

$$\mathcal{N}_{m}$$

NATURAL, style of writing: The way the individual normally writes. A natural sample would be one which was not written for analysis, or for inspection by some person seen by the writer as having authority. Natural behavior in general is typical for that person, or generally unselfconscious.

NEED: An emotional or organic state requiring satisfaction or fulfillment; a hunger. It is the basic motivating force of most drives (qv).

Need for Attention (trait): Probably the most common trait in human nature; the need or drive to be noticed and admired for what you are or what you have accomplished. Where the writer feels his own resources are inadequate (usually because he is not getting as much attention as he needs, or is getting the wrong kind) he will usually resort to some pretense (qv) to attract notice or admiration. This reaction is indicated in script by the use of some unusual and often unoriginal formation; the most common is the circled i-dot:

$$\overset{\circ}{\mathcal{i}} : \; Sometimes \; I \; think$$

Other unusual formations in the script provide clues to the cause of this form of insecurity. See also: ORNAMENTATION.

NEGATIVE INDICATOR: Any script formation which defines an attribute detrimental to the writer's well-being. "Negative" in this sense does not mean bad, anti-social, or sinful: it is some factor or behavior pattern which puts unnecessary roadblocks in the writer's path, depletes his energy, undermines his relationships with others, puts him on the wrong track, and/or results in his achieving unwanted results (which results can often be the exact opposite of goals he set out to achieve). As with positive attributes, it is usually self-reinforcing (qv); unlike positive attributes it is also, more often than not, unconsciously motivated (see: MOTIVATION). A negative trait or characteristic may exist as an underlying need or drive in the writer's makeup (as, for example, insecurity); or it may take the form of a single reaction or behavior pattern that exists as an inappropriate response to a need or drive (as, need for attention).

NORMAL: In reference to letter shapes and writing style, normal refers to a traditional, or generally accepted, technical way of writing them (see: SCHOOLFORM). In reference to individual reactions or behavior patterns, normal means customary for or natural to *that writer* (see: HABIT; CHARAC-TERISTIC). In reference to human behavior in general, there is no such attribute. "Normal" in this sense represents an average, not an ideal, and is unlikely to be demonstrated by any one individual. See also: GUIDELINES; SOCIALIZED BEHAVIOR.

OPEN FORMATION: Any penstrokes with space left between the beginning and the ending point, leaving an entrance or an egress; in the script alphabet, these are normally cup formations. Open formations are an indicator of receptivity (and sometimes honesty); i.e., openness of expression. (Chapter 7)

OPEN OVALS: Circular or oval-shaped formations, such as closed formations or loops, which are clearly formed and smoothly shaped, and show no internal penstroke formations. They may or may not also be open formations (qv). Open ovals are generally an indicator of honesty (qv).

Opinionated (attitude): Considering one's own views to be the only acceptable measure. Any angular script style is an indicator that the writer thinks for himself. However, this negative version of independent reasoning ability is shown by extreme angularity in the middle zone, translated as uncompromising rigidity in social areas.

Optimism (attitude): The feeling or belief that somehow, someway, everything will manage to work out for the best, and usually by itself. This is a general orientation rather than a passing mood. Its potential is shown in the upslanting t-bar or i-dot:

As a controlling factor (qv), optimism is indicated in script by a consistent upward flow in the baseline (qv).

ORGANIZATION: The overall structural co-ordination of a sample of handwriting; also, the sum of and relative usage of all trait indicators and penstroke formations. Script organization is a an indicator of the writer's ability to function effectively. See also: COMPLICATIONS; INCONSISTENCIES; and EXTREMES. (Chapter 1)

ORIGINAL/UNUSUAL FORMATIONS, in handwriting: Creative or unique use of penstrokes in forming letters and words. *Original formations* are those which have been designed by the writer to compliment his own script style or forward his actual intention (as; an alteration of connector strokes to assist flow). *Unusual formations* are those which do not fit with the script style (as; a single-letter change in tilt, single-stroke angularity in a roundhand, etc.). Either formation is considered positive if it assists the flow of script, and negative if it impedes script flow or obscures meaning. Use of original formations, whether positive or negative, is considered evidence of ingenuity (qv). The presence of unusual formations indicates that some extremely affective event has occurred in the writer's life or that some change may be taking place in his makeup. See also: ORNAMENTATION. (Chapter 7)

ORNAMENTATION: Decoration, design, or elaboration added to the basic letterform penstroke with the intent of making it more artistic, more attractive to the eye, or more fun to write. Ornamentation is a negative script indicator, in that it most definitely impedes the smooth flow of writing; it may or may not indicate a negative character trait. See also: ARTISTIC.

Pp

Pain: A continuous ache or suffering, physical or emotional, caused by some disorder or dysfunction which results from either illness or injury. Recovery or cure is generally not subject to the conscious control of the individual, although he may choose to ignore the presence of the pain. It is considered an *abnormal condition*, in that it is not based on or typical to the writer's own makeup or behavior.

Emotional pain usually falls into the category of an inflicted injury, real or imagined. It can be identified in script by the presence of some unusual formation (qv): a striking contradiction between the usage of an emotional indicator (often the pronoun I) and the rest of the script style. One such contradiction exists in American Schoolform style (the self-critical return-stroke angularity); here is another:

It's a comedy & I play the bad guy.

This script style "should not" show a left-tilting pronoun I; and the I itself, if it were vertical to right, would not show low ego-strength. Measured along its length, it is as tall as script capitals or taller, and at least as tall as most upper zone loops (except for mental reach indicators, which are normally much higher than other upper zone formations in an intellectual or spiritual script). This writer has not suffered ego-damage, but he has been badly hurt by an intense emotional experience, and is protecting his ego from any further such hurts by literally drawing his head into a shell. This type of emotional pain (and, in fact, most types of affective damage to the self-image), is usually the result of a negative experience with someone the writer loved very deeply. Emotional pain can also take more general forms, such as loneliness (an extreme right tilt with a squeezed-down or non-existent middle zone, or an extreme left tilt with an oversized middle zone, among others); look for it in scripts showing insecurity and especially withdrawal.

Physical pain shows up as a heavier dot on some part of the letter stroke. Where it shows up (what zone) indicates generally where on the body the pain is located:

a b g: would like to know

The dot, an ink blob, is caused by a sudden hesitation and/or sudden heavier pressure at that point on the penstroke, resulting from a stab of pain; the severity of the pain is indicated by the frequency of the dots.

Physical illness shows up in script as wavering or blotched letter forms (especially if accompanied by pain dots); or as a "hitching stroke," caused by a jerk of the pen and resulting from the physical dysfunction:

is of sample of how I normally

Not surprisingly, severe illness is often accompanied by other negative indicators. In such cases it is reasonable to assume that at least part of the script disorganization exists because a severely ill individual cannot smoothly control his physical reflexes. (Chapter 12)

Patient (trait): Unhurried and generally undisturbed by obstacles, delays, and/or the amount of extra effort it may take to do a job properly. Patience is indicated in script by even, medium pressure accompanied by careful attention to detail, as shown in precise placement of i-dots, t-bars, and punctuation:

t i: This is a sample of my writing.

As a combined trait, this even-tempered precision will also be accompanied by a general neatness (or tidiness) of style, and clarity of form. The writer whose patience extends to an understanding (or, at least, a tolerant acceptance) of other people's foibles will also show little to no signs of sensitivity in his script (see: Sensitivity). In an angular and/or mature script, patience indicates a careful planner. In a rounded and/or immature script, it usually indicates a slow thinker.

Impatience is indicated in a scrawled, careless style showing heavier and/or uneven pressure and word spacing. In its more positive aspects, such a script will generally show indicators for enthusiasm (qv) as well.

PATTERN, of behavior: A general or specific mode of conduct, generated by internal motivators and having their satisfaction as its goal. A personal way of acting or reacting.

PENSTROKE FORMATIONS: Shapes, designs or figures formed by the movement of pen on paper. In handwriting analysis, penstroke usage in forming letters and/or accessories to letters reveal unconscious motivators; their cumulative effect is shown in overall organization and the major trait indicators. (Chapter 7)

Perception: See: Mental Alertness.

PERSONALITY: The outer "I," or surface character. The social mask as presented by the individual to others. See also: PROJECTED SELF-IMAGE.

Pessimism (attitude): The feeling that no matter what you do, somehow everything is going to turn out for the worst. This is a general orientation, and not necessarily based on either unhappiness or depression. It is shown in script by a consistent downward flow to the baseline. See also: Depression; BASELINE.

Physical Health: See: Pain; Fatigue.

Planning Ability (characteristic): The ability to establish in advance the method by which a predetermined goal will be achieved; also called goal-oriented planning. It is indicated in script by t-bar balance, margin balance (see: MARGINS), good organization, and evidence of personal self-control.

PLAY: An unstructured and self-determined activity which permits the individual to experiment with skills, abilities and possibilities. In handwriting, some forms of ornamentation (qv) or other evidence of experimentation with penstroke shapes with the purpose of exploring their possibilities are evidence of play; in general penstroke analysis, play is the conscious intention of doodling (qv).

POSITIVE INDICATOR: Any script formation which defines an attribute beneficial to the writer. A positive trait or characteristic is one which helps the writer to cope; which enables him to work effectively, deal with obstacles, get along well in his environment, and achieve—or proceed toward—his goals; and/or which provides a means by which he can develop and exploit his own individual potential(s). See also: NEGATIVE INDICATOR; ORGANIZATION.

Possessiveness (attitude): An unreasonable desire to have or retain owner-ship of some person or object. This attitude is a combined form of materialism and greed when it refers to objects, and of jealousy and greed in reference to other people. See: Jealousy; Materialism; Greed; and Acquisitive.

POTENTIAL: Anything possible or in the making as opposed to something actual or realized. See: TALENT; HANDWRITING.

Practical (attitude): Preferring the actual to the speculative; applying knowl-edge or experience to some concrete end and largely unimpressed by the theo-retical, ideal, or abstract. Practical thinking and goals are indicated by loopless or narrow-looped ascenders and descenders, especially in a clear, well-orga-nized, script style:

The lack of emotional involvement demonstrates the writer's interest in how a thing or a piece of information can be used, rather than in the thing or knowledge for its own sake. When this direct, no-nonsense approach exists in a less than well-organized script, it may be expressed as bluntness, or uncom-promising (opinionated) behavior. An **impractical** (or unmanageable and inef-ficient) approach is shown not in wide loops so much as in a script loaded with unnecessary accessories.

Prejudice (attitude): The anti-social version of clannishness; unreasonable bias in reference to some other person, object or idea which does not take into account the actual nature or attributes of that other. In its actively harmful form (**bigotry**), it includes the intention of injury or damage to that other which is neither self-protective nor based on any rational cause. Prejudice is indicated by a combination of left-swinging, knotted lower zone loops (see: Clannish) and a rigid angularity in the middle zone.

PRESENTATION: The overall specifications, or mechanical technique, used in writing a sample of script. Interpretation of presentation includes analysis of margins and writing materials. See: MARGINS; IDIOSYNCRASIES. (Review II)

PRESSURE: The physical, muscular force put behind the pen as it is moved along the paper. Measured by both *density* (darkness and thickness) of pen-strokes, and by the *impression* (or indentation) made by the pen on the paper.

Script pressure is an indicator of both physical health and vitality, and of emotional force or determination. (Chapter 5)

PRE-STROKES: See: END-STROKES.

Pretense (characteristic): Claiming to be or presenting yourself as something other than what you are, either to attract admiring notice or to conceal some truth about yourself. Usually a form of insecurity. Pretense is indicated in script by decorative ornamentation, especially when it obscures letters or words; the use of attention-getting unoriginal formations such as the circled i-dot; and over-blown or exaggerated initial capitals, where internal capitals (qv) show low confidence. A variation of this characteristic is also indicated by a signature which differs in some deliberate way from the text style. See also: Projected Self-Image.

Pride (characteristic): Self-respect; a reasonable appreciation of your own capabilities and accomplishments, and a respectful evaluation of your own potentials. Healthy pride is indicated in script by a tall, vertical to controlled-right pronoun I. This formation is usually accompanied by confident capitals as well:

The pronoun I can be slightly larger than other capitals in the script and still retain its positive aspect. Its height, form, and pressure, however, must remain consistent throughout the sample to measure true self-respect. Where the internal pronoun is smaller than the initial I, it indicates a bold front with no real self-confidence. Where the initial I is smaller, it indicates that the writer is playing himself down (is more self-confident than he is willing to let others know); the second usage may often be a kind of courtesy, though it is usually a self-protective camouflage (see also: Pretense). If the pronoun I is too heavily pressured (in relation to the general script pressure), very much larger than other letters or capitals, or over-used (appears often), it is an indicator of **conceit** (or, if loopless, of **arrogance**). When it is inflated or flourished, it indicates **egotism** (pretenses to a pride that does not in fact exist), and is a form of insecurity. See also: Confidence; Emotional; and Internal Self-Image.

PRINTING: Non-cursive writing; the formation of individual letters in a nearly upright position and with no connectors or letterform penstrokes allowing for connectors; also called *block printing*. Printing is often used by a writer to ensure clarity of message, or because a given printed form is simpler or faster than the cursive (see: SCRIPT); as, printed insertions in a cursive style. Printed insertions may also be used where the cursive form of a letter is unfamiliar or unknown to the writer. A printed sample, especially block style (evenly formed and very plain) does not reveal enough about the writer to be used for an effective analysis of character and personality.

Procrastination (trait): The tendency to put things off or leave a job unfinished; general lack of carry-through. It is indicated in script by t-bars which stop left of stem:

If combined with added complications in the body of the script (as; extra knots or ties), the procrastination may be inadvertent (i.e., due to a tendency to get bogged down in unnecessary details, or even to perfectionism). See also: Impulsive; KNOTS AND TIES.

Projected Self-Image: The social mask; the writer as he wishes to be seen by others. It is illustrated in handwriting by the signature style. Any difference between the signature and the text style indicates the mask is different from the actual makeup of the writer. See also: PERSONALITY; Pretense. (Chapter 9)

PRONOUNCED USAGE: In handwriting, repetition and/or over-emphasis of any trait indicator or penstroke formation. The more frequently a given script factor appears in any sample, or the greater the emphasis on that factor in relation to the rest of the sample, the more important it is for or to the writer.

PUNCTUATION: See: ACCESSORY, necessary.

REASONABLE USAGE: *This is not a value judgement.* Reasonable usage is indicated by the employment of reasoning ability on the part of the user. An unreasonable need or drive, for example, is one that the writer cannot rationally expect to have satisfied under the circumstances in which it operates. In analysis, the determination of whether or not a given attribute is reasonable is made on the basis of script organization. If the usage is reasonable *for that writer*, it will show up as a positive indicator. See also: ORGANIZATION; EXTREMES.

REPRESSED ATTRIBUTES: Elements of the individual's makeup which he refuses, consciously or unconsciously, to recognize or make use of; repression is the prevention of natural or normal expression. The effect of repression can result in negative behavior patterns for which the individual himself may not be able to find rational explanations and over which he may have no conscious control. In its positive aspect, repression is the deliberate control of a negative trait, and is indicated in script by the appearance of an indicator for that trait in a de-emphasized form, usually in a well-organized script. Evidence that negative repression exists may show up in script in certain types of contradictory indicators or unusual formations. See also: Pain (emotional); HANDWRITING.

Reserve/Reticence (attitude): Cautious expression; a holding back of some part of self. Generally, *reserve*, which implies an intellectual decision, is indicated by a controlled-right tilt, and *reticence*, which is less voluntary (and can include the concept of diffidence), is indicated by a controlled-left. In any style of script, the predominance of closed formations also indicates the presence of this attribute. See: CLOSED FORMATIONS; OPEN FORMATIONS.

ROUNDHAND: A script style in which the majority of penstroke formations have a smoothly curved outline or form. There are basically three different roundhand styles in handwriting: (a) *traditional roundhand* (American Schoolform is a version of this style), in which curves are formed on all sides of the letter as logical to the script flow; (b) *garland writing*, which shows pointed tops and rounded bottoms; and (c) *arcade writing*, which shows rounded tops and pointed bottoms:

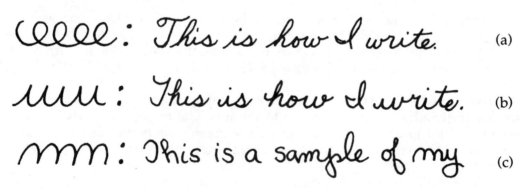

Rounded writing in general indicates cooperation, warmth, and often slowness of thought and perception (it does take longer to write this way!). *Traditional roundhand*, with its evenness and grace of flow, indicates a certain perception of design and consistency of usage on the part of the writer; in effect, an eye for appearances, which may be either self-centered or other-oriented, depending on other signs in the script. *Garland* writing tends to be a much more graceful and flowing style than arcade. If written quickly, showing upper and lower zone extensions, and/or indicating some personal independence, the garland writer can be genial, socially oriented, and usually projects a charming attitude—but he is very alert to his own self-interest. *Arcade* is a much more stylized (or, affected) script style, and also slower to write. Arcade writers tend to be more gentle in nature and slower thinkers than garland writers and are often very insecure. See also: ANGULAR; SCRAWLED. (Chapter 8)

$\mathscr{Ss}$

SAMPLE, of script: Any specimen of handwriting; especially a specimen which is used for analysis. In graphology, samples fall into two classes: (1) *natural samples*, which are done by the writer of his own volition and for his own purposes; and (2) *test samples*, which are done by request for analysis purposes, and which follow certain mechanical guidelines laid down by the analyst. For purposes of definition, samples of handwriting done with the understanding that someone will be judging its quality or appearance (as; penmanship exercises done by schoolchildren) are also considered "test samples"; samples in which the content will be under consideration, rather than the presentation, are "natural" (as; a handwritten job application). In short, if someone tells you how they want you to write and/or present it, it is not a natural sample. Of the two classes, the natural sample is considered superior in terms of an accurate portrayal of character and personality. See also: TEST CONDITIONS.

Sarcasm: See: Critical.

SCHOOLFORM: The style of script taught in and encouraged by a public or private school system; also called Schoolbook Writing. Schoolform styles vary from nation to nation; private schools' styles may also differ perceptibly from those taught in public school systems. Any Schoolform presents a picture of the "ideal" national or cultural personality (or idiomatic form of self-expression); the preferred Schoolform style and other social/mental disciplines taught at the same time will reinforce each other to give the young student an internal image of what kind of person he is supposed to grow up to be. Despite national differences, any Schoolform teaches a uniform style, or, one consistent within itself (i.e., good organization is emphasized in all penmanship lessons). Script indicators and penstroke formations have the same meaning no matter what the original Schoolform.

In graphology, variation from Schoolform is the first evidence of personal independence of thought and behavior, in that the writer's emphasis is transferred from doing the job exactly the way he was told, to getting the job done the best way he can. For most writers, conformity to Schoolform takes an extra effort both in terms of curbing natural impulses, and in terms of the sheer feat of memory required to reproduce letter forms exactly as they were first taught to write them (You don't think so? Make a Schoolform capital Q and a lowercase z without looking back at the lettering chart); this is especially true for little-used letter forms. Careful reproduction of Schoolform, if Schoolform is not the writer's natural style, indicates that the intent of the sample is to present a picture of law-abiding, traditional-values-oriented cooperation.

The style of Schoolform writing used for the purpose of comparison in this text is modern American Schoolform. (Chapter 7; Chapter 10)

SCRAWLED WRITING: A very rapid handwriting style in which letters are scribbled or carelessly shaped. In its extreme form, letters tend to "tail off," or flatten out almost entirely. Like any other form, scrawled writing may or may not also be irregular, awkward, or tangled. Script-flow impediments in this style, however, are generally considered more negative than in either angular or rounded writing; scrawled writing is an indicator of haste and/or a general lack of concern for appearances, so any impediments to that haste, or any (internal) concern for appearances indicates a certain lack of honesty. See also: ANGULAR; ROUNDED. (Chapter 8)

SCRIPT: Used in this text specifically to designate *cursive writing*, or "running hand." Script is writing formed with strokes joined to make words, and using letter shapes designed to make such joining convenient. See also: PRINTING.

Secretive (trait): A pronounced form of reticence (see: Reserve/Reticence); furtive in communication, or having the intent to escape observation. While it is concealment to an extent, being secretive is not a form of dishonesty, but rather an attempt to retain personal privacy (in a right tilt: withdrawal), or escape observation (in a left tilt: insecurity), and usually resulting from a basic distrust of others or their motives. Along with closed formations, it is indicated in script by tight, small letters in the middle zone, especially if the script as a whole is large:

The smaller, tighter, or more scrawled the middle zone formations, the greater the insistence on personal privacy, and the less likely the writer is to share his real feelings or to trust others with his secrets.

Self-Confidence (characteristic): Faith in your own ability to accomplish what you set out do to, *and* the belief that you have both the ability and the right to choose your own goals. Faith in self is considered in analysis the single most positive script factor, in that it is the most effective in enabling the writer to cope. A healthy ego is indicated in script by a large, vertical to controlled-right pronoun I (see: Pride) with positive pen pressure, especially if consistent throughout the sample. A pronoun I three times the size of the middle zone is not considered excessive (unless ornamented or peculiarly emphasized in some way). The narrower the loop, the less sensitive the writer is to external events, and the less vulnerable to the real or imagined reactions of others.

Self-Conscious (attitude): Aware of, involved with, and often embarrassed at your own behavior, particularly in social contexts. Conscious self-awareness is indicated by inflated loops in the pronoun I:

I: I like doing different

In general, this formation in a right-tending script (or pronoun) indicates that the writer is "on stage," with himself as audience. He would also enjoy talking about himself or hearing complimentary comments on his appearance or performance. The left-tilt inflated I is used by a writer who is more of an embarrassment to himself. He has the same needs as the right-tilt writer and may exhibit similar behavior, but he tends to writhe internally at intervals over what he views as making a fool of himself. Both formations indicate an emotional dependence for ego-support on other people's reactions, and are often a *cause*, as well as a result, of insecurity.

Self-Control (potential): The ability to make the most of your best attributes and put the lid on your negative ones. It is indicated in script by good organization in general, and by such deliberate self-disciplinary indicators as good spacing, precision i-dots and punctuation, and balanced t-bars, especially if found in quick writing. Self-control in the sense of the mind ruling the reactions (self-discipline) is also indicated to varying degrees by any vertical to controlled-right or controlled-left tilt.

Self-Doubt (attitude): A generally agonizing uncertainty regarding the validity (or "correctness," both morally and in practical terms) of decisions made or actions contemplated or taken. It is usually caused by conflict with or a lack of usable guidelines (qv), and is indicated in script primarily by a wavering or erratic baseline.

SELF-IMAGE: The picture, for good or bad, that the individual holds of himself; his own opinion of his value as a person. See also: Confidence; Self-Confidence; and Internal, Projected, and Comparative Self-Image. A positive self-image (or; Ego-Strength) is one which enables the writer to cope effectively despite setbacks, failures (or successes!), and the real or imagined reactions of others. In general, ego-strength is defined as the ability to retain intact one's own self-image and therefore function effectively in face of disturbing events or unpleasant criticism regarding that functioning. The quality of an individual writer's self-image will be found in the formation used to write the pronoun I. (Chapter 9)

Selfish (trait): The inability or unwillingness to share yourself or your possessions with others; it is generally based on insecurity, but see also: Secretive. For different versions of this trait, see: Greed; Materialistic; Secretive and Jealousy.

SELF-REINFORCING: Any attitude or behavior pattern which is encouraged or increased by its own repetition (or, more simply; the more it's done, the more you do it). A self-reinforcing trait or reaction may be negative or positive, but it always "proves" itself. For example: (negative pattern) Given an individual who believes no one likes him, and chooses to put on a false front in an attempt to be better liked. Finding that others avoid him even more, he may redouble his pretenses because he is unaware that it is the false front they are avoiding, and he will be more convinced than ever that it is himself they dislike. In its negative form, therefore, a self-reinforcing trait or reaction is an inappropriate behavior pattern (one that results in a different or even opposite effect than whatever the individual hoped to accomplish); in its positive form, a self-reinforcing reaction is the choice of an appropriate behavior pattern (one that achieves and/or reinforces the desired result). See also: POSITIVE; NEGATIVE.

Sensitivity (emotional state): An acute awareness of the reactions of others, real or imagined, to yourself or your behavior. It is indicated in any pronounced to extreme tilt, left or right, especially if the script shows excessive looping (emotional). **Hypersensitivity**, one of the most difficult emotional reactions for the individual to cope with, is like a raw wound. The writer responds with emotional pain to any behavior of others, often misjudging their intent (as; taking as a criticism some action not even directed at him); and any slight, disapproval, or insult, whether or not it is intended or even exists, is salt in the wound. Hypersensitivity is indicated in script by excessive looping, specifically if found on letters where no loops "should" be, such as the d or t stems:

The wider the loops, the greater the pain; the more often they appear, the more susceptible the writer is to hurt. See also: Pain (emotional), and Self-Conscious.

Sensual (physical state): Highly susceptible to stimulation of the senses, especially physical stimulation (i.e., the sense of feel); also, having or subject to strong erotic drives which, if expressed, may lead the individual to over-indulgence in sex, food or drink, or the use of artificial stimulants. Strong physical needs, which may also be expressed as material drives, are indicated in script by inflated lower-zone loops; if the sensuality is purely physical (i.e., not sublimated into or satisfied by material drives), it will show up in the middle zone as a blotted, ink-filled loop, such as in the e:

In a positive script, these loops indicate the writer who simply enjoys physical stimulation. In a script showing lack of self-control, he may be letting these (certainly natural and important) drives run away with him; accompanied by signs of guilt, as many of these indicators are, he may be making an unreasonable attempt to suppress them. See also: Sexual Hangups.

Sexual Hangups (emotional state): Unreasonable or unwarranted feelings of guilt caused by the existence of normal sexual drives and/or normal physical needs. This attribute qualifies as other-inflicted emotional pain, since proscriptions against the normal expression of sexual drives are imposed on (taught to) the individual. It is indicated in script by twisted or oddly formed lower zone loops:

[handwriting sample: "for your analysis of my"]

This is the writer who accuses himself of "perversion" or "unnatural drives" because of guilt feelings about his or her sexual needs. The formations are as likely to be found in the handwriting of an individual who has never stepped outside society's "acceptable norms" but who has been taught that sexual needs are "dirty," as it is to be lacking in the script of a writer who disobeys those learned strictures in some way, but who has come to emotional terms with his or her sexuality. Again:, signs of guilt in the handwriting *do not* necessarily mean that the writer has acutally done anything to feel guilty about. Note that the twisted return (as on the "g" on the right) may also indicate either a guilty or an intense craving for artificial or addictive stimulants (as; drugs or alcohol).

Sexual frustration is quite another matter. Physical deprivation of one form or another exists in an astounding majority of handwriting styles. It is indicated by incomplete returns in the lower zone; the lower on the stem the return, the less physical satisfaction the writer is getting, *according to his individual needs* (and each person's needs are quantitatively different):

[handwriting sample: "is the way I normally write."]

This type of return reveals any kind of unfulfilled physical drive, whether for sex, food, drink, or money. **Sexual preferences** (as; heterosexuality/homosexuality, etc.) *cannot be determined from a sample of script*, any more than biological sex (male or female) can be.

Shyness (emotional state): A tendency to be easily frightened by, and hence to avoid, other people's social approaches or demands. It is based on insecurity and sometimes low ego-strength, and is indicated in script by a controlled to pronounced left tilt. As with timidity (the inability to assert yourself), this style of script may also show weak or hesitant t-bars. See also: Fear.

SIGNATURE: The name of any person written by his or her own hand. See: Projected Self-Image. (Chapter 9)

SIZE, in handwriting: Refers to both the actual height of individual letters in a sample of script (as measured with a ruler), and the amount of space the sample as a whole takes up on a page. This second measurement is influenced by spacing between letters, words, and lines, as well as individual letter width. Script size is an indicator of the writer's range of feeling and interests; how much room he allows himself, occupies, or needs in order to express or be himself. (Chapter 4)

SOCIAL ATTITUDES: The individual's general emotional orientation toward others; both in terms of what he grants them as their right to expect of him and the stance he takes to defend those rights he prefers not to grant. Social attitudes in general are indicated in script by marginal precision (see: MARGINS). Formality, or propriety is shown by "correct" margins (as measured against generally accepted rules for different styles of written communications); a more relaxed, or casual attitude by a presentation which is reasonably well organized but does not attempt to follow accepted guidelines; and a total lack of regard for other's opinions or requirements by a presentation which has no recognizable format at all. See also: FORM. (Review II)

SOCIALIZED BEHAVIOR: Conduct or action subject to, in accordance with, or making use of predetermined and generally agreed-upon rules. Handwriting is a form of socialized behavior; in fact, a very complex form, with very specific rules. In addition to handwriting, this behavior includes use of courtesy titles or forms in speech (Sir, Madam, etc.), observance of suggested dress codes for specific social gatherings, etc. Its actual purpose is not to confine the individual to unnatural acts, but to provide him with an expedient and recognizable means of demonstrating his intentions toward others. In effect, the individual's use of or refusal to use socialized behavior patterns is an indicator of his social attitudes (qv).

STEM: The main or supporting stroke of a letter, such as the ascender of a d or t; the "up-down" (covered) stroke usually retraced on a return.

Stingy: See: Thrift.

STRESS: The graphological word for **tension**: severe to unbearable nervous strain, affecting both emotional equilibrium and physical health. It is caused primarily by vulnerability to external forces or events, and is indicated in script by variable indicators (qv); the inability to choose, much less follow, a coherent course of action. See also: INCONSISTENCIES.

Stubborn: See: Tenacity.

STYLE: See: ORGANIZATION.

Suicidal (emotional state): A death wish directed at the self; in its extreme form, a murderous rage turned inward. Whether the writer is just beginning to think about self-destruction as a possible solution to his problems, or has already begun to plan for it, this is always a dangerous state; whatever the degree of suicidal intent, the writer needs immediate professional help. Its potential is shown in script as a combination of emotional pain, withdrawal, despondence and depression, low-self-esteem and confused thinking, and—always—as fear:

This is the individual who blames himself—and hates himself—for an inability to cope with circumstances which are not reasonably within his control. See also: Pain (emotional); Depression; Confusion; and Fear. For its anti-social equivalent (i.e., the same rage, often with the same causes, turned outward), see: Cruelty.

TALENT: A potential for adept use of some skill or ability. Both a readiness in learning such skill and a natural disposition or tendency toward using it. Note that talent does not indicate the possession of the skill; that comes with training and practice.

Talkative (trait): Chatty; enjoying and employing the use of conversation without necessarily transmitting or needing to transmit any actual information. Like receptiveness, it is shown in open ovals in the middle zone, particularly in a right-angled script. For two different aspects of this trait, see also: Honesty; Insincerity.

TANGLED SCRIPT: Awkward, irregular, and usually illegible writing characterized by the use of a variety of unnecessary accessories and especially the tendency of penstrokes, letters, and words to run into or over each other, either horizontally (on the same line) or vertically (between lines). It is an indi-

cator of confused and irrational thinking in general, and one of the most negative indicators in handwriting, since it suggests an inability to think or act
coherently. For a sample of this type of style, see: Suicidal. (Chapter 1)

Temper (emotional state): A sudden surge of emotion, usually anger; a temporary but intense expression of feeling. It is indicated in script by sudden
surges of heavy pen pressure; and, if anger is the cause, by sudden slashing
strokes on t-bars or terminals:

Normally (or spontaneously) expressed, temper can be a positive indicator
(even if uncomfortable for others to deal with!), as it tends to relieve the pressure which caused it (it's a means of letting off steam). Too tightly controlled
or too often expressed, it becomes either a negative or an anti-social indicator.
See also: Anger.

TEMPERAMENT: The normal emotional attitude or tendencies of the individual; general and usual frame of mind as a combination of overall emotional qualities.

Tenacity (trait): Holding power, or general stick-to-itiveness; the tendency or
ability to remain immovable once a decision has been made. The script indicators for this trait are: (a) knots; (b) ties; and (c) hooked terminals:

(a)   (b)   (c)

Where the knot is placed inside an oval or loop, especially in the middle
zone, it also shows secrecy (as; the diplomatic loop: a holding onto secrets or
counsel); a knot that raises the height of a (middle zone) letter, as in the second sample above, indicates pride as the source, and turns the trait into an
attitude; and a stroke that swings back into self shows **stubbornness** (or,
determined defense of your own position). In general, the ability to stick to
your guns is a healthy trait, but when pronounced it can interfere with the
ability to function. For example, the tendency to get tied up in non-essential
details, shown in our second sample as tenacity based on pride, can have the
writer running around in circles. This writer may consider himself something

of a perfectionist, but that doesn't change the fact that not only does it take him twice as long to get a job done, he's also not doing it as well as he would *without* the extra strokes. See also: ACCESSORY (unnecessary).

TEST CONDITIONS: An artificial situation established by a researcher with the intent of obtaining, for the purpose of examination or trial, data of a known quality and/or of a specific, and predetermined, type. See also: SAMPLE. Results obtained under test conditions may not be reliable in actual (or, natural) situations.

Thought Clarity (characteristic): The ability to reason coherently and express the results of that reasoning in a comprehensible fashion. It is indicated in handwriting by a clear, legible, and simple (or, generally unadorned) writing style.

Thrift (trait): Careful and economical management of available resources; the purposeful and reasonable ability to make the best use, or get the most use, out of whatever you have to work with. It is indicated in handwriting by any small script style; narrow letters in a larger script also indicate the awareness of saving (either time or materials). Carried to extremes (and based on insecurity) thrift becomes frugality or **stinginess**, a penny-pinching attitude which does not actively satisfy the original need or drive (i.e., it does not enable the person to get more use out of his resources, but less, since he is less willing to make use of them). This fear of doing without someday is indicated in script by small, narrow, cramped writing with little to no margins; the writer who uses every available inch of space on a page.

Timid: See: Shyness.

TIES: See: KNOTS AND TIES.

TRAIT: A distinguishing quality of character, mind, or emotion; an individual attribute which influences behavior.

TRAIT INDICATOR: A formation in handwriting which reveals the presence of an attitude, characteristic, or potential in the makeup of the writer. Each indicator reveals the presence of a single trait or need (as; a pronounced-right tilt indicates emotional dependence on others); similar indicators are usually grouped in the study of handwriting analysis (as; all script tilts indicate basic reactions to other people). A single indicator shows a potential or a need; it does not by itself describe what the writer does or is able to do about it. Probable behavior patterns are inferred by combining the interpretations of related indicators or penstroke formations found in one sample of handwriting (i.e., those formations which describe reactions to the same characteristic or need). See also: MAJOR TRAIT INDICATORS.

TYPES OF SCRIPT: Classification of script types is an aesthetic judgement and should be made with care; if you find it difficult to make this judgement, the analysis can be accurately completed without it. Basically, there are three general categories which may be found in either organized or disorganized, unadorned or flamboyant, styles of writing. They are: (a) Graceful; (b) Awkward; and (c) Crude. The samples shown below were deliberately chosen to demonstrate just how close they can sometimes be:

This is a sample of the way (a)

This is a sample of the (b)

This is a sample of (c)

A **graceful** script is practiced; it flows smoothly, and shows superb control of the writing instrument, if nothing else. It indicates that the writer is sure of his penmanship ability, and/or comfortable with the task of writing (or the writing situation in which he finds himself). It also indicates a basic skill confidence in general; if capitals do not, then the writer is someone who simply feels comfortable and sure of himself in familiar tasks or situations. As a style, it can range from very simple, to deliberately decorated. Where the style does show varying degrees of artistic (qv) formations, the writer may be interested in the impression his penmanship makes on others; but he is primarily concerned with satisfying his own sense of aesthetics (which is why this type of script can also indicate artistic potential or appreciation). A truly graceful script can appear well-organized (i.e., look like it must be controlled), even when it is not.

An **awkward** script looks unpracticed, and sometimes is. Children's handwriting is almost always awkward for just that reason. In an adult's writing, this is a style which appears either clumsy (as in our second sample), or illiterate, which it may or may not be; and which can look disorganized, even when it's not. It indicates that the writer is uncomfortable with himself or the (writing) situation. An awkward script may indicate either a lack of writing skill, or a lack of skill confidence in general (i.e., the writer who makes hard work of getting a task accomplished, or a generalized feeling that he may not be the "right man for the job"). In many cases, and especially if the script is well organized and generally unadorned, this type of script is also an indicator of honesty and lack of pretenses.

A **crude** script very often is disorganized; if not, it will still show many negative indicators. Almost a cross between the first two styles, this *is* clumsy writing that is attempting to be impressive; and with or without the kind of flourishes this sample shows, the writer's purpose is neither the skill nor the message; he needs attention and appreciation. What kind of attention he wants depends on how he does it. If his writing is deliberately unattractive or difficult to read, he's being inconsiderate (thumbing his nose at others). If he's crude with flourishes, he wants admiring notice for qualities he feels, or fears, he does not possess. Without flourishes, and especially if lacking signs of sensitivity, he may be anything from a loudmouth to a bully. In any case, his handwriting style is (you guessed it) a form of insecurity. Crude writing does not necessarily indicate a crude person, though it very often indicates an individual who lacks the skill or the insight to accomplish his purposes. See also: Vulgarity.

Uu

UNUSUAL FORMATIONS: See: ORIGINAL/UNUSUAL FORMATIONS.

Unpredictable/Unstable (characteristic): Emotional and/or behavioral fluctuation which follows no rational or recognizable pattern, and which apparently cannot be traced to any specific cause. Variation in any of the major trait indicators (qv) is an indicator for this type of emotional disorientation. If pronounced (indicating instability), the writer himself may not be able to tell what he will do next. This characteristic is both a cause and effect of stress (qv).

USAGE, in graphology: The way penstrokes are formed or shaped, and the way they are joined or fitted together within a single sample of script; the way the writer makes use of those penstroke formations which make up letters and words.

Vv

Vanity/Conceit (attitude): An unreasonable concern with or interest in yourself (vanity); a highly inflated opinion of your own self-worth (conceit). Unlike egotism, which is an attempt to bolster a weak self-image, vanity assumes, at least on a conscious level, that the self-value perceived does in fact exist. This superiority complex is indicated in script by some combination of two or more of the following indicators (see sample, below):
 (a) over-inflated capitals (the braggart: claiming capabilities which may not even exist);
 (b) ornate, artificial forms (the show-off: these are the abilities he's claiming);
 (c) looped beginning strokes (emotional involvement concentrated inward on the self);
 (d) ballooned or over-inflated upper and lower zone loops (grandiose plans and goals);
 (e) excessive flourishes or scrolls (attention-getters: on the order of "look

what I can do!"); and

(f) an ornate or underscored signature (emphasis on personal identity):

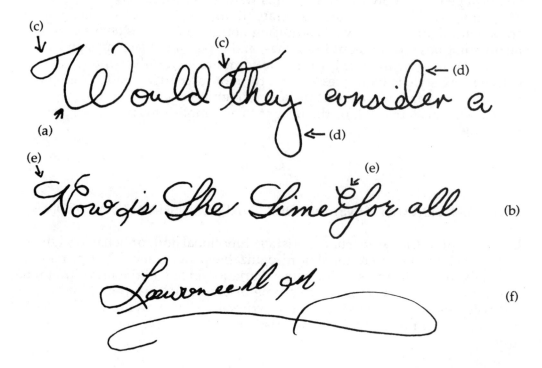

Vanity is more often self-deceit than insecurity, but it does derive from an unconscious recognition that somehow the unemphasized and unadorned self is inadequate, or that actual skills are not worth much, and you will find evidence of insecurity or extreme sensitivity in these styles if you look closely enough. **Conceit** is more other-oriented, and often expressed in an anti-social manner as well; the attempt to tell others you are better than they are assumes some quality in yourself or your social grouping that those others lack. The capping t-bar in our first sample shows a potential for this attitude, as does the underlined and flourished signature; conceit may also be found in script styles showing clannishness or bigotry. See also: REPRESSED ATTRIBUTES.

VARIABLE INDICATORS: Specifically, inconsistent usage of the major trait indicators, as; a combination of left and right angle, large and small size, etc. Variation is an indicator for stress and instability. See also: INCONSISTENCIES. (Chapter 1)

Versatility (potential): In general, showing a variety of aptitudes or abilities; in script, demonstrating the ability to vary the use of some common thing to suit varying circumstances or needs. A single indicator in handwriting for this potential is variation in t-bar formations, especially where that variation is used to adapt or include this penstroke into the flow of script:

The t-bar is an extra stroke and requires an interruption of script flow to execute, but it is a necessary accessory to script. Where it is reshaped to meet the needs of script flow, the writer is avoiding or lessening the interruption without omitting the t-bar. Other original formations which promote rapid script flow while retaining clarity also indicate this potential; note also that the backswing connector stroke on the second two t-bars is a knot formation, indicating that some part of versatility involves a certain degree of stubbornness. See also: Ingenuity; Unpredictability.

Vindictive (attitude): The anti-social form of bitterness (qv); a generally expressed vengeance-seeking for wrongs, real or imagined, experienced by the writer. Downturned initial or terminal hooks show a potential for this attitude (see: Bitterness; Critical; Cruelty); the vindictive script will usually also show dagger or heavy-pressured club-shaped terminals (anger), and a general disorganization:

As a combined trait, the vindictive script will also show: (1) sudden pressure strokes (temper); (2) rigid angularity, particularly in the middle zone (uncompromising, unfeeling); and, very often (3) the domineering t-bar, capping the middle zone. These are all danger signs (i.e., indicators of other abusive tendencies); if pronounced in the script, and especially if combined with an extreme right tilt, the possibility exists that they may take some explosive form. See also: Anger; and Pain (emotional); and, compare this sample to Suicidal.

Vitality (physical state): General physical good health and emotional well-being, and the basis of the ability to persevere or endure. It is indicated in script by consistently firm pen pressure.

Vulgarity (characteristic): Offensively ill-bred or coarse in manner or expression. Vulgarity is primarily indicated in script by crude writing (see: TYPES OF SCRIPT), when that style is not tempered by any signs of a need for approval. This type of script shows a total lack of concern for the opinions or sensibilities of others. Vulgar writing will generally contain one of all of the following elements: (1) ugly or ungainly forms of various kinds; (2) exaggerated forms, especially if crude; (3) blotchiness, showing haste or carelessness; (4) illegibility, missing accessories, and bad spacing; and (5) irregular and narrow (or no) margins:

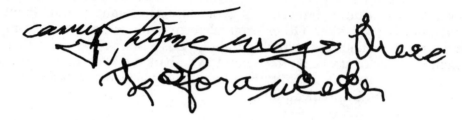

As with a crude style, vulgar script does not necessarily mean a vulgar person. Whether or not the writer is actually ill-bred depends on both the presence of exaggerated crudities (which means he's doing it on purpose), and the context in which the sample was written. A blotchy, illegible scrawl which lacks exaggerated accessories (as; in the t-bars, above), especially if found in a personal notebook and/or at the end of a very long sample of writing, may still show a total lack of concern for the amenities but (and especially if it was not written for others to see) can often be simply the result of hurried carelessness or even writer's cramp. In general, the judgement "vulgar" refers to the appearance of the writing, and not the nature of the writer.

$$\mathcal{W}w$$

Warmth (attitude): A genuine affection for others and a welcoming pleasure in their company. It is indicated in script by a controlled right tilt (preference for social contacts which is not based on emotional dependency), especially if the style retains at least some roundness in the middle zone.

WHITE SPACE: See: MARGINS.

Will power: See: Ambition; Energy; Determination; PRESSURE.

WIND-UP STROKES: See: END-STROKES/PRESTROKES.

Withdrawal (attitude): A drawing into your shell; an emotional retreat from social contacts or painful situations. Withdrawal is indicated in a left-leaning script style; or, in penstrokes, by any flow which moves left or inward. See also: Pain (emotional).

WORD BREAKS: The separation of a single word into segments, either by the elimination of a connector, or by the insertion of a printed letter. Also called *intuitive breaks*. Note that this definition does not include any word breaks created by hyphenation, either at the end of or in the middle of a line. Word breaks in script indicate the occurrence of intuitive flashes (or of thoughts which interrupt the thought being written about). If a word break occurs at a hyphenation point (a syllable break) in longer words only, it indicates logical thinking; if word breaks occur at technically logical points (as; where it makes sense in terms of manual reach to lift the pen off the paper; also usually in longer words but not necessarily at syllable breaks), they are one indicator of ingenuity. Too many word breaks, especially in a disorganized script and largely confined to very short words, may indicate the inability to keep on track.

Worry (emotional state): A state of emotional harassment generally due to concern for the outcome of a situation beyond the individual's control. Where pronounced, worry is the basis of anxiety (see: Insecurity), and a cause of tension (see: Stress). Worry (and a corresponding feeling that the writer lacks situational control) is first indicated in script by the appearance of prop strokes and other pre- and end-stroke accessories. In general, pre-strokes indicate hesitation and a need for reassurance, and tailing off strokes represent delaying tactics. Combined with indicators for sensitivity, dishonesty, or insecurity, worry signs can also indicate fear.

$$\mathcal{X}x,\ \mathcal{Y}y,\ \mathcal{Z}z$$

YOU-ME FORMATIONS: See: Comparative Self-Image.

ZONES: The physical areas—highest, central, and lowest—into which letters or parts of letters fall. Handwriting is mechanically divided into three zones: the *upper zone* (ascenders), which formations indicate the writer's intellectual/spiritual interests and orientation; the *middle zone* (or, script body), which indicates social attitudes; and the *lower zone* (descenders), which indicates material interests or physical drives. Formations in the different zones can also indicate physical problems or dysfunctions in the corresponding areas of the body (see: Pain, physical). (Chapter 6)

Conclusion

Listed below, in alphabetical order, are 116 traits and characteristics which can be determined with a reasonable amount of accuracy from a sample of handwriting. This "trait list" can be used as an additional worksheet for a mini-analysis, aptitude analysis, or even as a quick means of identifying attributes and attitudes for the GPA. All traits in this list have been explained and defined in the Glossary.

Analysis Note

Trait lists are a useful analysis tool but, as mentioned earlier, you should avoid using these highly significant words when writing up your analysis. The best way to describe attributes you identify in a sample is to use the definition instead of the word. *Sensitive*, for example, is defined as susceptible to external stimuli, and that's what it means; but for many people, it connotes sympathetic or empathetic. If your subject is sensitive, he needs to know exactly in what way. You tell him that he is easily affected, and often hurt, by what other people do or say, and—particularly if he is hypersensitive—gently point out that he should try to remind himself when something does hurt him that perhaps it was not intended to. In all cases, and for all attributes, your analyses will do no good unless you can explain clearly and unmistakably exactly what you found in a sample of script.

Note also that neither the trait list nor this Glossary is a valid substitute for really knowing and understanding the meaning of penstroke formations found in script. In the final analysis, your ability to interpret penstroke and script formations for yourself (*without* looking it up) is what will make you a good graphologist.

TEST YOURSELF

As you have seen, most attributes contain elements of other attributes, or are influenced by them: which should not surprise you, since you know that every person is a composite of all his inherent qualities and lifetime experiences, and that handwriting pictures the interrelationships of these many different facets of character and personality.

To demonstrate that, we've got one more practice exercise for you to try. The five samples which follow our trait list were all used to illustrate specific traits or characteristics described in the Glossary; the entry they illustrated is given in brackets. But they don't illustrate only that one trait. You list as many other traits, characteristics, potentials or attitudes as you can identify in each sample; to test your own knowledge, work from the trait list instead of referring back to the text. The samples are on page 306. Our answers are in Appendix B.

TRAIT LIST
Attributes and Attitudes Revealed in Handwriting

1. Acquisitive
2. Adaptable
3. Affable
4. Affection
5. Aggressive
6. Altruism
7. Ambition
8. Anger
9. Argumentative
10. Artistic
11. Ascetic
12. Athletic
13. Bitterness
14. Bluntness
15. Calculating
16. Careless
17. Clannish
18. Concentration
19. Confidence
20. Conformity
21. Confusion
22. Conscientious
23. Cooperative
24. Critical
25. Critical Judgement
26. Cruelty
27. Decisive
28. Defensive
29. Depression
30. Determination
31. Diplomacy
32. Dishonesty
33. Dominant
34. Emotional
35. Emotional Stability
36. Energy
37. Enthusiasm
38. Evasive
39. Exaggeration
40. Extravagant
41. Fatigue
42. Fear
43. Frustration
44. Generosity
45. Greed
46. Gregarious
47. Guilt
48. Gullible
49. Honesty
50. Humor
51. Imagination
52. Immaturity
53. Impulsive
54. Inconsiderate
55. Independence
56. Inferiority
57. Inflexible
58. Ingenuity
59. Inhibition
60. Insecurity
61. Insincerity
62. Intuition
63. Irritability
64. Jealousy
65. Kindliness
66. Laziness
67. Literalness
68. Logical
69. Love
70. Materialistic
71. Maturity
72. Mental Alertness
73. Need for Attention
74. Opinionated
75. Optimism
76. Pain, Emotional
77. Pain, Physical
78. Pain, in Illness
79. Patient/Impatient
80. Pessimism
81. Planning Ability
82. Possessiveness
83. Practical
84. Prejudice
85. Pretense
86. Pride
87. Procrastination
88. Reserve/Reticence
89. Secretive
90. Self-Confidence
91. Self-Conscious
92. Self-Control
93. Self-Doubt
94. Self-Image
95. Selfish
96. Sensitivity
97. Sensual
98. Sexual Hangups
99. Sexual Frustration
100. Shyness
101. Suicidal
102. Talkative
103. Temper
104. Tenacity
105. Thought Clarity
106. Thrift
107. Unpredictable
108. Vanity
109. Versatility
110. Vindictive
111. Vitality
112. Vulgarity
113. Warmth
114. Will Power
115. Withdrawal
116. Worry

SAMPLE ONE: (ANGER)

tell me what you think

SAMPLE TWO: (ASCETIC)

This is how I form my handwriting.

SAMPLE THREE: (DECISIVE)

I told you yesterday

SAMPLE FOUR: (GULLIBLE)

but do you know what

SAMPLE FIVE: (VULGARITY)

every time we go there.
for a week

APPENDIX B

Answers to Chapter Quizzes

Note: There are *always* other signs in a sample of script, but the samples shown in the chapter quizzes were chosen or reshaped to show the indicators listed here. If you have other answers as well, that's fine: but to be correct, you should have these.

CHAPTER 1: Organization (pp 3-14)

SAMPLE ONE
> *Positive:* Steady, level baseline (also: consistent slant)
> > Meaning: Reasonably sure of ability to make decisions; clear objectives
> *Negative:* Pronounced to extreme (left) slant
> > Meaning: Over-reacts in this area (Afraid of others; unable to relate)

SAMPLE TWO
> *Positive*: Consistent letterform usage /OR/ Consistent size and spacing
> > Meaning: Consistent behavior /OR/ self-control (comfortable with lifestyle choices)
> *Negative*: Unnecessary penstrokes or additions to the letterform; ornamentation
> > Meaning: indecision, pretense, confusion and/or poor communication

SAMPLE THREE
> *Positive:* Moderate slant
> > Meaning: Controlled reactions (to others)
> *Negative:* Variable size and spacing
> > Meaning: stress (in lifestyle situation or choices)

SAMPLE FOUR
> *Positive*: Consistent size and spacing (it's tight, but consistent!)
> > Meaning: Self-control; knows his own mind in this area

Negative: Extreme pressure /OR/ Variable pressure
　　　Meaning: Over-reacts in this area /OR/ stress, frustration

SAMPLE FIVE
　　Positive: Clarity/simplicity of form /OR/ Moderate slant
　　　　Meaning: Self-control; clear thinking /OR/ good control in this area
　　　　　　　(good communication)
　　Negative: Variable baseline
　　　　Meaning: Stress in this area (emotional ups and downs, self-doubt)

CHAPTER 2: Baseline (pp 15-27)

SAMPLE ONE
　　Direction: Level
　　Shape: Reasonably steady; pronounced internal sag
　　Analysis: Realistic; has clear objectives; very unhappy about some spe-
　　　　cific situation or event

SAMPLE TWO
　　Direction: Upslant
　　Shape: Reasonably steady; minor sag; internal bounce
　　Analysis: Outwardly optimistic, but may have some doubts (baseline
　　　　waver is minor sag); has clear objectives; finds something amusing

SAMPLE THREE
　　Direction: Level
　　Shape: Reasonably steady; internal sag
　　Analysis: Realistic; has clear objectives; unhappy about some specific situ-
　　　　ation or event

SAMPLE FOUR
　　Direction: Downslant
　　Shape: Reasonably steady; pronounced internal sag
　　Analysis: Pessimistic; has clear objectives; very unhappy about some spe-
　　　　cific situation or event

SAMPLE FIVE
　　Direction: Level
　　Shape: Pronounced baseline waver, not yet erratic
　　Analysis: Realistic; has doubts about objectives and/or feels insecure
　　　　about ability to achieve goals

CHAPTER 3: Angle (pp 29-44)

SAMPLE ONE
　　Angle: Variable vertical (mostly vertical, with controlled left and some pro-
　　　　nounced left; some swings right)
　　Attitude: Trying to be self-contained, but probably from shyness or fear;
　　　　may want friends

SAMPLE TWO

> *Angle:* Variable (right to left swings)
> *Attitude:* Isn't sure how to react to others; some fear, some need, trying to be self-sufficient

SAMPLE THREE

> *Angle:* Variable right (controlled to pronounced right; vertical inserts on capitals only)
> *Attitude:* Would (like to) be self-contained, but has a strong need for others

SAMPLE FOUR

> *Angle:* Extreme left, just over the border from pronounced
> *Attitude:* Generally distrusts others

SAMPLE FIVE

> *Angle:* Vertical
> *Attitude:* Generally uninvolved with others

CHAPTER 4: Size (pp 45-61)

SAMPLE ONE

> *Size:* Starts medium-small, ends small; inconsistent letter width; occasional word-spread or word cramping, with spread dominant
> *Range:* This is a writer who is trying to grow. Not comfortable in a conventional setting; for the most part, feels the need for more room, but also sometimes considers withdrawal. Stress, confusion over how to meet needs.

SAMPLE TWO

> *Size:* Small to extremely small; width and spacing reasonably consistent; occasional word-spread
> *Range:* Isolated, precise, able to concentrate; general tendency to shut everything out except specific interests; word spread may be either opening up or closing up

SAMPLE THREE

> *Size:* Very large; reasonably consistent width and spacing, with a tendency to narrow in
> *Range:* Expansive and outgoing; some minor signs that writer may have a tendency to take on too much; basically over-excitable with not enough time for everything

SAMPLE FOUR

> *Size:* Large; letter width and spacing medium
> *Range:* Outgoing, enthusiastic, but may have taken on too much

SAMPLE FIVE
> *Size:* Medium growing to medium-large; letter width proportional but gradually spreading
> *Range:* Still adaptable, but needs more elbow room; range of interests appears to be growing

CHAPTER 5: Pressure (pp 63-74).

No questionnaire.

CHAPTER 6: Zones (pp 75-91)

SAMPLE ONE
> *Zone Usage:* Middle zone de-emphasis; lower zone concentration
> *Variations:* Sporadic short descenders, sporadic longer ascenders
> *Analysis:* Physical drives are strongest, though probably sometimes curbed. Very little interest in close personal relationships or responsibilities. Intelligence and reasoning ability utilized, but secondary to physical drives. Writer is going through some changes/testing of priorities

SAMPLE TWO
> *Zone Usage:* Fairly balanced; slight lower zone emphasis
> *Variations:* All within reasonable limits
> *Analysis:* Fairly flexible; balanced lifestyle with a greater emphasis on sensuality, physical or material drives

SAMPLE THREE
> *Zone Usage:* Middle zone emphasis
> *Variations*: are in size, not zones; the entire letter size alters
> *Analysis*: Very family and security-oriented; family-social-community needs take priority. Slightly immature

SAMPLE FOUR
> *Zone Usage:* Lower zone emphasis; upper zone secondary
> *Variations:* Within reasonable limits
> *Analysis:* Physical drives pronounced. Writer can think when he has to; little or no interest in social relationships

SAMPLE FIVE
> *Zone Usage:* Variable, with lower-zone emphasis
> *Variations:* Throughout, and between zones
> *Analysis:* Physical drives strongest; confusion over intellectual or social priorities. This writer is going through growing pains

CHAPTER 7: Penstrokes (pp 95-122)

SAMPLE ONE
> *Penstroke Description:* Extra knots = added complications; t-bar stops short

of stem = doesn't finish what he starts

Trait: Procrastination, based on a tendency to get involved in unnecessary complications

SAMPLE TWO

Penstroke Description: Downturned hooks on t-bar (combined with critical i-dots) = vicious; sharp lower zone terminals = anger

Trait: Cruelty (especially in a disorganized script!); with other-oriented script, possibly vicious

SAMPLE THREE

Penstroke Description: Openings on closed formations with deep double looping = insincerity; added loops on d and e = sensitivity

Trait: Scared (this is the *reason* for the insincerity)

SAMPLE FOUR

Penstroke Description: Upturned hook on prestrokes = acquisitive; extra knots = stubborn

Trait: Greedy

CHAPTER 8: Capitals and Script Form (pp 123-141)

SAMPLE ONE
Capitals
Relative height: Barely tops the middle zone
Idiocyncracies: Fairly simple, flourished connector
Meaning: Not much confidence, and a need to connect with others
Connectors
Usage: Both logical and intuitive word breaks
Meaning: Ability to find his own solutions; flashes of insight
Script Form:
Shape: Basically rounded, some angularity on m's and n's
Meaning: Generally cooperative, but starting to think for himself; mentally alert. (Note: This roundhand is an arcade style; see Glossary: ROUNDHAND)

SAMPLE TWO
Capitals
Relative height: Barely tops middle zone; shorter than ascenders
Idiocyncracies: Schoolform decoration
Meaning: Low confidence; desire to please
Connectors
Usage: No word breaks
Meaning: Literal-minded
Script Form
Shape: Roundhand; some angularity on m's and n's
Meaning: Generally cooperative; starting to think for himself

SAMPLE THREE
  Capitals
    Relative height: Consistent with script size
    Idiocyncracies: Graceful in form and connector usage
    Meaning: Confident, also artistic and/or wants to please
  Connectors
    Usage: No word breaks
    Meaning: Literal-minded
  Script Form
    Shape: Angular
    Meaning: Thinks for himself

SAMPLE FOUR
  Capitals
    Relative height: Twice the middle zone, despite middle-zone emphasis
    Idiocyncracies: None: plain and printed
    Meaning: Confident, straightforward
  Connectors
    Usage: Word breaks and printed insertions
    Meaning: Intuitive and practical
  Script Form
    Shape: Roundhand
    Meaning: Cooperative, wants to please

SAMPLE FIVE
  Capitals
    Relative height: Smaller than ascenders; less than twice the middle zone
        (smaller than script size)
    Idiocyncracies: Swashbuckling; flourished style
    Meaning: Not much confidence, and a need to show off (this writer is
        putting on a bold front)
  Connectors
    Usage: Sporadic word breaks; most words connected
    Meaning: Literal-minded but disorganized
  Script Form
    Shape: Scrawled, but decorated and complicated
    Meaning: Trying to show off

CHAPTER 9: Identity Words (pp 143-166)

SAMPLE ONE
  Analysis: Low self-esteem
    Poor self-image (based on pronoun I); resents authority figures (based
    on small "W" in last name and also smaller "Sir" in address), but recog-
    nizes their potential power (larger and decorated-y in "your")

SAMPLE TWO
  Analysis: Needs attention

(Based on flourished script and signature; underlining in signature); basically insecure (small pronoun I)

SAMPLE THREE
Analysis: Low self-esteem, expressed as exaggerated humility.
Basically aware she has worth (pronoun I), but very low self-esteem (lack of capitals in signature)

SAMPLE FOUR
Analysis: Wants to be noticed
(larger signature than script); tends to believe what he's told about himself (open cup on pronoun I)

APPENDIX A: TRAIT LIST (pp 239-306)

SAMPLE ONE
Used to illustrate: ANGER
Additional traits: argumentative; bitterness; critical; depression; emotional pain; energy; *honesty*; hostility; temper; unstable

SAMPLE TWO
Used to illustrate: ASCETIC
Additional traits: concentration; confidence; (very) conscientious; critical judgement; determination/high aspirations; emotional stability; energy; honesty; *impulsive* (note the t-bar); inflexible; patient; practical; pride; withdrawal

SAMPLE THREE
Used to illustrate: DECISIVE
Additional traits: Athletic; affection; confidence; conformity (Schoolbook); conscientious; generous; kindliness; warmth; will power

SAMPLE FOUR
Used to illustrate: GULLIBLE
Additional traits: adaptable; affectionate; co-operative; honesty; insecurity; literal-minded; self-doubt; sensitive; sensual; talkative; unpredictable; worry; some withdrawal

SAMPLE FIVE
Used to illustrate: VULGARITY
Additional traits: Calculating; careless; clannish; confusion; dishonest; frustration; inconsiderate; opinionated; emotional pain; prejudice indicated; pretence; stubborn pride; temper; unstable—which means that in fact, this sample *is* likely to indicate a vulgar behavior pattern

☾ REACH FOR THE MOON

Llewellyn publishes hundreds of books on your favorite subjects! To get these exciting books, including the ones on the following pages, check your local bookstore or order them directly from Llewellyn.

ORDER BY PHONE

- Call toll-free within the U.S. and Canada, 1-800-THE MOON
- In Minnesota, call (612) 291-1970
- We accept VISA, MasterCard, and American Express

ORDER BY MAIL

- Send the full price of your order (MN residents add 7% sales tax) in U.S. funds, plus postage & handling to:

  Llewellyn Worldwide
  P.O. Box 64383, Dept. K390-5
  St. Paul, MN 55164–0383, U.S.A.

POSTAGE & HANDLING

(For the U.S., Canada, and Mexico)

- $4.00 for orders $15.00 and under
- $5.00 for orders over $15.00
- No charge for orders over $100.00

We ship UPS in the continental United States. We ship standard mail to P.O. boxes. Orders shipped to Alaska, Hawaii, The Virgin Islands, and Puerto Rico are sent first-class mail. Orders shipped to Canada and Mexico are sent surface mail.

International orders: Airmail—add freight equal to price of each book to the total price of order, plus $5.00 for each non-book item (audio tapes, etc.).

Surface mail—Add $1.00 per item.

Allow 2 weeks for delivery on all orders.
Postage and handling rates subject to change.

DISCOUNTS

We offer a 20% discount to group leaders or agents. You must order a minimum of 5 copies of the same book to get our special quantity price.

FREE CATALOG

Get a free copy of our color catalog, *New Worlds of Mind and Spirit*. Subscribe for just $10.00 in the United States and Canada ($30.00 overseas, airmail). Many bookstores carry *New Worlds*—ask for it!

Visit our web site at www.llewellyn.com for more information.

The New Palmistry

How to Read the Whole Hand and Knuckles

Judith Hipskind

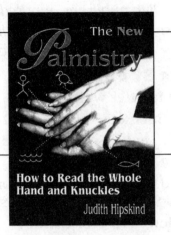

Ten years ago professional palmist Judith Hipskind made a shocking discovery. On the back of a client's hand, and in the knuckles specifically, she saw lines and symbols that revealed as much—if not more—than the palm lines she had studied for some 15 years. Over the next decade, Hipskind researched the knuckles and received verification from hundreds of surprised and satisfied clients on the remarkable accuracy of her amazing new system.

In this groundbreaking book, Hipskind shares her discoveries so you, too, can easily read the secrets in the whole hand. We all know our future, and the subconscious mind records its information through the nerve supply to the knuckles. Your own hands contain incredibly clear answers to your questions about the immediate future of your career, finances, relationships and health. Learn about the people in your life—significant others, your boss or the person in the office next to you. Discover whether or not there will be difficulties ahead that can be worked out with advance warning, and find out whether your current efforts are leading to success.

1-56718-352-2

336 pp., color photos, 5¼ x 8, softcover   **$12.95**

Instant Handwriting Analysis
A Key to Personal Success

Ruth Gardner

For those who wish to increase self-awareness and begin to change some unfavorable aspect of their personality, graphology is a key to success. It can help open our inner selves and explore options for behavior change. With practice, one can make graphology an objective method for giving feedback to the self. And it is an unbeatable channel for monitoring your personal progress.

Author Ruth Gardner makes the process quick and easy, illustrating how letters are broken down vertically into three distinctive zones that help you explore your higher philosophies, daily activities and primal drives. She also explains how the size, slant, connecting strokes, spacing, and amounts of pressure all say something about the writer. Also included are sections on doodles and social graphology.

Instant Handwriting Analysis provides information for anyone interested in pursuing graphology as a hobby or career. It lists many resources for continuing study, including national graphology organizations and several correspondence schools.

0-87542-251-9

159 pp., 7 x 10, illus., softcover **$15.95**

Tarot for Beginners

*An Easy Guide to Understanding
& Interpreting the Tarot*

P. Scott Hollander

The Tarot is much more than a simple divining tool. While it can—and does—give you accurate and detailed answers to your questions when used for fortune-telling, it can also lead you down the road to self-discovery in a way that few other meditation tools can do. *Tarot for Beginners* will tell you how to use the cards for meditation and self-enlightenment as well as for divination.

If you're just beginning a study of the Tarot, this book gives you a basic, straightforward definition of the meaning of each card that can be easily applied to any system of interpretation, with any Tarot deck, using any card layout. The main difference between this book and other books on the Tarot is that it's written in plain English—you need no prior knowledge of the Tarot or other arcane subjects to understand its mysteries, because this no-nonsense guide will make the symbolism of the Tarot completely accessible to you. You will receive an overview of of the cards of the Major and Minor Arcana in terms of their origin, purpose and interpretive uses as well as clear, in-depth descriptions and interpretations of each card.

1-56718-363-8

352 pp., 5¼ x 8, illus.   **$12.95**